The
Reference Shelf®

The Transformation of American Cities

CABRINI COLLEGE LIBRARY
610 KING OF PRUSSIA ROAD
RADNOR, PA 19087

The Reference Shelf
Volume 87 • Number 5
H.W. Wilson
A Division of EBSCO Information Services

Published by
GREY HOUSE PUBLISHING
Amenia, New York
2015

922373397

The Reference Shelf

The books in this series contain reprints of articles, excerpts from books, addresses on current issues, and studies of social trends in the United States and other countries. There are six separately bound numbers in each volume, all of which are usually published in the same calendar year. Numbers one through five are each devoted to a single subject, providing background information and discussion from various points of view and concluding with an index and comprehensive bibliography that lists books, pamphlets, and articles on the subject. The final number of each volume is a collection of recent speeches. Books in the series may be purchased individually or on subscription.

Copyright © 2015, by Grey House Publishing, Inc. All rights reserved. No part of this work may be used or reproduced in any manner whatsoever or transmitted in any form or by any means, electronic or mechanical, including photocopy, recording, or any information storage and retrieval system, without written permission from the copyright owner. For subscription information and permissions requests, contact Grey House Publishing, 4919 Route 22, PO Box 56, Amenia, NY 12501.

Publisher's Cataloging-In-Publication Data
(Prepared by The Donohue Group, Inc.)

The transformation of American cities / [compiled by] H. W. Wilson, a
  division of EBSCO Information Services.

   pages : illustrations ; cm. -- (The reference shelf ; volume 87, number 5)

   Includes bibliographical references and index.
   ISBN: 978-1-61925-694-1 (v. 87, no. 5)
   ISBN: 978-1-61925-689-7 (volume set)

   1. Cities and towns--United States--History--21st century. 2. City and town life--United States--History--21st century. 3. Urban ecology (Sociology)--United States--History--21st century. 4. United States--Social conditions--21st century. 5. United States--Economic conditions--21st century. I. H.W. Wilson Company. II. Series: Reference shelf ; v. 87, no. 5.

HT123 .T73 2015
307.76/0973

Printed in Canada

Contents

3

Economy and Industry

4

Crime and Policing

5

Architecture and the Arts

6

Politics and Education

Preface

After a half-century of economic stagnation and population loss, signs of an American urban renaissance have become evident in the 2010s. Long maligned as dangerous and polluted, cities have in recent years experienced dropping crime rates and are increasingly popular as laboratories for sustainable development. Though the revitalization trend is new and potentially transient, city planners, administrators, politicians, and urban activists are enthusiastically embracing this increase in popularity and promoting cities as vibrant centers for diversity, cultural exchange, and social/political innovation.

What Is a City?

Size matters in cities. While definitions vary, the size and density of a population is one of the primary characteristics dividing cities from towns and villages. According to the United States Census Bureau (USCB), any community with a population of more than 50,000 people is defined as an "Urbanized Area (UA)," while communities with 2,500–50,000 residents are called "Urban Clusters (UCs) and communities with fewer than 2,500 are classified as "rural." When the Census Bureau first began distinguishing urban and rural areas, any community with more than 2,500 was considered "urban," but the subsequent growth of suburbia since the 1950s necessitated new definitions. The Census Bureau's Office of Management and Budget makes another population distinction between "metropolitan" areas, which are defined by having a "core" urban area with more than 50,000 residents, and "micropolitan" areas, which have urban cores of between 10,000 and 50,000.[1]

In practice, communities with less than 50,000 residents have little in common with America's largest cities like New York (pop. 8.4 million)[2] or even smaller cities like Raleigh, North Carolina (431,746).[3] Though difficult to define, the urban feel that has come to define "cityhood" in the American imagination is largely a matter of population density. The size and density of the population causes cities to grow vertically, with families and individuals living close together in more diverse communities and a unique aesthetic in the form of the city skylines. Vibrant downtown districts provide urban residents with access to diverse dining, artistic, and recreational options, which in turn inspire more and more new residents to come to cities looking to expand their social, cultural, artistic, and professional experiences through the unique urban milieu. From a qualitative, rather than quantitative perspective, the density and diversity of urban populations gives cities a sense of vibrancy, with an ineffable energy and dynamism that has come to represent the visceral feel of city life.

Another way to define cities is in terms of "importance," which can be measured in a variety of ways. While cities have long been important in terms of economic influence and as administrative centers for government, cities are also hubs for culture. From the metropolitan art and theater scenes to the numerous linguistic, recreational, and artistic innovations created within diverse urban populations, cities set the tone for cultural development around the nation. Though cities have changed through decades of growth and decline, the importance of cities as hubs for cultural development has endured, and today, cities are leading a new phase in human culture: the digitization revolution and search for sustainable development that are determining the shape of the next era in both urban and American life.

History and Development of Cities

Archaeologists have found evidence of the first "cities" in remnants from the Nile Valley, Indus Valley, and Mesopotamia as early as 7,500 years ago. The ancient city of Babylon, for instance, housed a population of at least 250,000, while ancient Rome (between 400 BCE and 100 CE) had a population as large as 650,000.[4] The earliest cities were cultural and economic centers, established and developed to facilitate travel and commerce between agricultural centers. Until the mid-1800s, only an extremely small portion of the population, usually estimated at between 4 to 7 percent, lived in cities. The Industrial Revolution, a series of economic and labor developments inspired by new discoveries in manufacturing and technology, drastically changed the demographic environment of the United States. As manufacturing and other industrial jobs became more common in cities, residents flocked from rural areas for work. This growth then facilitated the growth of service industries to provide for growing urban populations. Steam-powered ships and locomotives further fueled the urban boom by making cities more important for shipping and trade.[5]

From the mid-1800s to the mid-1900s, urban communities around the world grew faster than rural communities. Population growth and density inspired vertical growth, leading to the first skyscrapers, and also to the characteristic downtown districts and financial districts associated with cities today. Locomotives and steamships, replaced later with gas-powered vehicles, made it possible for corporations to grow to national scale, selling products manufactured in one area to consumers around the country. This growth continued with the popularization of the automobile and the development of interstate highways connecting cities and towns.[6]

In a phenomenon known as the Great Migration, more than 6 million African Americans moved from the rural South to cities in the North, West, and Midwest between 1910 and 1960. This exodus was motivated by the desire to escape racial prejudice in the South and to capitalize on the growth of urban industry around the country. When African Americans moved into these cities, however, they encountered northern prejudice, and racial tension and conflict ensued.

From the end of World War II to 1975, the United States saw the greatest increase in economic growth in history and a rise in the standard of living and overall affluence. At first this money was concentrated in cities, but with the growth of the highway system and the ability of most white families to own at least one car, many people decided to move to the suburbs and pursue the American dream of houses with yards and white picket fences.

The mid-decades of the twentieth century marked a turning point in American urban history. The "deindustrialization" of the United States in the 1970s, when American companies began to move plants abroad, had particularly adverse effects on cities, which lost good jobs, the tax base, and people. By the 1980s, American cities had lost nearly a quarter of their peak populations, with a subsequent reduction in economic growth as many companies also moved to the suburbs to seek cheaper property and the labor force of growing suburban populations. Ultimately, this transformation led to urban blight, economic stagnation, homelessness, and poverty in urban areas.[7]

These depressed economic conditions exacerbated racial tensions, and in the 1960s and 1970s, a number of cities, like Cleveland, Detroit, and Newark, experienced urban riots. Racial prejudice and the riots contributed to the mass movement of white families away from American cities into the suburbs, in a phenomenon now called white flight.

Whereas cities were seen as hubs of economic and social opportunity in the early twentieth century, by the 1970s cities were increasingly associated with economic depression and crime. This perception motivated further waves of migration into the suburbs, which in turn increased urban decay. This process continued into the 2000s, with suburban growth outpacing urban growth as individuals raising families continued to move into suburbs seeking safer, cleaner environments or opportunities for employment. Over fifty years, the first suburbs located near city centers became increasingly urbanized and racially diverse, which then stimulated further waves of migration into new suburbs further and further from city centers.

In the 2010s, cities have begun slowly to regain some of their former economic and cultural prominence. In part, the new wave of urban growth has resulted from young adults in the Millennial generation whose interest in living in city centers has led to an urban renaissance. Demographers have also found that older generations, after having raised children in the suburbs, are returning to cities to benefit from the more diverse cultural and recreational options available in urban environments. Population growth alone also leads to urbanization as more and more residents flock to suburbs, thereby increasing demand for "urbanized" housing options and amenities. Therefore, many formerly quiet, semirural communities on the edges of cities have become extensions of residential and business corridors linked to cities. As of 2015, the U.S. population was growing at a rate of 0.73 percent, with a baby born every 8 seconds, and a population of more than 300 million. As this rapid growth continues, both cities and suburbs become more dense and diverse, essentially leading to a convergence between urban and suburban communities.[8]

From Blight to Hope

Though crime in American cities has fallen since the 2000s, public perception has not changed in concert, and a majority of Americans still believe that life in suburbs is superior to life in cities.[9] Changing this public perception is the difficult job of the politicians, developers, and urban advocates struggling towards urban renewal. Demographic trends indicating an increased interest in urban life show that young Americans increasingly value population and cultural diversity; have more interest in the amenities and recreational options of cities; and are more comfortable with smaller living spaces, congestion, and the other inconveniences associated with higher density.

Capitalizing on the tastes of a new generation of consumers, cities around the nation are working to change public perceptions, investing in downtown revitalization efforts aimed at showing that cities are the ideal "laboratories" for economic, environmental, and social innovation. For instance, urban governments have promoted technological development in cities while also providing tax and other incentives for entrepreneurs looking to revitalize blighted areas or to fill needed niches in the city's services and amenities. Small cities like Pittsburgh, once seen as a polluted, blue-collar city with little appeal to young residents, have invested heavily in green infrastructure, shifting urban environments into increasingly self-sufficient communities where individuals interested in environmental activism and sustainable living are beginning to concentrate.[10] Larger cities like Chicago and Boston have likewise made major steps toward reducing crime; improving quality of life; and investing in sustainable architecture, power, and other infrastructure.[11]

In 2015, it remains unknown whether the urban renewal will be lasting or transient. It also remains to be seen whether the resurgence of interest in urban living will dissipate as more and more young adults begin having children. The current state of cities therefore is one of cautious hope, with urban renewal advocates enthusiastically pursuing development, knowing that the next decade could see a return to previous patterns of decline.

Challenges and Changes

In the nineteenth century, the Industrial Revolution resulted in the massive economic growth of the working and middle classes; in the late twentieth and early twenty-first centuries, the Digital Revolution is once again changing urban economies and creating a proliferation of new jobs, this time particularly in white-collar industries. While urban job markets are growing, digital age industries provide fewer job opportunities due to automation in manufacturing, the shift towards digital rather than physical products, and outsourcing. For instance, the newspaper and magazine industries, having shifted to digital formats and shared content, now employ only 10 percent of their former workforce. Currently, there are few effective strategies for creating working-class job growth, especially in cities where the high cost of living and property values complicate efforts to create economic growth. The plight of the American working class is one of the key issues in the struggle to combat poverty, which is a national epidemic that contributes to crime and decay and affects urban and rural populations alike.

Over the first decade and a half of the twenty-first century, economic disparity has grown, and correspondingly, class conflict has become a prominent issue in American politics and especially in American cities. The Occupy Wall Street protest movement provides an example of popular dissatisfaction with economic inequity in American society and the "wealth gap" between the nation's richest and poorest populations.[12] Likewise, cities have become the main locale for the controversial "education reform" movement, as typified by the growth of charter schools.

For contemporary urbanites, and especially those invested in renewal, fostering new priorities around such key challenges as educational quality, economic justice, and environmental sustainability will be crucial to improving the quality of city life for current and future generations.

Micah L. Issitt

Notes

1. Census Bureau, "2010 Census Urban Area FAQs."
2. "Population-Current Population Estimates," NYC Gov.
3. "Raleigh Demographics," City of Raleigh.
4. Morley, "Population Size and Structure." 42–43.
5. Frey and Zimmer, "Defining the City," 14–16
6. "Rise of Industrial America, 1876–1900," Library of Congress.
7. Jackson, *Crabgrass Frontier*.
8. Schlesinger, "The 2015 U.S. and World Populations."
9. Mathis, "Overall, Americans in the Suburbs Are Still the Happiest."
10. Williams, "Why Pittsburgh Is a Front-Runner in Sustainable Development."
11. Eversley, "Hard-knocks Cities are Working on a Comeback."
12. Moyers, "The Great American Class War."

1
Green Initiatives, the Environment, and Natural Resources

© Rick D'Elia/Corbis

Phoenix Spokes People organize awareness and improvement of bicycle-friendly roads through the center of Phoenix. One of the group's fun events is Bike to the Ballpark, to see the Arizona Diamondbacks. Photographed August 8, 2014.

The Greening of American Cities

Is it possible to create a city that is sustainable and exists in harmony with the surrounding environment? This is the goal of the eco-city, a theoretical model of urban planning and operation that seeks to reduce the environmental impact and enhance the sustainability of urban environments. While engineers, scientists, politicians, activists, and other innovators have been pursuing this agenda since the 1960s, interest in eco-cities has expanded in the twenty-first century as issues like climate change, oceanic degradation, loss of species, and the rising cost of petroleum have pushed environmental issues to the forefront of the public debate.

Environmentalism and the Eco-City Concept

In 1969, a portion of the Cuyahoga River running through Cleveland, Ohio, caught fire, the result of a high level of combustible pollutants floating within the effluent. Though the river had caught fire on numerous other occasions (recorded first in 1868), in 1969, American popular culture was on the verge of an environmental awakening, and the widely publicized event was strange and shocking enough that it became a galvanizing moment in American environmentalism. The Cuyahoga fire inspired the federal government's Clean Water Act, but more important, it inspired hundreds of American citizens to get involved in local environmental issues.[1]

Fossil fuels like petroleum and natural gas, are the products of ancient carbon-based materials (plants, animals, fungus) decomposing within the Earth's crust. Combusting coal, gas, and oil creates heat and energy that is used to create electricity and to power machines. Fossil fuels propelled human society through the Industrial Revolution but environmentalists gradually realized that burning fossil fuels also creates pollution, including "greenhouse gases," like carbon dioxide, that permeate the atmosphere and pollute both the air and water. The gradual realization of the environmental degradation caused by fossil fuels became the primary focus of environmentalism in the 1970s and remains one of the chief environmental issues of the twenty-first century.

The concept of the "eco-city" is often attributed to the nonprofit Berkeley, California, group Urban Ecology formed in the mid-1970s by activist Richard Register.[2] Register and colleagues created urban green projects that included city gardens, tree plantings, urban farming programs, and campaigns against known sources of environmental pollution like automobiles. The organization began publishing the journal *Urban Ecology* in the 1980s and helped to organize the first national and later international conferences for those interested in sustainable urban development.[3]

In the 1990s, Canadian environmentalist Bill Rees coined the term *environmental footprint* to refer to the impact of a person or group on the nonhuman environment.[4] This led to the idea of the "carbon footprint," which attempts to mea-sure the carbon-based pollutants associated with a person, city, or country. Since the 1990s, "carbon footprints" have become a major focus in environmentalism and the idea of creating "low carbon" or "carbon neutral" cities is central to evolving eco-city concepts.

According to the 2015 sustainable cities report from the Amsterdam-based Ar-cadis consulting company, no North American city has yet to make it into the "top ten" sustainable cities in the world. However, Boston, Massachusetts (ranked 15), and Chicago, Illinois (ranked 19), provide examples of cities that have made sig-nificant strides, incorporating public policy and grassroots initiatives to enhance sustainability and reduce environmental impact.[5]

Getting Out of the Greenhouse

Two of the most significant environmental issues of the modern age are climate change and air pollution, and both are intimately linked to transportation. Envi-ronmental Protection Agency (EPA) research indicates that burning fossil fuels for transportation produces 27 percent of greenhouse gas emissions in the United States. Burning fossil fuels to produce electricity is the most significant source, producing more than 67 percent of greenhouse gases.[6] In addition to controversial climate change concerns, greenhouse gases have been demonstrably linked to a variety of health issues including higher levels of cancer; respiratory illnesses; and a variety of minor health concerns like fatigue, cold and flu outbreaks, and nasal congestion.[7]

Air pollution is often higher in urban areas due to the concentration of homes and vehicles. To combat automotive pollution and the peripheral issue of traffic congestion, city governments, environmentalists, and politicians have attempted to encourage alternative modes of transportation, including cycling, walking, carpool-ing, and mass transit. Both in Europe and the United States, "cycling" for commut-ing and urban transportation has become a popular trend in the 2010s. The benefits of cycling are considerable, promoting exercise while simultaneously reducing traf-fic congestion and pollution. Cycling and walking are more popular in cities that have "segregated" or "protected lanes" to protect bicycle and pedestrian traffic from automobiles. In 2015, all 50 states and the District of Columbia had active pro-grams to promote cycling. Among the more innovative efforts are "bicycle sharing" and "bicycle rental" programs that allow commuters to rent a bicycle for temporary use. Philadelphia's "Indego" Bike rental program[8] provides an example, using a com-bination of corporate and municipal investment to create a network of bike rental stations across the city. [9]

According to the U.S. Census Bureau, the number of commuters using bicycles in the United States doubled between 2000 and 2013 (from 488,000 to 882,198). The enthusiasm of cycling culture gives the impression that urban bicycling consti-tutes a transportation "revolution," though the actual impact of cycling on traffic is modest. In 2013, less than 2 percent of commuters used bicycles to get to and from work and estimates indicate that more than three times as many Americans walk rather than using a bicycle for commuting.[10]

Cycling and walking are only viable options for individuals without mobility restrictions and are only useful within a range of environmental conditions. Other alternative transportation methods are therefore necessary and many cities therefore promote mass transit alternatives. In many of America's greenest cities, municipal governments have created programs to decrease the environmental impact of public transportation. In Boston, for instance, the city spent $3.25 million to modify five hundred school buses to reduce carbon emissions. This and similar green initiatives have resulted in Boston being ranked as one the most ecologically efficient cities in the United States.[11] Some cities have considered more radical environmental initiatives to reduce traffic. For instance, city administrators in Hamburg, Germany, have considered plans to ban automobiles completely from the city by 2034.[12] While Hamburg's car-free proposal is a radical example, reducing automobile traffic is essential to creating sustainable cities.

Addressing pollution from the electricity industry is an even more complex issue than combating automotive pollution. The only viable strategy is to invest in the production of alternative energy technology like solar, wind, geothermal, and tidal/wave power. With sufficient investment, the entire energy needs of a nation can be derived from alternative sources. For instance, research from the National Renewable Energy Laboratory suggests that the United States could derive 20 percent of consumer electricity from wind power alone by 2030.[13] U.S. cities lag significantly behind European cities in this regard. In 2014, wind-based electricity exceeded oil-based electricity in Europe, and major cities like London and Copenhagen were aggressively incorporating alternative technology into city planning.

Solar energy production has been increasing in the United States and, between 2000 and 2014, solar energy output increased from 170 megawatts nationwide to over 20,000 megawatts, which is sufficient to provide electricity to more than 4 million average-size homes.[14] Efforts to increase alternative energy production have met with resistance from lobbyists supporting the fossil fuel industry, but have also met with opposition based on a variety of other concerns. For instance, proposals to build an offshore wind power facility 4.8 miles from the Massachusetts coast have been stalled by an influential lobby representing less than 1 percent of the population who object to the project on the basis that the wind turbines will ruin the scenic views for coastal property owners.[15]

Water and Land Management

Another essential step in building eco-cities is protecting the quality of water moving within and through urban areas. This includes metropolitan lakes, rivers, creeks, and coastal areas, but it also applies to sewage and rainwater. Cities are nodes of pollution and produce thousands of gallons of waste that filters into natural reservoirs and water systems. To combat this, the Environmental Protection Agency has created a list of recommendations, called "green infrastructure," for urban businesses, property owners, and governments interested in water preservation. The EPA's green infrastructure programs include botanical installations, such as planting trees and plants in key areas and preserving, restoring, and protecting ecosystems essential to water management like flood plains, swamps, and wetlands. In addition, the EPA recommends a variety of architectural modifications, like permeable pavement and the installation of rain barrels, that can help to preserve water.[16]

Rain barrels, PVC or wooden barrels that capture rainwater and runoff, provide an example of a relatively simple device that has a major impact on water preservation. EPA reports indicate that a single rain barrel can save a homeowner 1,300 gallons of water during peak summer months, and can be used to water plants or lawns or for a variety of other uses. The EPA also recommends installing green roofing, in which a portion of a rooftop is covered in a waterproof membrane and used for planting grass or other plants. Green roofing saves energy by insulating buildings, reducing air pollution, and helping to purify rainwater before it infiltrates the soil and flows to nearby bodies of water.[17]

Strategic urban planning can also have a significant positive impact on the biological diversity of urban ecosystems. For instance, when planting trees or plants, environmentalists recommend choosing native species that are known to occur naturally in the area. Landscaping with indigenous plants provides microhabitats for native animals and oases that can help to allow migratory species to move through, rather than around, cities.[18]

Another innovative use of urban space is the creation of urban agriculture programs in which community lots, rooftop space, and urban yards are used to grow food rather than decorative plants. The U.S. Department of Agriculture studies in 2011 and 2012 indicate that undernourishment is a significant problem in American cities as urban residents often live in food deserts without affordable access to healthy fruits and vegetables.[19] The urban agriculture movement seeks to address this issue by transforming unused or underutilized space into productive agricultural centers. Urban agriculture also increases green spaces that reduce pollution, utilize and preserve rainwater, and contribute to better air quality. Innovative programs like urban beekeeping and rooftop gardens to supply restaurants provide examples of how the creative use of space is contributing to an emerging evolution of the eco-city concept.

Building eco-cities is a long-term goal and the United States, though progressing toward sustainability, lags behind many European and Asian cities in terms of energy and infrastructure investment. With global environmental issues like climate change looming and population growth leading to increased congestion, demand for resources, and pollution, popular interest in sustainable development has never been higher. It remains to be seen however, how long it will take for environmental concerns to inspire the difficult, substantive economic and legislative changes needed to create truly sustainable cities.

Micah L. Issitt

Notes

1. Rotman, "Cuyahoga River Fire."
2. Caprotti, Eco-Cities and the Transition to Low Carbon Economies, 15–19.
3. Urban Ecology, "History."
4. Stoli, "Global Carbon Footprints," 21–22.
5. "Sustainable Cities Index," Arcadis, 2015.
6. "Sources of Greenhouse Gas Emissions," EPA, Jun 2015.
7. "Ambient (Outdoor) Air Quality and Health," WHO.
8. "Indego," 2015.
9. Baskas, "Bike-sharing Booming in US Cities."
10. McKenzie, "Modes Less Traveled."
11. "Transportation Under Greenovation," City of Boston.
12. Eisentein, "A Ban on Autos?"
13. "Large Scale Offshore Wind Power in the United States," NREL.
14. Pentland, "Top 16 U.S. Cities for Solar Power."
15. Williams and Whitcomb, Cape Wind.
16. "What Is Green Infrastructure?" EPA.
17. "Green Roofs," EPA, 2013.
18. "Going Native," NC State University.
19. Coleman-Jensen, et al., "Household Food Security in the United States 2011."

The Best Bike-Sharing Program in the United States

By Tom Vanderbilt
Slate, January 7, 2013

If you had been handed, a decade ago, a map of the U.S. and asked to predict where the novel idea of bike sharing—then limited to a few small-scale projects in a handful of European cities, might first find its firmest footing, you probably would have laid your money on a progressive hub like Portland or Seattle or the regional poles of walkable urbanism, New York or San Francisco—all of which were scoring higher, those days, in surveys like *Bicycling* magazine's list of most bikeable cities. But today, the nation's largest, most successful bike-share program—in terms of size, ridership, and financial viability—is in Washington, D.C. How did D.C. accomplish this unlikely task?

The program was essentially born late one night, two decades ago, in a library.

Paul DeMaio, an urban planning student at the University of Virginia, was doing Internet research ("pre-Google," he notes) when he stumbled upon images of By-Cyklen, a new "city bike" program launched by the city of Copenhagen. Enthralled by the idea, he visited the city, learned what he could about the system, and, eventually, distilled his findings into a master's thesis on bike sharing. Which had about as much impact as the typical master's thesis. "No one was picking it up," he recalls over coffee at D.C.'s Union Station. "I was so upset. But as a 22-year-old, what are you going to do?"

And so the idea, in the U.S. at least, lay dormant, as DeMaio left school and went to work on traffic-calming projects for the city of Alexandria, Va. But DeMaio nurtured the idea, one of a small band of enthusiasts in the world of bike advocacy and in the fringe of city transportation departments, as it rose to prominence in Europe with popular programs like Paris' Velib and programs in Stockholm and Amsterdam, among others. And then one day he was talking with a local colleague—Jim Sebastian, the bicycle coordinator with D.C.'s Department of Transportation. The district's contract for bus shelter advertising was coming up for renewal. "I said, 'Hey Jim, this is what they're doing in Europe—they're offering bike-sharing services as part of an outdoor advertising contract.'" The DDOT, then led by Dan Tangherlini, got behind the idea. And, so tucked into the many-page request for proposals was, he says, a "very short mention of bike sharing." One hundred bikes, 10 stations.

From Slate, January 7 © 2013 The Slate Group. All rights reserved. Used by permission and protected by the Copyright Laws of the United States. The printing, copying, redistribution, or retransmission of this Content without express written permission is prohibited.

And so, in 2008, a few decades after DeMaio's Copenhagen epiphany and a few years after the RFP—Clear Channel, the winner of the bus shelter contract, "wanted to get all their bus shelters out first, and then. . . look into this weird bike thing," jokes DeMaio—Smart Bike DC launched. It was, by most accounts, a noble failure. There were too few stations and bikes to form a meaningful and useful network. The system offered only long-term memberships, rather than offering short-term access via credit card. In fact, it didn't take credit cards at all (so much for capturing the tourist market). Building stations took a lot of time and money. DeMaio himself says he used it only a handful of times.

But D.C. had launched the first commercial bike-sharing program in a major U.S. city, so the idea was planted. And even as Smart Bike was foundering, the ground was being laid for a new, larger, *regional* bike-share system. DeMaio, who now runs his own transport consultancy (and who, in a historical irony of sorts, recently worked on a newly reinvigorated bike-sharing program for the city of Copenhagen), began talking about an improved bike-sharing system with Chris Hamilton, the head of the Commuter Services Bureau of the transportation division in Arlington County, a portion of Virginia just over the river from D.C. "He basically said, 'Why aren't we doing this yet?'" says DeMaio. Dennis Leach, Arlington's transportation director, also signed on. "He's a bike commuter," says DeMaio, "and when we bring him an idea of how we can make bicycling in Arlington better, he jumps at it."

In D.C., Gabe Klein, a former VP at car-sharing pioneer ZipCar and political neophyte, was appointed head of the DOT. He had an "action agenda," as he calls it, with more than 100 items on it—one of which was to launch a larger bike-share system. "Having come from ZipCar," says Klein, now transportation commissioner for the city of Chicago (which, like New York, is launching a big bike-share system this spring), "I knew that any sort of nodal business was only as effective as the number of nodes you have." While SmartBike was useful in terms of getting early adopters onboard and the public used to the idea, it was a trip to Montreal, with its Bixi system, that hinted at what a bike-share system could look like. SmartBike stations, Klein says, "were a construction project. It took months. You had to get PEPCO [the local electrical utility] out there, it had to be wired." Bixi's stations, by contrast, were solar-powered and modular. Where it could take three months to build a SmartBike station, Bixi stations could be set up in three days.

Shortly after his appointment in 2008, Klein, who had worked with Arlington County on ZipCar, began conversations on creating a regional bike-share system. It soon became clear that Clear Channel, which had sponsored the SmartBike experiment, was out. He then went to Adrian Fenty, D.C.'s newly elected, and popular, mayor, and said he wanted to launch a new, larger bike-share system. "He said three things. Number one: Can it be the best out there? I said yes. Can it be the biggest in the U.S.? I said yes. Can you build it such a way that it will be cost-neutral to the city? I said I think so."

Launching a sponsorless bike-share system intended to break even, or even make money, was unprecedented. And having no sponsor made raising capital a challenge, but D.C.-area governments scavenged for the money. "We got lucky," says DeMaio. In Arlington, the Virginia Department of Rail kicked in $200,000; a business-improvement district in Crystal City matched that. The county chipped in more. In D.C., the government used money from the Congestion Mitigation and Air Quality (CMAQ) improvement program. It also tapped its own innovative revenue stream. Through an "enterprise fund" within DOT—funded by things like parking revenues (which, Klein says, had gone up some 400 percent thanks to new technologies like "pay by phone")—Klein says there was "money to match the ongoing growth of the program." Bike sharing, like all politics, is the art of the possible.

And so in 2010, Capital Bikeshare—which has now grown to more than 1,700 bikes and nearly 200 stations, with 8,000 trips a day, across D.C., Maryland, and Virginia—was born. That D.C has been a leader in American bike sharing is somewhat surprising. But D.C. has some inherent qualities that helped make this success possible: A relatively healthy number of cyclists (and an active cycling advocacy scene), a young (and getting younger) population, and a robust tourist market. D.C., notes Klein, is also unique in terms of being a city that is not part of an overseeing state, giving it a certain autonomy. (Much of the resistance, adds Klein, came at the *federal* level, e.g., the National Park Service not wanting bike-share stations on its property.)

But all this kindling needed the continued sparking of progressive planners and policymakers having conversations—at conferences, in offhand remarks at the end of meetings—about this ephemeral, *European* idea. And it helped that the political climate was encouraging. "To be honest," says Klein, "under another mayor, it wouldn't have launched." As it happened, Fenty lost his bid for re-election just as the system was getting off the ground. "That's why it's important to be aware of your time limits," says Klein, adding that the system launched a little over a year after his fateful trip to Montreal.

The project also benefited from Klein's entrepreneurial bent. "I was obsessed with every detail. I wanted the website to really resemble a car-sharing website. The biggest compliment we got was that people were flabbergasted it was being run by the city. They thought it was like ZipCar, a completely private operation."

And, arguably, before bike sharing could succeed in D.C., it had to fail. This, says Harriet Tregoning, the District's Director of Planning, is itself a valuable lesson. "This should be really encouraging to other policy entrepreneurs in the urban space: That you basically can't be an innovative city if you're afraid to fail," she says. "We're delighted that we now have a wonderfully successful bike-share system built on the lessons of a not-so-great initial system."

Just getting a system up and funded is hardly the end of it, of course. It has to work, on any number of levels, from user-interaction to network viability to system legibility. On a drizzly December morning, I performed my own test. Just off the Acela, I call up the Spotcycle app on my phone (here's another key: data transparency) and locate a station a block away from Union Station that is showing plenty of availability. There should, of course, be a bike-share station just *outside* the station, a visible connection—the main lesson transportation should draw from behavioral economics is: *Make it easy*. The more steps—either transactional stages, or literally, walking—required, the less attractive the choice becomes. But in a few minutes, I have joined Capital Bikeshare and am pedaling toward its operational headquarters to meet Eric Gilliland, Capital Bikeshare's general manager, in a warehouse not far from the Nationals stadium.

One of the ironies of bike sharing is the most important role in the company, even more than the bike mechanics, is that of the driver. "This is our biggest employment category," says Gilliland, as he leads to me to the "rebalancing room." In an ideal world (or mathematical model), the supply and demand of trips and bicycles would be in equilibrium—as I left Union Station on that bike, another commuter would be pulling up with a bike of his own to drop off. In reality, though, people's individual trips rarely coincide to maximize network efficiency. After an average Nationals baseball game, for example, says Gilliland, more people want to leave on Capital Bikeshare bikes than arrived that way. "They just don't want to bother with the crowded Metro," he says. For reasons like

> **... D.C. has some inherent qualities that helped make this success possible: A relatively healthy number of cyclists (and an active cycling advocacy scene), a young (and getting younger) population, and a robust tourist market.**

this, Capital Bikeshare's sweep teams spend their days moving bikes around, by van. The morning crew makes sure downtown docks are empty, to accommodate the incoming tide; the late-morning crew shifts bikes back to the neighborhoods ("to give people another opportunity to use the bikes"); the afternoon crew brings bikes downtown for the evening commute.

The system is not without its weaknesses. Work by David Daddio has shown, for example, that many stations are underused, and that a station's success depends largely on five factors: The age of its nearby population; the density of retail outlets (and in particular liquor licenses); the proximity of Metrorail stations; distance from the center of the system itself; and, essentially, the presence of a lot of white people. Gilliland says Capital is trying to counter the demographic skew, not just through geographic expansion, but in a partnership with Bank on D.C. to provide bike-share access to the "unbanked" —i.e., people who don't have credit cards, which are necessary to use the system.

By one important measure, however—revenue—the system is succeeding. While the money from usage fees—cyclists pay a general membership fee, and then pay a bit extra if they want to use a bike for extended periods of time—does not begin to dent the capital costs, says Gilliland, "on an operational basis there are probably six to eight months a year where D.C is actually making money." That sort of "farebox recovery," as planners call it, would be the envy of any transit system. Not that profits should be viewed as an end goal, adds Gilliland. "This is a public good; you don't expect it to make money."

To help defray the costs of expansion, the city, led by its planning department, has been encouraging the funding of bike-share stations by private developers, ranging from a new Wal-Mart in the District to a development by the Shooshan Co. in the Ballston section of Arlington. As D.C. planning head Tregoning explains it, developers, in exchange for a concession—say, having to build fewer "structured parking spaces," agree to pay for a bike station near their property. In a city where only 60 percent of the population has access to a car, says Tregoning, developers are keen to avoid "getting stuck with the parking," i.e., building more parking spaces than they want to in order to comply with mandatory minimums.

In the end, with a lot of intensive groundwork laid, a kind of virtuous circle takes over. You don't have to spend much money marketing the system because, as Gilliland says, "the way most people find out about the bikes in the stations is seeing the bikes in the stations. When it's a busy nice day in the summer, they're all over the place. The stations and bikes themselves are our best advertisement." Installing new stations also becomes more streamlined. "Now, more and more people know what it is," says DeMaio, "so when we go out into the neighborhoods we don't have to spend as much time talking about what it is, but rather we talk about where we want to locate stations." And, gradually, a novel idea promoted by enthusiastic staffers at the lower levels of government begins to become a norm. "There's such a buzz around bike sharing" says DeMaio. "If you were to go to a city and they don't have recycling, you'd think, 'Where am I, in the 1970s?' It's just one of those amenities that you've come to expect, and I think that's definitely becoming true for bike sharing in the U.S."

Streetcorner Serenade for the Public Plaza

By Michael Kimmelman
The New York Times, May 31, 2013

In Brooklyn, the No. 3 subway line ends at New Lots Avenue, where passengers descend from the elevated tracks to what used to be a nasty intersection, trafficked by prostitutes, drug dealers—"You name it," as Eddie Di Benedetto, the owner of Caterina's Pizzeria, put it the other day. Not long ago, a coalition of local merchants and community leaders turned to the New York City Department of Transportation, which runs a program to make traffic circles, triangles and streets into pedestrian plazas.

The department brought in some potted trees and chairs, closed off a short street and voilà, what had been a problem became a boon. Since the plaza opened last summer, crime has plummeted, Mr. Di Benedetto told me, crediting the local police precinct. He heads the New Lots Avenue Triangle Merchants Association.

"People use the place all the time now, meaning the area is watched and safe," he said. "I've had my pizzeria since 1971, so I can tell you, this is a renaissance."

Cities need public spaces like plazas. For years they have mostly been planned from the top down. In New York, zoning laws have carved many of these spaces from commercial developments, which have been given bonuses to include them. Mayor Bloomberg is pushing a new proposal to rezone east Midtown, near Grand Central, that is a variation on this same old trickle-down theme.

But fresh thinking has focused on cheap, quick, temporary and D.I.Y.-style approaches to creating public space—among these, curbside "parklets" in San Francisco and a communal farm on what had been a derelict parcel in the middle of Phoenix. "Small steps, big changes," as Janette Sadik-Khan, the New York City Department of Transportation commissioner, described the logic of plazas like that at New Lots.

And guess what? A beer garden made out of freight containers on an empty plot turns out to be a lot more popular and better for a city than a sad corporate atrium with a few cafe tables and a long list of don'ts on the wall.

As more and more educated Americans, especially younger ones, are looking to move downtown, seeking alternatives to suburbs and cars, they're reframing the demand for public space. They want elbow room and creative sites, cooked up by the community or, like the plaza program, developed from a democratic mix of top-down and bottom-up governance.

From The New York Times, May 31 © 2013 The New York Times. All rights reserved. Used by permission and protected by the Copyright Laws of the United States. The printing, copying, redistribution, or retransmission of this Content without express written permission is prohibited.

The other day I visited Michael Bierut, whose design firm, Pentagram, has drawn the maps that accompany the new bike-share program. Pentagram's New York office faces Madison Square Park. Mr. Bierut remembered when the plaza program started to take over the pedestrian-unfriendly territory where Broadway crosses Fifth Avenue, just next to the park. Traffic patterns improved, but he still thought the city was nuts to create plazas from concrete islands marooned between busy boulevards when there was already, right there, one of the most gorgeous parks in the city.

"Was I wrong," he said, laughing.

The plazas outside his building are mobbed on warm days, with people even toting Shake Shack burgers out of the park to sit next to all the traffic—partly for the view (the Flatiron building one way, the Empire State Building the other) but also for the reason people gravitate to Trafalgar Square in London or the Piazza del Campo in Siena, Italy.

To be in the middle of things.

"It's why we congregate near the kitchen at a dinner party instead of in the living room," said Andy Wiley-Schwartz, who directs the Department of Transportation's plaza program. "That's where you see people coming and going to the fridge to grab a beer and watch stuff happen."

Nationwide, people moving downtown want to be in on the mix, too; they want pedestrian-friendly streets, parks and plazas. And smart cities are responding, like Dallas, whose Klyde Warren Park opened downtown last year atop the Woodall Rodgers Freeway, where it burrows for a few merciful blocks below ground. The place was buzzing when I passed by one recent weekend. In Phoenix, where nearly half of all city lots are vacant, the mayor, Greg Stanton, lately chose an empty 15-acre parcel—an eyesore in the heart of town—for an urban park and garden where nearby residents, mostly immigrants,

> As more and more educated Americans, especially younger ones, are looking to move downtown, seeking alternatives to suburbs and cars, they're reframing the demand for public space. They want elbow room and creative sites, cooked up by the community or, like the plaza program, developed from a democratic mix of top-down and bottom-up governance.

can grow vegetables, for their own tables or to sell at local farmers' markets.

And in San Francisco, the city government has been renting out curbside parking spaces, long term, on the condition they be turned into parklets. Most involve little more than benches and shrubs. But the best have become elaborate interventions, with landscaping, platforms, even mini-mini-golf. I spent a morning watching kids play and adults sunbathe in a parklet outside Fourbarrel Coffee on Valencia Street. Los Angeles and Philadelphia, among others, have recently started parklet programs. New York is trying it out, too.

In the Hayes Valley neighborhood of San Francisco, I also came across a project called Proxy, which recovers the land left behind where a highway had been. After the Central Freeway was taken down, residents petitioned the mayor to do something with a few of the vacant lots it left behind. Douglas Burnham, a local architect who runs the firm Envelope A+D, proposed Proxy: a shifting, temporary campus of modified shipping containers hosting retailers, art galleries and cafés.

Crowds flock to hang out at the Suppenkuche's Biergarten, a scene at night. The architecture is simple. The vibe is friendly. The changing layout conforms to a neighborhood in flux. Local merchants feared Proxy would steal customers away. Instead, it has brought people to the neighborhood.

Back east, retailers in Times Square saw a similar influx after the plaza program closed Broadway to cars. Carmageddon didn't happen; business boomed. Commercial rents in Times Square have doubled during the last year alone.

All these New York plaza projects haven't come up roses. Neighborhoods mostly request plazas with an agreement to look after them; poorer communities, without Business Improvement Districts, have sometimes had trouble with the maintenance.

To aid them, Ms. Sadik-Khan said, the Transportation Department is working with the Horticultural Society of New York and the nonprofit ACE Programs for the Homeless to develop a jobs initiative in which ex-convicts and homeless people provide horticultural services and general upkeep. Communities pay on a sliding scale for the help. It remains to be seen if it delivers.

The process of construction is that the department first lays out the plazas (Pearl Street in the Dumbo area of Brooklyn, for example) with temporary materials. Then the city's Department of Design and Construction takes over, as do outside architects, including well-known and young firms like Snohetta (Times Square), RBA GROUP and DSGN AGNC (Corona, Queens) to consult with local representatives on the final results.

Not surprisingly, bottom-up design usually works better than trickle-down. That east Midtown rezoning plan I mentioned, which the Bloomberg administration is trying to ram through the City Council before the mayor's term expires, would be a bonanza for commercial developers who want to erect giant office towers on Park Avenue and around Grand Central Station. But even as it portends to radically reshape the neighborhood, it treats the public realm (mass transit as well) as an afterthought.

There's a half-baked idea to transform some of Vanderbilt Avenue into a pedestrian street and a plan for public space being drawn up with consultants. In return for the right to build extra big buildings, developers would contribute to a city-run fund that, someday, might act on that plan. It remains a backward approach to addressing public needs.

We've seen what happens the old way. During the early 1960s, zoning codes in New York created privately owned public spaces, or POPS. There are now more than 500 of these plazas, arcades, and atriums—spaces that often nobody wanted, least of all the developers who built them in exchange for gaining millions of extra square feet and other valuable zoning concessions.

I spent a day last month touring sites with Jerold Kayden, an urban planner and Harvard professor. The City Planning Commission has tried in recent years to improve standards and upgrade certain locations, working with outsiders in some cases. Mr. Kayden took me to what had been an especially grim atrium near 62nd Street and Broadway that, with Lincoln Center's patronage, has been turned into the David Rubenstein Atrium, expertly redesigned by Tod Williams and Billie Tsien. There are regular concerts and café tables next to gadget-charging outlets. I chatted with four women running a small dance company in Inwood who meet there every week for the usual reason: to feel in the middle of things, they said.

These public spaces more or less operate on the honor system, so owners take advantage. At Trump Tower, public benches that the building is obliged to provide have been replaced by a sales counter hawking Trump merchandise, and there was no furniture, though promised, on the public terraces. J. P. Morgan Chase, which owns 383 Madison Avenue, has blocked off a lobby that is a public through-space, claiming security concerns. Guards shooed me out the door when I asked whether the building's owners had obtained permission from the city.

Since Occupy Wall Street took over Zuccotti Park, another POPS, owners have drawn up ever more restrictive lists of rules. At 120 Park Avenue, across from Grand Central (years ago the Whitney Museum had a branch there; now it's desolate), a guard stopped me from taking a photograph; at 590 Madison Avenue, formerly the IBM Building, the nicest of the indoor sites, you can't play cards.

New Yorkers deserve better, and have paid for it. As with the rest of the public realm, the priority ought to be public service. Ms. Sadik-Khan is right: Improving public space doesn't always take much. It's good for business. It's good for people.

It's common sense.

Ten Urban Experiments That Your City Should Adopt

By Sasha Abramsky
The Nation, March 4, 2015

It's become all-too-fashionable in recent years to say that American politics is "broken," to throw one's hands up in horror and mutter about stalemate, paralysis, the outsize influence of Big Money and all the other demons of Washington, DC. And, federally, that may well be the case. Yet, at the city level, politics is a whole different ballgame, with a generation of progressive mayors pushing big-picture reforms on a scale not seen in years. As a result, many regions are being remade for the better around creative approaches to the environment, mixed-income housing, transport, employment, schooling, health and food.

Seattle has garnered international attention with its move to increase the city-wide minimum wage to $15 an hour, achieved after socialist Councilwoman Kshama Sawant pushed the issue to the fore during her 2013 campaign, and after her victory convinced Mayor Ed Murray of the electoral benefits of embracing the higher wage. In its wake, San Diego, San Francisco and many other cities have moved toward far higher minimum wages than those guaranteed both federally and at the state level.

Portland, Oregon, meanwhile, has long been renowned for pioneering investments in public transport, creating near-total access to buses and light rail, and helping secure its place as one of the country's most livable cities. And in New York, Mayor Bill de Blasio has pioneered a universal prekindergarten program, offering a preschool place to any child whose parents want it. In September 2014, more than 50,000 kids began attending city-run and city-funded prekindergartens, and the number is expected to rise next year to more than 70,000. Many of America's other large cities, including Seattle, Denver, Boston, San Francisco, Los Angeles, Chicago and DC, are also moving toward universal preschool access.

But the city-level changes in America go far beyond these headline-generating moves. Often out of the public spotlight, hundreds, if not thousands, of creative programs and policy experiments are being pushed in cities from Honolulu to Miami, Chicago to Houston. Ideas range from the distribution of free laptops to kids in poor neighborhoods, as in parts of Miami, to innovative public-health strategies to contain the spread of hepatitis and HIV among intravenous drug users in Albuquerque, to Cleveland's well-publicized support for the worker-owned Evergreen Cooperative.

From The Nation, March 4 © 2015 The Nation Company, LLC. All rights reserved. Used by permission and protected by the Copyright Laws of the United States. The printing, copying, redistribution, or retransmission of this Content without express written permission is prohibited.

Here are ten urban experiments that have resulted in major changes in the lives of residents. While not generating the headlines of Seattle's minimum-wage increase or New York's preschool guarantee, they nonetheless merit attention, both for their stand-alone promise and their potential to inspire copycat programs that shift the terrain across the country. "It's like turning a paddle ship," says John Duda of the Democracy Collaborative, which has been working with the city of Jacksonville, Florida, to forge a Community Wealth Building Roundtable. "You do it slowly, but if it works, the results will be very important."

Detroit's Urban Gardens

Long considered a near-apocalyptic example of what happens when a big city hits the skids and goes into a steep population decline, Detroit has become home to a vast network of urban farms and gardens. Out of dystopia is emerging, in some neighborhoods, a strangely utopian social experiment.

The transformation of Detroit's abandoned lots into sustainable green spaces started as a somewhat inchoate phenomenon, the farms begun by desperate residents simply trying to survive. But in recent years, urban farming has coalesced into a more organized movement with a fair degree of political clout, the farmers represented by an array of organizations. The Garden Resource Program, which supplies information as well as seeds and vegetable transplants to residents who want to start farming, supports 1,400 farms and gardens in Detroit alone, growing everything from tomatoes to apples. Some even host cattle and goats.

While the city administration was initially hostile, it has recently embraced this trend, realizing that the farms may be Detroit's last, best chance to convert abandoned lots back into something productive. A staggering 200,000 parcels of land were vacant in the city and its surrounding area in 2012. A year later, the City Council passed a zoning ordinance allowing agriculture within the city limits. Farmers' markets are now emerging, and restaurants have started selling meals cooked with city-grown produce.

Philadelphia's Land Bank

Like many other old East Coast and Rust Belt cities, Philadelphia has long been pocked by vast tracts of blight. The best estimates place the number of vacant or abandoned lots between 30,000 and 40,000. These buildings have, historically, ended up owned by numerous different city agencies, with an utter lack of coordination characterizing the process.

The term "land bank" can make one's eyes glaze over. But, in fact, the land bank movement represents an important effort to tackle both urban blight and the ongoing impact of the foreclosure epidemic. And it has been embraced by New York State, Michigan and a number of other locales.

The Philadelphia Land Bank, which is the country's newest big-city land bank, could end up in charge of more than 8,000 buildings, creating a huge opportunity to regenerate long-neglected neighborhoods as well as to preserve affordable housing in gentrifying districts. It is backed by a $4 million starting budget and brings together an array of community and business groups, as well as city agencies. And it has a comprehensive plan to convert these lots to uses that will benefit the community: affordable housing, community centers, urban gardens and so on. Rick Sauer, executive director of the Philadelphia Association of Community Development Corporations, summarized the goal: "Get the property to folks who are going to put it to productive use, and get the property back on the tax roll."

New Orleans's Jack & Jake's and California's Fresh Approach

Although the Big Easy is one of America's great culinary centers, diabetes and obesity have long plagued the city and, in particular, its poor residents. Many parts of town, especially after Hurricane Katrina wiped out local businesses, are food deserts, lacking ready access to healthy foods.

Entrepreneur John Burns has sought to change this. With the help of funding from progressive social impact investors and the city, his company Jack & Jake's has opened several large wholesale outlets since 2011 that work with local farmers and fishermen to get healthy food into grocery stores and restaurants. In early spring, the company is set to open a 27,000-square-foot market–cum–food court in an abandoned schoolhouse in the Central City neighborhood. If the strategy works, it will open low-cost stores featuring healthy alternatives to junk food—both fresh produce and prepared local dishes—in poor, diabetes-ravaged communities throughout the South and Appalachia. "This model is attractive," argues Burns, "because it's not the traditional grocery store model."

All of this is part of a broader strategy to prioritize social impact investments in post-Katrina New Orleans and to convert disused warehouses, schools and other large spaces into hubs for economic activity in poor neighborhoods. Will it work? The Big Easy still has a long way to go. But if it can find a way to tackle the obesity and diabetes epidemics that afflict its impoverished communities, that will be its own kind of triumph.

With the same goals in mind, Los Angeles, San Francisco and other California metropolises have chosen a different strategy to get healthy food onto the plates of low-income residents. The California Market Match Consortium's Fresh Approach programs take the economic sting out of buying fruits and vegetables by providing poor Californians with $5 worth of free produce every time they spend $10 of CalFresh benefits (the state's version of food stamps) at a participating farmers' market. In 2013, CMMC released a report showing that, since the program's inception in 2009, the use of CalFresh benefits at farmers' markets had grown by 171 percent. In other words, poor Californians are getting healthier food thanks to this effort.

Austin's Smart Housing Program

The Lone Star State's progressive capital has bucked the car-centric, economically segregated design of other big Texas cities, promoting affordable mixed-income housing development anchored by easy access to public-transit systems. And, since

Austin is now the second-fastest-growing city in the United States, that's no mean achievement.

Under SMART (which stands for Safe. Mixed income. Accessible. Reasonably priced. Transit oriented), the more units a developer sells or rents at prices affordable to a family earning less than 80 percent of the city's median income, the greater the percentage of fee waivers the city gives. Once 40 percent of units in a given development are "affordable," the city waives all of the developer's fees. What makes Austin's program more interesting, however, is that it's not just about affordability; it's also about access. Built into the SMART codes are requirements that SMART-qualified housing be within a half-mile of a bus route. That's a slightly less stringent requirement than the program initially had, but still one that keeps Austin a public transit–centered city as it expands.

Atlanta's East Lake Public Housing Redevelopment

Austin isn't alone in pushing for creative, mixed-income solutions to the housing crunch. In Atlanta, the area of East Lake, once home to one of the city's largest public-housing tracts, has been redeveloped by a group called Purpose Built Communities (PBC). With a mixture of public and private funding, large swaths of desperately poor and dangerous public-housing blocks—the biggest contiguous swath of public housing in the South—have been replaced by low-rise, mixed-income neighborhoods, along with new schools and businesses.

The East Lake changes have been successful in large part because they have taken place with the support and engagement of local residents. How was that support won? By the city, under then-mayor Shirley Franklin, committing not to push the existing residents out of the neighborhood—as has happened elsewhere when public-housing tower blocks have been replaced by mixed-income, low-rise dwellings—and by a participatory process that brought local residents to the table when changes were broached. Franklin has since become president of PBC.

Salt Lake City's Housing Program for Homeless Veterans

In January 2014, Salt Lake City, the capital of Utah—a state that is hardly known for its progressive vision—made history by becoming the second city in the country to end homelessness among military veterans. (Phoenix was the first.) How did Salt Lake City do it? While other urban hubs were busy passing laws to arrest people for panhandling or sleeping in public, Salt Lake City opted for the more humane, and ultimately more practical, approach of providing homes for its homeless vets. Inspired by the "housing first" philosophy, the program aggressively links homeless men and women with housing—by finding and building apartments—while also providing access to counseling and other support services.

Salt Lake City's experiment is part of a still more ambitious statewide housing first program, which is working to provide permanent homes to 2,000 chronically homeless residents, many in the urban environs of Salt Lake City. Somewhat counterintuitively, Utah has found that providing homes to the homeless, and then

> While the city administration was initially hostile, it has recently embraced this trend, realizing that the farms may be Detroit's last, best chance to convert abandoned lots back into something productive.

helping with mental health treatment and job searches, comes in many thousands of dollars cheaper than leaving homeless men and women to cycle in and out of jails, prisons, hospitals and shelters. According to the best estimates, the cost of housing a homeless person averages about $12,000 a year, whereas the cost of leaving a person to the streets can climb to more than $20,000 a year.

Burlington's Champlain Housing Trust

Back in the mid-1980s, progressive politicians in Burlington, Vermont, began fearing that the influx of moneyed homeowners from the big East Coast cities was making their town unaffordable to local residents. So they decided to act: they formed a Community and Economic Development Office, which then put up $200,000 in seed funds for a city land trust that began buying up local properties, selling them at subsidized rates and reinvesting profits in more properties.

The intent? To build up, over a period of decades, a large stock of homes rented or owned by low- and moderate-income locals at below-market rates, with the land trust putting up a percentage of the initial purchase price in exchange for a share in the profits when the owner eventually sells the home. To help maintain these homes, the housing trust also provides residents with low-cost loans for repairs and for environmental upgrades. And, to ensure that the homes stay affordable from one owner to the next, owners have to sell at a designated price: what they paid originally, plus 25 percent of the appreciation in value that the house would have had on the open market. In other words, say a house was bought originally for $100,000, but is now worth $200,000. When the owner sells back to the housing trust, the trust only has to pay $125,000. Think of it as akin to rent stabilization, but for homeownership. Roughly 2,000 individuals and families are now in the city's Housing Trust homes.

Chicago's Green Roofs

When the word "environmental" is bandied about, one doesn't immediately think "Chicago." Yet when it comes to green roofs, the Windy City has led the way for more than a decade (though in recent years its dominance has been challenged by New York; Portland; and Washington, DC). Its transformation began more than fifteen years ago, after Richard Daley, who was mayor, visited Europe in the wake of a heat wave in Chicago that had killed upward of 700 people. There he saw innovative urban environmental planning, including the widespread use of green roofs, and came back inspired to emulate some of the design ideas pioneered in Copenhagen and various German cities. His first big move was to transform City Hall's roof in 2001 into a garden made up of tens of thousands of plants. At the same time, the city enacted incentives for developers, from speeding the permit process to offering grants, and allowed green-roofed buildings to have additional floor space.

Citywide, there are now over 500 green roofs (amounting to 5 million square feet), and Michael Berkshire, the green projects administrator for Chicago's Department of Housing and Economic Development, says the city's heat-amelioration and water-absorption plans extend far beyond roofing, to the laying of permeable pavements, the planting of rain gardens designed to soak up excess water, and the growing of "urban forests." "We're looking at all forms of green infrastructure," Berkshire explains, "adding vegetation wherever we can within the urban landscape."

Boulder's Carbon Tax

Nine years ago, Boulder, Colorado, voters passed the country's first carbon tax, electing to charge themselves roughly $7 per metric ton. The tax covered all electricity usage in the city, although homeowners who use alternative energy sources, such as wind power, qualify for rebates. In 2009, the city increased the tax rate another few dollars per ton.

While the program hasn't been the financial windfall some predicted, generating less than a third of the anticipated revenue, it has still cut emissions by well over 100,000 metric tons per year. And the money raised has been plowed back into energy-efficiency investments.

Boulder's tax has been recognized internationally by climate activists, and modified versions of the program have been implemented in other US cities. The program remains popular: in 2012, 82 percent of residents voted to keep the carbon tax for five more years. In a uniquely Boulder-esque twist, the city recently responded to Colorado's legalization of marijuana by imposing an extra carbon tax on industrial-scale pot producers.

New-Age Central Parks

By Rutherford H. Platt and Peter Harnik
Planning, July 1, 2015

City parks don't just happen; each is a unique blend of nature, technology, design, culture, politics, and vision. Many European city parks are remnants of former royal estates. Examples include London's Hyde Park and Regent's Park, Jardin des Tuileries and Jardin du Luxembourg in Paris, Berlin's Tiergarten, and Vienna Woods.

American cities, lacking such aristocratic legacies, have had to fabricate parks out of colonial commons in New England, former military sites like San Francisco's Presidio, filled land such as Chicago's lakeshore, distinctive natural or scenic sites, or simply nooks and crannies of underused land.

An early notable example in the U.S. was the audacious 1858 Greensward Plan for Central Park by Frederick Law Olmsted and Calvert Vaux, which transformed 843 acres of rocky wasteland into the world's best known urban park. That masterwork in turn spawned an urban parks movement that endowed American cities with hundreds of parks and landscapes designed by Olmsted and his successors until the 1970s.

That era is over: Big new parks on the scale of Central Park aren't feasible today. One attempt to convert a former military base into a 1,300-acre Great Park in Orange County, California, has been tangled in design and financing issues. The winning design for Governors Island in New York Harbor may be as innovative as Greensward in its day, but the island can only be reached by ferry. One of us (Harnik) has documented how parks now are cobbled together in surprising places like rooftops, landfills, cemeteries, freeway decks, and stormwater channels.

While the size and complexity of the great Olmsted parks can't be replicated today, a new generation of much smaller but hugely successful facilities may claim to be "new-age Central Parks." This judgment is based not on whether they look Olmstedian; most do not. Rather, the resemblance lies in their audacity: How bold are they in concept and execution and how inventively do they use available scraps of urban space and serve diverse people?

The audacity of Central Park was reflected in such factors as:

- **VISION**: advocacy by New York civic leaders to set aside a "central park" before Manhattan Island was fully built out
- **OPPORTUNISM**: New York City's timely purchase of underused land in the path of development as a site for the future park

Copyright 2015 by the American Planning Association. Reprinted by permission of Planning magazine.

- **INGENUITY**: creative adaptation of legal authorities, technology, financing, and landscape design
- **TENACITY**: confronting bureaucracy and politics, requiring leaders and activists with unusual creativity, stamina, and political skills
- **HUMANISM**: in Olmsted's words, welcoming "vast numbers of persons brought closely together, poor and rich, young and old, Jew and Gentile."

With these indicators in mind, we now visit some of our favorite "new-age Central Parks," beginning in New York City, close to the mother lode.

New York and Vicinity

Since the 1980s, much of New York City's waterfront has been transformed from a no-man's-land of derelict piers and warehouses to a green fringe of exciting new parks and bikeways. Unlike the Chicago lakeshore parks, which are managed chiefly by one agency (the Chicago Park District), New York's waterfront is a hodgepodge of diverse facilities, each with its own history, physical obstacles, vested interests, design features, funding sources, and administrative structure.

Riverbank State Park is one of the city's busiest but least known newer parks. It occupies the 28-acre rooftop of the North River Sewage Treatment Plant, which extends 600 feet into the Hudson River at the edge of Harlem. The park originated as "compensation" to offset the environmental injustice of placing the city's biggest sewage plant on the doorstep of one of its poorest communities.

Designed and constructed over 15 years (1978–1993) by Dattner Architects and ABB Landscape Architects, Riverbank features an Olympic-size swimming pool, basketball and tennis courts, garden plots, a year-round skating rink, cultural center, restaurant, and a 2,500-seat athletic complex. Modeled on Tokyo's Arakawa Nature Park, it demonstrates the feasibility of locating a park above municipal infrastructure and folding its capital cost into the overall project budget. Riverbank State Park attracts about four million visitors a year.

Continuing downstream, the west side of Manhattan is lined by eclectic old and new parks: Riverside Park, originated by Olmsted and completed by Robert Moses in the 1920s; Riverside Park South, donated by Donald Trump in the 1990s as a condition for approval of a high-end residential complex; Hudson River Park, built and managed by a state-created authority after defeat of a massive highway and park project (Westway) in the 1980s; Battery Park City, with 36 acres of public parks provided by the BPC development authority; and Battery Park, a historic common ground dating back to Dutch settlement in 1623.

Just inland from Hudson River Park, the renowned High Line snakes around former lofts and warehouses now going upscale at a dizzying pace. The High Line is a showcase of new-age park creation. An abandoned 1.45-mile rail viaduct on Manhattan's Lower West Side provided the opportunity. The vision to convert it into a linear public park, modeled on the Promenade Plantee in Paris, originated with neighborhood residents Robert Hammond and Joshua David, who founded the Friends of the High Line Greenway, Inc. in 1999.

Some $50 million from the city and even more in private donations funded an international design competition in 2003. The winning concept by James Corner Field Operations in partnership with Diller Scofidio+Renfro and Piet Oudolf has transformed the rusty viaduct into an elevated ribbon of walkways, gardens, casual seating, and public art—entirely removed from traffic and offering glorious views of the city and the Hudson River.

As a public-private partnership, the High Line is city-owned but by the well-financed Friends of the High Line. Now open for its entire length, the High Line is jammed with residents and tourists, in good weather and bad. Surrounding neighborhoods are exploding in value and new development is going up at a scale perhaps not seen since Central Park itself was built.

Just across the East River from lower Manhattan, the acclaimed Brooklyn Bridge Park, which won a 2014 National Planning Excellence Award for Urban Design from APA [American Planning Association], is shoehorned onto a 1.3-mile strip of waterfront and abandoned piers bordered on the inland side by the Brooklyn Heights Promenade and the Robert Moses–era Brooklyn-Queens Expressway. BBP's modest 85 acres (one-tenth the size of Central Park) is offset by inventive design and stunning views of the Manhattan skyline, with the Brooklyn Bridge and Manhattan Bridge arching overhead.

The vision for the park came from a community group, Friends of Fulton Landing (later renamed the Brooklyn Bridge Park Coalition), when the Port Authority of New York and New Jersey decided in 1984 to divest some obsolete waterfront properties. In 2002, the coalition persuaded the city and state to establish the BBP Development Corporation to design, build, and operate the park. Public agencies contributed $360 million toward its construction, but operating costs were to be generated mostly from concession revenue and high-end real estate development.

Under the 2005 BBP master plan by Michael Van Valkenburgh Associates, the challenging site (including its piers) has been transformed into a collage of small hills, lawns, trees, playgrounds, sports fields, food vendors, wetlands, a pocket beach, boat ramps, and the 1920s-era Jane's Carousel, restored and donated by a local couple, Jane and David Walentas.

In October 2012, when Hurricane Sandy slammed the new park with a 13-foot storm surge, thousand-pound concrete planters became floating objects, low-lying electrical and mechanical equipment was disabled, and some playgrounds and landscaping were damaged. But the Van Valkenburgh plan anticipated sea-level rise in its selection of park elevations, soil types, vegetation, tree placement, and edge design, and timely sandbagging narrowly saved Jane's Carousel.

The unusual practice of funding a parks operation from real estate development inside its boundaries remains controversial. In April 2015, completion of a luxury residential building was stayed by court order pending the outcome of a lawsuit by a neighborhood group, Save the View Now, which fears the project will obstruct views of the Brooklyn Bridge and Midtown Manhattan. Eighty miles north of Times Square, the Hudson River is spanned by another audacious new park: the Walkway Over the Hudson. In 1889, the Poughkeepsie-Highland Railroad Bridge opened as the longest bridge in North America and the only Hudson River span south of Albany at the time. Until closed by a fire in 1974, the 1.28-mile bridge was a vital route for trains bringing coal from Pennsylvania to New England.

Due to be scrapped, the decrepit bridge attracted the attention of Poughkeepsie resident Bill Sepe, who saw an opportunity to create a level-grade bike and walking route high above the most scenic reach of the mid-Hudson Valley. In 1992, Sepe and a local attorney founded Walkway Over the Hudson to promote the project.

Seventeen years later, at a cost of $38 million (substantially provided by the Dyson Foundation in Millbrook, New York), the bridge reopened as the Walkway Over the Hudson State Historic Park. Now paved, lighted, and handicap accessible, the span is the world's longest elevated walkway—and one of the highest at about 200 feet above the river and the Poughkeepsie riverfront. A 21-story high-speed elevator, completed in 2014, connects the walkway deck with a riverfront park and train station beneath it. Some 700,000 people visit the walkway annually.

Ironically, both the walkway and the High Line benefited from a kind of making-the-best-of-it audacity. Each used obsolete structures that were too big to tear down. (Simply removing the elevated viaduct in Manhattan would have cost Consolidated Rail Corporation about $30 million.) The new park facilities were in effect "Plan B" concepts to save the government from expensively tearing down a huge, orphan structure.

Around the Country

Chicago's much admired 30-mile chain of lakefront parks was long interrupted by a gaping void of parking lots and train tracks east of the city's Loop, its downtown business district, so named for the elevated train tracks that encircle it.

In 1997, Mayor Richard M. Daley, reportedly looking down at the unattractive scene from his dentist's office, resolved to seize a golden opportunity to convert this beleaguered site into a world-class park. His germ of an idea, implemented by a formidable public-private partnership, led to the construction of Millennium Park on a 25-acre platform above a new parking garage. At $475 million (split

> The new park facilities were in effect "Plan B" concepts to save the government from expensively tearing down a huge, orphan structure.

about fifty-fifty public and private), Millennium is the most expensive city park ever created, but the investment has already stimulated billions of dollars in nearby real estate construction and tourist spending.

When it opened in 2004, Millennium Park attracted more than 1.5 million visitors in its first six months, lured by its many delights: the wading pool between digital towers at Crown Fountain, a native-plant horticulture garden, a mirrored sculpture (Cloud Gate, usually called "the Bean"), a sinuous pedestrian bridge and outdoor performance extravaganza (both designed by Frank Gehry), and a bicycle station for commuters.

Located downtown, Millennium Park established a new public focal point and center-city destination, and thousands of high-end apartments and condos have since been constructed within sight of it. Its role as a free and democratic playground for millions of people is in the best Olmsted tradition.

Also downtown and connected to Millennium Park by the Gehry bridge, the 25-acre Maggie Daley Park is named for the late wife of the former mayor. Opened [in the spring of 2015], it reenvisions a corner of the enormous lakefront Grant Park, where seldom used tennis courts and formal gardens have been replaced with climbing walls, undulating hills, an ice skating ribbon, and inventive, adventuresome play spaces.

There's a great new park in Dallas, too, although its genesis came at a painful moment for the city. When the Boeing Corporation announced the relocation of its headquarters from Seattle to Chicago in 2001, the news hit Dallas like a bombshell. Dallas had been a contender and was accustomed to winning these kinds of competitions, especially when up against older Rust Belt cities. But Boeing let it be known that it was the quality of urban living—including parks—that had tipped the balance to Chicago.

Dallas's powerful corporate community immediately began refocusing from simple growth to complex placemaking. And the city sprang into action on both the public and private fronts. Among many parks that have grown from these initiatives, the most transformative has been Klyde Warren Park, designed by the Office of James Burnett and built on a deck over the Woodall Rogers Freeway.

Barely five acres in size, the park packs in a load of spaces from dog park to event lawn, to reading and games courtyard, to jogging trail, to performance pavilion, to restaurant, along with more than 300 trees and 900 shrubs. Further, the park links downtown office towers and cultural icons with the arts district and residences situated in uptown.

Because the park has healed the 50-year-old gash of the below-grade freeway, it has stimulated downtown high-rise housing, something quite rare in Dallas. Named for the nine-year-old son of the park's biggest benefactor, Klyde Warren Park is certainly not Olmstedian in design or in conception, but it is having the kind of impact on real estate and city shaping that the best of the greensward parks did more than a century ago.

Klyde Warren Park is not the first park to be built on a deck over a highway—the earliest on record was built in New York City in 1939—but it is quickly becoming the most influential since Seattle's Freeway Park opened to great fanfare during the nation's bicentennial year in 1976. The concept of a green and social oasis in the middle of a human and architectural bazaar is so novel and intriguing in formerly white-bread Dallas that it has become the place to see and be seen, just as Olmsted's more bucolic parks first were 150 years ago.

Not to be outdone in the new city park competition is Houston, Dallas's friendly rival. Already home to 445-acre Hermann Park (with the city's zoo and an iconic lake) and 1,466-acre Memorial Park (whose three-mile running track gets 10,000 users a day), Houston now boasts a new 12-acre gem in the bull's-eye center of its downtown. Called Discovery Green, the $182 million park was carved out of former parking lots and several streets that the city decertified and donated to the assemblage.

Funded about one-third publicly and two-thirds privately, the park is chock full of things to see, use, and experience—a playground, interactive fountain, dog park, café, putting green, kayaking pond, model boat basin, ice skating rink—and, like Klyde Warren, has stimulated a localized development boom, including the first downtown apartment tower built in 50 years. Discovery Green is located near the city's gargantuan Convention Center—the kind of facility that is usually the kiss of death for its surrounding neighborhood—but with 1.2 million park visitors a year, it thus far has held its own against the needs of out-of-town conventioneers with other things on their minds.

Thanks to aggressive programming by the indefatigable Discovery Green Conservancy, the park is being adopted by Houstonians as their own special place. Although the number of children living downtown is still small, the Houston Independent School District schedules numerous field trips to the park, and Discovery Green is frequently encircled by yellow buses while students play in the water, listen to music, learn ecology, picnic, or happily take part in other activities.

Other cities are making their marks with high-profile parks as well. Cincinnati has invested $120 million its downtown front. Smale Riverfront Park is a dramatic 45-acre destination that includes a stage and event lawn, an adventure playground, a carousel, a stairway that incorporates a light show, two interactive fountains, a striking Civil War monument to the Black Brigade, tree groves, a meditative labyrinth, a bike center, and a brewpub. (Future phases will include a marina and a boat dock.)

Cincinnati has, in fact, boasted an exemplary park system for many decades, but since the hilly city is segmented into dozens of insulated neighborhoods, each with its own special green space, there has been no central park that all citizens could share as owners. Smale Park, located in Cincinnati's front yard, between the baseball and football stadiums and facing the iconic Roebling Bridge, solves that problem in a way that would make Olmsted proud. Fittingly, despite the high-tech nature of some of the amenities, the park's most memorable and coveted features are the gently swinging steel benches with their alluring vistas of the Ohio River and Kentucky in the distance.

Small but Mighty

Not every city park can or should be as iconic as Millennium Park or the High Line. Older city neighborhoods are often served only by scruffy, down-at-the-heels parks in dire need of help. The "new-age Central Parks" summarized in this article represent the most audacious level of park creation in the finest Olmsted tradition. But even the humblest city park may be revitalized through neighborhood initiative, supported by public and private funding.

The New York Restoration Project founded by Bette Midler has revitalized many neglected parks in distressed neighborhoods of New York City. While not

world-class showcases, such revived parks may also reflect the humanitarian in-
stincts of Frederick Law Olmsted and his successors. Nearly two centuries after his
birth, creating and revitalizing city parks is a crucial part of making urban America
more green, healthy, equitable, and humane.

Aging Pipes Are Poisoning America's Tap Water

By Alana Semuels
The Atlantic, July 29, 2015

Melissa Mays looks around the emergency room at a frail, elderly man in a wheelchair and a woman with a hacking cough and can't quite believe she's here. Until a few months ago, she was healthy—an active mother of three boys who found time to go to the gym while holding down a job as a media consultant and doing publicity for bands.

But lately, she's been feeling sluggish. She's developed a rash on her leg, and clumps of her hair are falling out. She ended up in the emergency room last week after feeling "like [her] brain exploded," hearing pops, and experiencing severe pain in one side of her head.

Mays blames her sudden spate of health problems on the water in her hometown of Flint. She says it has a blue tint when it comes out of her faucet, and lab results indicate it has high amounts of copper and lead. Her family hasn't been drinking the water for some months, but they have been bathing in it, since they have no alternative.

"It set off a train wreck in my system," Mays told me, sitting in the emergency room. Later, doctors would put her on beta blockers after finding problems in the arteries around her brain.

In the past 16 months, abnormally high levels of e. coli, trihamlomethanes, lead, and copper have been found in the city's water, which comes from the local river (a dead body and an abandoned car were also found in the same river). Mays and other residents say that the city government endangered their health when it stopped buying water from Detroit last year and instead started selling residents treated water from the Flint River. "I've never seen a first-world city have such disregard for human safety," she told me.

While Flint's government and its financial struggles certainly have a role to play in the city's water woes, the city may actually be a canary in the coal mine, signaling more problems to come across the country. "Flint is an extreme case, but nationally, there's been a lack of investment in water infrastructure," said Eric Scorsone, an economist at Michigan State University who has followed the case of Flint. "This is a common problem nationally— infrastructure maintenance has not kept up."

© 2015 The Atlantic Media Co., as first published in The Atlantic Magazine. All rights reserved. Distributed by Tribune Content Agency, LLC

Indeed, water scarcity in the parched West might be getting the most news coverage, but infrastructure delays and climate change are causing big problems for cities in the North and Midwest, too. Last summer, hundreds of thousands of people in Toledo were told not to drink tap water because tests showed abnormally high levels of microcystins, perhaps related to algae blooms in Lake Erie. Microcystins can cause fever, headaches, vomiting, and—in rare cases—seizures. Heavy rainfall has caused backups in the filtering process at overloaded water-treatment plants in Pennsylvania, and so residents are frequently finding themselves under advisories to boil water. And Chicago, which installed lead service lines in many areas in the 1980s, is now facing a spike in lead-contaminated tap water.

In 2013, America received a "D" in the drinking-water category of the American Society for Civil Engineers' Report Card for America's Infrastructure. The report found that most of the nation's drinking-water infrastructure is "nearing the end of its useful life." Replacing the nation's pipes would cost more than $1 trillion. The country's wastewater infrastructure also got a "D" grade.

Like many cities in America, Flint has lost residents but still has to provide services like water and sewer and road maintenance within the same boundaries. All while bringing in less tax revenue to pay for it. Flint has not had the money to spend on crucial infrastructure upgrades, and has left old pipes in place for longer than most engineers would recommend. Water prices are rising in Flint, like they are in lots of other cities, but the quality of water is getting worse, not better.

Flint has financially struggled for longer than most American cities. The birthplace of General Motors, the city began having problems in the 1980s and 1990s when GM started closing plants. By 2001, its unemployment rate was 11.2 percent, which grew every year until it reached 25 percent in 2009. Families began to seek opportunity elsewhere, leaving behind empty homes. As the city's population declined, it struggled to come up with the revenue to provide basic services such as police and fire coverage for residents. The water system, though, was still a "cash cow," said Scorsone, the professor, so Flint borrowed from the water authority to pay its city bills.

Flint has been buying water from Detroit since 1967. The Detroit Water and Sewer Department, in the booming postwar years, expanded its services, adding 1,000 square miles of territory. But as the population began to shrink in both Detroit and Flint, fewer customers were left to pay for infrastructure and services. Detroit began raising rates, but Flint didn't pass those rate increases on to customers because residents were struggling economically and politicians worried they'd get voted out of office, said Scorsone. That meant that little to no money was spent on infrastructure upgrades.

In 2004, Detroit charged Flint $11.06 per million cubic foot of water. By 2013, it was charging $19.12 per million cubic foot, a 73 percent increase.

"It's a combination of bad management and bad economics," Scorsone said.

By 2011, Flint had a $15 million deficit and Michigan Governor Rick Snyder appointed an emergency manager to take control over the city. It was a move that upset many, since emergency managers are used to replace elected officials such as city councils and mayors and have widespread authority, but less connection to residents. In 2012, Michigan voters repealed an emergency-manager law that had allowed emergency managers to take over troubled cities and school districts. But the state legislature then passed a different, and more far-reaching, emergency-manager law later that year. A group of citizens, including some from Flint, filed a lawsuit arguing that the law violated their constitutional right to equal protection. In November, a judge allowed the suit to go forward.

Unwilling to pay rising Detroit water costs, Genesee County, where Flint is located, decided to work with other Michigan counties to build a pipeline from Lake Huron to mid-Michigan. But the pipeline, called the Karegnondi Water Authority, won't be completed until late 2016. So in 2013, Flint decided that until the pipeline was finished, it would pump water from the Flint River, treat it, and sell it to residents. The plan would save the city much-needed money: The annual cost to treat water from the Flint River is $2.8 million, said Howard Croft, the city's public-works director. Buying water from Detroit, on the other hand, costs $12 million a year.

But making river water safe for public use is a much more difficult task than treating reservoir or lake water. Rivers are subject to runoff and the water quality can change quickly with air temperature or heavy storms. Flint found this out as soon as it turned off the pumps from Detroit and started pumping its own water in April 2014.

Residents said they noticed the difference almost immediately. Melissa Mays says her water started smelling like rotten eggs, and had a strange tint when coming out of the faucet, sometimes blue, sometimes yellowish.

Claire McClinton, a GM retiree, said her house began to smell like garbage. Another resident, Bethany Hazard, says her water started coming out of the faucet brown and smelling like a sewer, and when she called the city to complain, she was told the water was fine.

The water was not fine. First, tests showed there was fecal coliform bacteria in the water, and the city had to issue numerous boil advisories to citizens. In response, engineers upped the amount of chlorine in its water, leading to dangerously high levels of trihalomethanes, or TTHMs, which put Flint in violation of the Clean Water Act. TTHMs are especially dangerous when inhaled, making showering in hot water toxic.

By October, GM, which still has a plant in Flint, had started noticing that the water was corroding parts of its engines. The plant switched off the Flint water, and started trucking in water from elsewhere. It asked the city for permission to use water from Flint Township, rather than the city of Flint (Flint Township was still buying water from Detroit), and switched back to Detroit water, said spokesman Tom Wickham.

LeeAnne Walters didn't notice any changes right away. But a few months after the switch, she noticed that her children were getting rashes between their fingers, on their shins, on the back of their knees. Her four-year-old son, who has a compromised immune system, started breaking out into scaly rashes whenever he swam in their salt-water pool, which he'd used since birth. Then Walters' 14-year-old son got extremely sick and missed a month of school.

So she sent her water off to Marc Edwards, a Virginia Tech environmental engineering professor who had forced the CDC to admit it had misled the public about the amount of lead in D.C.'s water.

Edwards was shocked when he found that Walters' lead content was 13,000 parts per billion. The EPA recommends keeping lead content below 15 parts per billion.

"At first I didn't believe the results because they were the worst I'd ever seen, and I've seen a lot," Edwards told me.

None of the samples Walters sent were safe to drink. Some had lead content of 200 parts per billion. Over 30 samples, the average lead content was 2,000 parts per billion, which meant that no matter how long Walters let her taps run, it still would have been toxic. This could easily have been causing the health problems that Walters and her children were experiencing.

"Lead is the best known neurotoxin, it adversely impacts every system in the human body," Edwards told me. "Certainly it could have caused children's lead poisoning."

The city says it does not know why so much lead was found in Walters' pipes, but Edwards has a theory: Many cities have lead pipes, and when water sits in those pipes, the lead can leech into the water. So cities usually add corrosion-control chemicals, such as phosphates, to keep the lead out of the water. But because Flint didn't take such precautions when they began pumping their own water, "the public health protection was gone," Edwards says.

The water situation has made people furious with the city, and with the emergency-manager system of government. Residents say Flint first learned about the high levels of TTHMs in May 2014, but didn't inform residents until January. City meetings have devolved into a mob of angry residents yelling at the emergency manager.

> **Indeed, water scarcity in the parched West might be getting the most news coverage, but infrastructure delays and climate change are causing big problems for cities in the North and Midwest, too.**

"We still don't have a true democracy," said Claire McClinton, the retiree. "As soon as [the emergency manager] sets foot in your city, your local government is gone." In March, Flint's city council voted to "do all things necessary" to once again purchase water from Detroit, but the city's emergency manager nixed the vote, calling it "incomprehensible." The emergency manager stepped down in April, announcing that the city was on firmer financial footing, but one of his last orders was that the city council could not change any of his orders for a year, including the order to switch to Flint water.

Flint last week sent out yet another notice that tap water had higher than acceptable levels of TTHMs. There are currently two lawsuits pending about the water issues, one of which questions the city's financial accounting; another demands that the city go back to Detroit water because Flint's water quality is so poor.

Many Flint residents have a visceral reaction to the water problem, and have focused their attention on the emergency manager, on their city's finances, and on the unfairness of their situation.

"How many times can they kick the people who live here?" Melissa Mays asked me in frustration.

But it's not one emergency manager, or one bad decision about pumping water from the Flint River that has led these problems—and that might be the scariest part of all. Neglected infrastructure is really to blame, but it's not quite as satisfying to blame old pipes as it is to blame the people in charge. And the city's financial woes have a lot to do with its shrinking population, but it's hard to blame the people who left in hopes of finding employment or a better life elsewhere.

Eroding infrastructure isn't unique to Flint. Things just broke down there first.

In a report released to its members last month, the American Water Works Association warned that many utilities across the country won't have the money to perform much-needed infrastructure upgrades over the upcoming decades. Utilities are seeing water sales declining as households and commercial clients become more efficient, but, like Flint, still have to provide the same infrastructure as before with less revenue.

"There is a gap between the financial needs of water and wastewater systems and the means to pay for these services through rates and fees," the report read.

"They don't have money to even do the best practices according to our currently lousy best practices," says Edwards, of Virginia Tech. "They have even less money than normal to address these very, very expensive problems."

And if utilities can't pay for much-needed upgrades, other cities might soon find themselves in the same situation as Flint.

Climate Change Crusade Goes Local

By Doug Struck
Christian Science Monitor, August 9, 2015

Florida's state leaders are running hard from climate change. The governor, Rick Scott, doesn't want state employees to even utter the words. Former Gov. Jeb Bush and US Sen. Marco Rubio, both Republican presidential aspirants, offer a medley of objections to scientists' calls for bold action on climate change.

Eric Carpenter shrugs. The director of Miami Beach's Public Works Department sits at his desk, poring over tables of high tides on his computer. He is calculating how many pumps he needs to buy to keep the city's streets from being flooded from a rising sea caused by climate change.

Under a broiling sun, he takes a visitor a few blocks from his office, to where contractors are pouring concrete to replace a section of a city street. The new roadway is being laid incongruously 2½ feet above the sidewalk cafe tables and storefront entrances at the old street level. The extra height is in preparation for the seas and tides that Mr. Carpenter already sees engulfing this section of Miami Beach.

In city after city in South Florida, local officials are dealing with climate change. So, too, are municipalities big and small across the United States. The same determination is evident among governors and legislators in more than two dozen states. And it is magnified worldwide: Surprising progress in grappling with global warming is coming from surprising nations.

This groundswell of action on climate change is producing solutions and often bypassing lagging political leadership. The gathering force of these acts, significant and subtle, is transforming what once seemed a hopeless situation into one in which success can at least be imagined. The initiatives are not enough to halt the world's plunge toward more global warming—yet. But they do point toward a turning point in greenhouse gas emissions, and ambitious—if still uneven—efforts to adapt to the changes already in motion.

"The troops on the ground, the local officials and stakeholders, are acting, even in the face of a total lack of support on the top level," says Michael Mann, a prominent climate scientist at Pennsylvania State University in State College, Pa. "The impacts of climate change are pretty bad and projected to get much worse if we continue business as usual. But there still is time to avert what we might reasonably describe as a true catastrophe. There are some signs we are starting to turn the corner."

From The Christian Science Monitor, August 9 © 2015 The Christian Science Monitor. All rights reserved. Used by permission and protected by the Copyright Laws of the United States. The printing, copying, redistribution, or retransmission of this Content without express written permission is prohibited.

Philip Levine, the mayor of Miami Beach, agrees. "We may not have all the answers," he says. "But we're going to show that Miami Beach is not going to sit back and go underwater."

• • •

Representatives from more than 190 countries will gather in Paris in December [2015] to try to agree on international strategies for dealing with climate change. They will be spurred by their own alarm at a succession of storms, droughts, and heat waves affecting millions of people on the planet, and by outside calls, such as the moral edict from Pope Francis, to care more about the world.

The record of past such meetings is not encouraging. But the representatives will arrive as progress on curbing greenhouse gas emissions, often overlooked, has been mounting:

- Wind and solar power generation are bounding ahead faster than the most optimistic predictions, with a fivefold increase worldwide since 2004. More than 1 in 5 buildings in countries such as Denmark, Germany, Sweden, and even Albania are now powered by renewable energy.

- The US saw its greenhouse gas emissions peak in 2007. They have fallen about 10 percent since, and are roughly on course to meet President Obama's pledge to reduce emissions in the next 10 years by about 27 percent from their peak.

- China, the world's largest carbon emitter, paradoxically leads the world in installed wind and solar power, and is charging ahead on renewables. China and the US ended their impasse over who is most responsible to fix global warming, agreeing in November to mutually ambitious goals. Experts say China already has cut coal consumption by 8 percent this year, and the environmental group Greenpeace says China stopped construction of some new coal power plants.

- Worldwide, carbon dioxide emissions, a principal component of greenhouse gases, did not grow in 2014, according to the International Energy Agency. Emissions remained flat even as the global economy grew—an important milestone.

- Coal-fired power plants are being replaced rapidly by natural gas plants, which are cleaner and emit half the greenhouse gases. Britain saw an 8 percent drop in greenhouse gas emissions last year, which is attributed to national energy policies, more energy efficiency, and the switch from coal.

- Tropical rainforests, which absorb carbon dioxide, are being cut down at a slower rate than in the past—13 million hectares per year, compared with 16 million in the 1990s, according to the latest figures from the United Nations Food and Agriculture Organization. That is still alarmingly high but shows progress, in part because of vows by big corporations not to buy palm oil grown on deforested lands. Brazil has made notable progress in reducing deforestation of the Amazon.

In the US, state and local governments are taking bold action even as the national discussion about the looming climate crisis remains paralyzed along political lines. In South Florida, for example, officials of four populous counties shun the rhetoric from GOP presidential aspirants and officials in the state capital and gather regularly to plot cooperative climate change strategy.

That group, the Southeast Florida Regional Climate Change Compact, is considered a national model for the kind of shoulder-to-shoulder effort needed to address the problem. They came up with an agreed estimate of sea level rise and identified the most vulnerable areas of the region, and now are plowing through more than 100 recommendations for action.

"There are no new funding sources coming down from the state or the Feds," says Susanne Torriente, assistant city manager for Fort Lauderdale, one of the participants of the compact. "Would it be good to have state and federal dollars? Yes. Are we going to wait until they act? No."

Their cooperation was born, essentially, on the back of a napkin. Kristin Jacobs, now a state representative who was a Broward County commissioner in 2008, was lamenting at the time that the 27 disparate municipal water authorities in the region could not agree on joint action. So she and others came up with the idea of getting local officials together in a classroom.

"We said, 'Let's have an academy,'" she recalls, and the Broward Leaders Water Academy began offering elected officials in South Florida six-month courses in water hydraulics and policy. It has now graduated "three generations of elected officials," she says.

Figuring out what to do about climate change—whether it is building up dunes on the beaches, raising the height of foundations, or shifting developments back from the coastline—takes a cooperative approach. "We couldn't do it by just saying 'this is the way it is'—the Moses approach," Ms. Jacobs says. "We had to do it with compliance and acquiescence and leadership."

Normally, direction on some of these issues might have come from state officials. But not in Florida. Not on climate change.

"We didn't have to worry about those who don't believe," Jacobs says. "At the end of the day, when the water is overtopping your sea wall, you don't really care that you didn't believe in climate change last week. You do believe in it this week."

• • •

Built on the edge of the sea, Miami Beach is one of the most vulnerable cities in the world to the vicissitudes of the ocean. Its boutique commercial district and canyons of pastel apartments sit on a sieve of porous limestone. The leaky footing was formed over the eons from accumulated seashells, coral, and fish skeletons.

Today the rock acts as a giant wick, giving the relentless ocean a route for subterranean attack. Seawater pushes in from underground and often gurgles to the surface in inconvenient places. On days of really high tides—even without any rain—the briny invasion turns some city streets into small lakes, snarling traffic and cutting off businesses. Locals call it "sunny day flooding."

The man charged with stopping the sea—or at least getting tourists and residents out of its way—is Carpenter, an affable engineer with a bur-

> **In city after city in South Florida, local officials are dealing with climate change. So, too, are municipalities big and small across the United States.**

ly physique. Carpenter took over the city's Public Works Department two years ago. His recurring nightmare is of rising seas, frequent storms, and "king" tides sweeping through Miami Beach—and doing it in full view of the world. He knows that whatever the city does—or does not do— to prepare for climate change will be tested soon on a stage before a global audience.

"What we do here is magnified because of who we are," he says. Miami Beach thrives on a global reputation for glamour, for cultural fusion, for beaches, for heat—from the sun in the day and its epicurean club culture at night. That's not an image that sits well with flooded streets. But the water is already coming.

As the Atlantic Ocean warms and expands, fed by melting polar ice caps, the seawater is pushing back into the 330 storm-water pipe outlets designed to drain rain from city streets. So Miami Beach is in the process of installing as many as 80 pumps, at a cost of nearly $400 million, to make sure the water flows outward.

"If the seas are continuing to rise, and the tidal events are higher than the inland elevation, we have to pump," says Carpenter.

The city plans to raise the level of 30 percent of its streets, encouraging businesses to abandon or remodel their first floors to go to a higher level. Carpenter says he wanted to go up nearly six feet, but town officials said "we are going too fast." So they settled on just over three feet.

"I don't think this is where we want to be long-term, but it's enough to get us through the next 10 or 20 years," he says, while standing on a new section of road at Sunset Harbor, looking down at the café tables on the sidewalk below, where the street used to be.

Mayor Levine echoes the importance of dealing with the future encroachment of the sea—now. "We did not ask for climate change or sea level rise," he says. "But we are the tip of the spear. We don't debate the reason why; we just come up with solutions."

Forty miles to the north, past Fort Lauderdale, Randy Brown and his utilities staff in Pompano Beach are also trying to halt the sea. Like the rest of South Florida, the coastal city of 100,000 residents is confronting the ocean above and below ground.

They are burying a new network of water pipes—painted grape purple— running to businesses and homes. The pipes contain sewer water that has been treated to remove the smell and bacteria and then siphoned from a pipe that used to discharge it into the sea.

Pompano Beach residents use the water for their lawns and gardens, bypassing the restrictive bans on lawn sprinkling. This recycled water then trickles down into the Biscayne Aquifer.

Cleansed as it sifts through the ground, it helps reduce the shrinking of the freshwater aquifer, which is being drawn down by the town's 26 wells and is threatened by underground salt water pushed inland by the rising sea level. Homeowners pay about two-thirds less for the recycled water than they do for potable water.

When city officials first laid out the program at a public meeting, bringing a cake to set a neighborly tone, "it was a fiasco. [Residents] called it dangerous," chuckles Maria Loucraft, a utilities manager.

Now, people "say they can't wait for it to get to their area," adds Isabella Slagle, who goes to public events with a mascot, a purple-colored sprinkler head with sunglasses, named "Squirt" by elementary school students.

Green lawns trump the political arguments over climate change, says Mr. Brown. "We don't say 'climate change,'" he admits. "It's 'protecting resources' or 'sustainability.' That way, you can duck under the political radar."

Some don't want to avoid the radar. Last October, the South Miami City Commission voted to create "South Florida" and secede from the rest of the state, in part because, they said, the state government in Tallahassee was not responding to their pleas to help them deal with climate change.

"It got a lot of press but nobody in the state took it very seriously," muses the mayor, Philip Stoddard, over a sandwich on the campus of Florida International University, where he is a biology professor. "But it did get people talking about climate change."

"My house is at 10 feet elevation," he adds. "My wife and I—our question is—will we be able to live out our lives in our house? I'm 58. We don't know. It's going to be a close one. If you look at the official sea level projections, they keep going up, which is a little disquieting. If you look at the unofficial projections, they scare the hell out of you."

While South Florida is a leader at local cooperation, officials in towns and cities across the country are struggling to react to a warming climate. Many municipalities have drafted action plans. Boston is converting its taxis to hybrids and requires new buildings to be built with higher foundations. Chicago is planting green gardens on city roofs to reduce the air conditioning needed to cool buildings. Seattle is helping residents install solar panels. Montpelier, Vt., vows to eliminate all fossil fuel use by 2030.

> "There are no new funding sources coming down from the state or the Feds," says Susanne Torriente, assistant city manager for Fort Lauderdale. . . "Would it be good to have state and federal dollars? Yes. Are we going to wait until they act? No."

Houston is laying down "cool pavements" made of reflective and porous material, and planting trees for shade.

Governors and state legislators across the country have gotten the message, too. While Congress will not debate the "Big Fix"—putting a price or a cap on carbon pollution—some states are already doing it. About 30 percent of Americans live in states that have rules capping carbon dioxide emissions and markets that allow companies to buy and sell carbon credits.

In addition, 28 states have set mandatory quotas for renewable energy from their electric utilities. Seven states have set ambitious targets for overall greenhouse gas reductions—California has promised a reduction of 40 percent below 1990 levels by 2030.

"The best thing Congress can do right now is stay out of the way," says Anna Aurilio, director of the Washington office of the nonprofit advocacy group Environment America. Between the state efforts and the executive orders by President Obama, she says, the US is on track to meet the administration's greenhouse gas goals.

"When we look at programs currently in place or set to be implemented, we can come close to the US commitment" of a 27 percent decrease in greenhouse gas emissions in 10 years, she says. "But we know we have to go much, much further."

To get near the goal of keeping average global warming at 2 degrees Celsius (3.6 degrees Fahrenheit) or less, climatologists predict that countries must largely abandon the fossil fuels that have driven technological societies since the Industrial Age—achieving an 80 percent reduction in greenhouse gas emissions by 2050.

That is an imposing goal, since billions of dollars are invested in new and existing fossil fuel power plants that can last 30 to 50 years. Even if solar or wind energy is cheaper than coal, oil, and natural gas, the owners of fossil fuel plants will be reluctant to abandon their investments. But the decisions are starting to come from the people, not just governments or corporations.

"When you have enough action taking place at the grass roots, sometimes that's a more effective means of implementing change on a large scale," says Penn State's Mr. Mann.

• • •

Nicole Hammer is one of the foot soldiers in the new war on global warming. A biologist, consultant, and former assistant director of a university center on climate change, she quit and decided to work with nonprofit groups, including the Moms Clean Air Force, an organization that campaigns to stem air pollution and climate change.

"I realized we have more than enough science to take action on climate change," she says while walking at an ecology park near her home in Vero Beach, Fla. "People who normally wouldn't be involved in environmental issues are starting to speak out."

She believes community involvement is the key to solutions, because the problems are felt most keenly at that level. "We have people in communities who have to put their kids in shopping carts to get across flooded streets to get food," she says.

"When you see that happening—and then you see people at high levels denying it—it's disappointing and it's incredibly frustrating."

Public outcry has helped close coal-burning power plants, which produce the dirtiest energy. Coal plants now provide about one-third of the electricity in the US—down from more than half in 1990. Tightening pollution standards and cheaper natural gas prices have prompted utilities to close 200 coal-fired plants since 2010, the Sierra Club estimates, and the trend would only accelerate under new clean air regulations unveiled by Obama in early August [2015].

Until recently, one argument against closing coal plants was that if the US didn't burn its own abundant coal reserves, they would just be exported to China. But Chinese authorities are so sobered by their public's resentment of the thick coal soot and industrial pollution that they are turning with startling speed to renewables. China reached a significant agreement with the US in November to cap its greenhouse gas pollutions by 2030, and further impressed experts in July by promising to ramp up renewables to provide 20 percent of its power, a sharp turn away from its pace of bringing a new coal power plant on line every 10 days.

"China has become a policy innovator," says Nathaniel Keohane, vice president of the Environmental Defense Fund, who worked on international climate issues in the Obama administration.

Other countries are plotting their own ways to curb greenhouse gases. Germany, Italy, Japan, and Spain are ramping up solar energy. France has embraced nuclear. Denmark, Portugal, and Nicaragua led in wind power in 2014. Brazil is adding hydroelectric plants as well as sharply reducing deforestation. Kenya and Turkey are tapping geothermal power. And smaller countries such as Costa Rica, Iceland, and Paraguay have found financial and tourism benefits in being at or very near "carbon neutral."

Still, the current projections from the Intergovernmental Panel on Climate Change on when the world will see a significant decline in global emissions vary widely—from about 2030 to after 2100—based on guesses of how countries respond. But the dramatic shift to natural gas in the US, and the racehorse expansion of hydraulic fracturing to get it, are demonstrations that if new technologies are profitable, industries can pivot quickly.

"We can make that turn," Mr. Keohane predicts. "Imagine the day when emissions are falling instead of rising. Imagine when we are winning rather than losing."

2
Cost of Living and Changing Demographics

© Art on File/Corbis

Children playing in a fountain at Jamison Square, a park in downtown Portland, Oregon, one of the more affordable, family friendly cities in the United States.

The Modern Urbanite

Each year, American cities attract millions of new residents coming from smaller American towns and communities or from countries around the world seeking the recreational, educational, and employment opportunities that are unique to urban environments. In the 2010s, after decades of slow growth, American cities are experiencing a minor renaissance. However, slow growth in urban industry and working-class employment threatens urban diversity, while inspiring the growth of suburbs as the new enclaves for working-class, immigrant, and poor families.

The Urban-Suburban Divide

Before the Industrial Revolution, less than 7 percent of Americans lived in cities, as most Americans worked and lived in rural, agricultural areas. The Industrial Revolution led to explosive job growth in cities, with thousands of new factories created to churn out innovative industrial products. From the 1850s through the 1920s, American cities grew rapidly, becoming the epicenter for American culture and commerce. As the cities grew larger and more congested, more and more Americans wanted a "middle ground," living close enough to take advantage of urban resources while enjoying the benefits of rural life, like larger lots, more spacious homes, cleaner air, quieter streets, and more green space.[1] The typical suburb "style" developed after World War II when developers like Abraham Levitt began creating housing projects marketed towards returning soldiers and their families. Historians believe that the "suburbanization" trend was a product of the uncertainty and trauma of the war era, as returning soldiers increasingly sought a quieter, more controlled way of life.

Levitt and imitators created a model that has remained common: single family detached homes, typically on large lots with driveways, garages, and front and back yards, built on curvilinear streets. Also characteristic is an extensive use of planted and heavily manicured green spaces that provide a more controlled approximation of rural green spaces.[2] The Interstate Highway System, established in 1958, fueled suburbanization, making it easier for individuals and families to commute into cities for work while living outside the city. For the postwar generation, and their children, the "baby boomers," the suburbs became the answer to the American dream, providing access to a quaint "town" feel without sacrificing the benefits of living near a city.[3]

The detriments of suburban growth, or "sprawl" as it became known, became a major topic among sociologists in the 1970s. The movement of white families away from cities significantly altered urban demographics and led to impoverishment as tax revenues that once fueled urban growth were increasingly diverted to the suburbs. From an ecological perspective, suburbs are the pinnacle of inefficiency: using a large amount of space for a small number of residents; replacing natural growth with invasive landscaping species; and accelerating pollution by encouraging car ownership and the establishment of new sewage, electricity, and gas utilities. Finally, nearby suburbs absorbed territories that might otherwise have been used to expand urban areas, effectively constraining the growth of cities.

In 2011, for the first time since before World War II, American cities grew faster than suburbs. Demographers began asking whether "generation Y," also known as the "millennials" (born in the 1980s and 1990s) would be the first generation to prefer cities to suburbia. As the largest demographic group since the baby boomers, millennial preferences will be a dominant force in American society over the next century. A 2014 report from the Nielsen group indicated that the population age 18–36, which consists of 77 million or 24 percent of the population, have greater tolerance for the "inconveniences" of urban life and favor a more vibrant, diverse, and heterogeneous environment.[4] According to Census Bureau data, 2.3 million Americans moved into cities between 2012 and 2013, marking the largest rate of urban growth since the 1960s. In addition to young millennials, studies also showed that a large number of "baby boomers" are returning to cities for their retirement, after having raised children in the suburbs.[5] However, contrasting research indicates that the majority of millennials prefer suburban housing as they begin raising families[6] and by 2014, population growth in suburbs had again eclipsed urban growth across the country.[7]

Even if most millennials eventually follow their parents and grandparents into the suburbs, millennial consumers have adopted different lifestyle preferences, leading to a trend towards "new urbanism," in which suburbs are increasingly becoming "city like" in architecture and planning. For instance, a reduced reliance on automobiles among millennials (from 73 percent in 2007 to 66 percent in 2011), has inspired suburban planners to incorporate mass transit and bicycling facilities.[8]

Millennials are also leading a renaissance in America's smaller cities as they seek a new "middle ground" between the sterile suburbs and the expensive, congested environments of larger cities. According to census data, in 2015, the United States had 10 cities with more than 1 million residents, and the populations of many smaller cities was growing almost as rapidly as suburbs. As small cities have grown, many have incorporated landscaping, planning, and design characteristic of suburbia, including a prevalence of single-family tract homes with larger lots, more green space, and more "suburban" isolation and amenities. Essentially then, the millennials are inspiring a convergence in which suburbs are becoming more like cities and smaller cities more like suburbs.[9]

Race and Income in the New Urbanist Environment

A March 2015 study from the University of Virginia's Demographics Research Group indicates that the structure of urban/suburban America has changed significantly since the 1990s. The traditional model of the 1960s was a "donut," with the city in the center surrounded by a ring of suburbs that tended to attract white, middle- and upper-class families. The "new donut" of the twenty-first century has an "urban core," comprising the downtown area, surrounded by an "inner ring," typically comprising the oldest suburbs within 4–15 miles of the city center. A new "outer ring" has developed with newer suburbs and "exurbs" that are far enough removed to be semirural. In the twenty-first century, individuals who would once have moved to inner ring suburbs, now move to the outer ring while the inner ring suburbs have developed to be more "urban" in design and in the diversity of their populations.[10]

The population of white middle- and upper-class families in cities declined by more than 16 percent from the 1960s to the 1990s, in a phenomenon that researchers and the media often called "white flight."[11] As businesses and job opportunities followed white families into the suburbs, many urban neighborhoods were left with poor, minority populations, an environment that came to be called "ghettos" in 1970s American pop culture. The idea of African American and Latino/Hispanic ghettos became so common in pop culture that the term "urban" became, in the 2010s, a controversial term used by outsiders to describe African American people or culture in the cities.[12]

Before desegregation, laws and regulations prohibited minority families from moving to suburbs and exurbs. The Supreme Court prohibited segregation in 1948 but white suburban communities continued to use legal and social tactics to discourage the settlement of minority and poor families. For instance, zoning restrictions prohibited apartments and smaller homes suitable for families operating on lower incomes. From the 1970s to the 1990s, as minority affluence increased, an increasing number of minority families moved to the "inner ring" suburbs. White flight then continued, with upper- and middle-class white families creating newer suburbs further from the cities. The suburb of Ferguson, Missouri, provides an example, as the proportion of African Americans living in Ferguson increased from 14 percent in 1980 to more than 69 percent in 2010, with minority families relocating from Northern St. Louis City, while white residents relocated to new outer-ring suburbs further from the city.[13]

Cost of Living and the Price of Decay

One of the factors limiting urban growth is the "cost of living," an economic measure that incorporates the cost of renting/purchasing property and the price of utilities and resources. Rental properties effectively support populations of low-income residents and laborers and provide an attractive option for young individuals building their careers. However, the cost of purchasing property within cities, especially in "city centers," can be prohibitive, inspiring sprawl as young families look for affordable housing. In 2015, smaller cities in the South and Midwest boasted the most favorable cost of living in the nation, though urban cost of living has increased in all areas since 2000.[14]

The increased cost of home buying and rising mortgage rates have created a trend toward renting rather than purchasing property. However, average rental costs increased by 12 percent between 2000 and 2010—the largest spike in any decade since 1960. In the nation's most popular cities, like New York and San Francisco, residents may pay upwards of 50 percent of their income toward rent. In addition, utility costs have increased, with renters and homeowners paying an average of 4 percent of their income towards utilities and leaving low- and middle-income families in the city with little resources for food or recreation.[15] Rising rental costs are complicated by availability, as many markets have seen sharp declines in vacancy with cities unable to meet residential demand. For instance, in Manhattan, vacancy rates were estimated at just 2.3 percent in 2015, thus discouraging relocation and immigration, which have long fueled population growth in the city.[16]

For most of American history, cities have been the most attractive destination for immigration. Census Bureau data from 2013, for instance, indicates that 51 percent of all foreign born living in the United States reside in just ten of America's largest cities. However, the number of immigrants settling in cities declined from 56 percent in 2000 to 51 percent in 2010. Smaller cities like Nashville, Tennessee, and Raleigh, North Carolina, saw major increases in immigrant populations, and the fastest growth in immigrant populations is occurring in American suburbs, a trend driven by the shift in American labor towards suburban factories and facilities.[17]

As young white residents return to cities, there has been an increasing trend towards gentrification, a phenomenon in which higher-income residents settle in poor or working-class communities that were subject to blight and decay during suburbanization and so have low property values. Real estate developers, following consumer demand, then begin purchasing abandoned and low-cost properties to create apartments, homes, and condos. This leads to a rapid increase in property value and the cost of living, which benefits home and property owners but also tends to push out working-class and low-income residents. As the process continues, the neighborhood changes, becoming a middle-class or upper-class neighborhood, with a subsequent decline in economic and racial diversity.[18]

Though cities need laborers to participate in maintenance, operations, construction, and services, industry and working-class populations have increasingly left cities for suburban environments. Ironically, though many who prefer urban living cite diversity as among the chief benefits of cities, urban renewal is often accompanied by an unintentional reduction in economic and racial diversity through the gentrification of neighborhoods and a reduction in employment opportunities. In some cities, like San Francisco, urban gentrification resulted in a "reverse donut," with upper-class families residing in the cities while working-class families and residents were pushed into surrounding communities.

Since the 1940s, some American cities have attempted to protect working-class residents from exploitation through "rent control" regulations that regulate rental prices in an effort to maintain affordable housing in certain neighborhoods or areas. Since 2000, voters in a number of cities have abolished rent control through public referendum, and the subject is highly debated in cities that maintain the practice. Despite objections from critics arguing that rent control discourages development and exacerbates urban blight, rent control has been an important key to supporting urban working-class, artistic, and immigrant populations. Supporters argue that without such controls on cost-of-living expenses, cities risk creating more gentrified, high-income neighborhoods while forcing out working-class families. Similar to many other controversies in urban politics and development, the fate of issues like rent control hinges on the relative value city residents place on economic and cultural diversity. While some advocate policies to protect working-class residents and neighborhoods in cities, others argue against any government regulation or intervention.[19] The debate will continue, as cities across the United States struggle with the question of how to encourage innovation and grow business without allowing the progress of the market to come at the expense of local populations.

Micah L. Issitt

Notes

1. Kushner, Levittown, 7–10.
2. Jackson, Crabgrass Frontier, 240–250.
3. Ames, "Interpreting Post-World War II Suburban Landscapes as Historic Resources."
4. "Millennials: Breaking the Myths," 2014.
5. Westcott, "More Americans Moving to Cities, Reversing the Suburban Exodus."
6. Hudson, "Generation Y Prefers Suburban Home Over City Condo."
7. Kolko, "Urban Headwinds, Suburban Tailwinds."
8. "Millennials Prefer Cities to Suburbs, Subways to Driveways," 2014.
9. Carlyle, "America's Fastest-Growing Cities 2015."
10. Juday, "The Changing Shape of American Cities."
11. Blakeslee, "'White Flight' to the Suburbs: A Demographic Approach."
12. Wacquant, *Urban Outcasts*.
13. "The Death of Michael Brown," *New York Times*.
14. Carlyle, "America's Most Affordable Cities In 2015."
15. "Rental Housing Affordability," 2011.
16. Carlyle, "San Francisco Tops Forbes' 2015 List of Worst Cities for Renters."
17. Wilson, "Immigrants Continue to Disperse, with Fastest Growth in the Suburbs."
18. "What Is Gentrification?," PBS.
19. Chen, "When Rent Control Just Vanishes; Both Sides of Debate Cite Boston's Example."

The End of the Suburbs

By Leigh Gallagher
Time, July 31, 2013

A major change is underway in where and how we are choosing to live. In 2011, for the first time in nearly a hundred years, the rate of urban population growth outpaced suburban growth, reversing a trend that held steady for every decade since the invention of the automobile. In several metropolitan areas, building activity that was once concentrated in the suburban fringe has now shifted to what planners call the "urban core," while demand for large single-family homes that characterize our modern suburbs is dwindling. This isn't just a result of the recession. Rather, the housing crisis of recent years has concealed something deeper and more profound happening to what we have come to know as American suburbia. Simply speaking, more and more Americans don't want to live there anymore.

The American suburb used to evoke a certain way of life, one of tranquil, tree-lined streets, soccer leagues and center hall colonials. Today's suburb is more likely to evoke endless sprawl, a punishing commute, and McMansions. In the pre-automobile era, suburban residents had to walk once they disembarked from the train, so houses needed to be located within a reasonable distance to the station and homes were built close together. Shopkeepers set up storefronts around the station where pedestrian traffic was likely to be highest. The result was a village center with a grid shaped street pattern that emerged organically around the day-to-day needs and walking patterns of the people who lived there. Urban planners describe these neighborhoods, which you can still see in older suburbs, as having "vibrancy" or "experiential richness" because, without even trying, their design promoted activity, foot traffic, commerce and socializing. As sociologist Lewis Mumford wrote, "As long as the railroad stop and walking distances controlled suburban growth, the suburb had form."

Then came World War II, and the subsequent housing shortage. The Federal Housing Administration had already begun insuring long-term mortgage loans made by private lenders, and the GI Bill provided low-interest, zero-down-payment loans to millions of veterans. The widespread adoption of the car by the middle class untethered developers from the constraints of public transportation and they began to push further out geographically. Meanwhile, single-use zoning laws that carved land into buckets for residential, commercial and industrial use instead of having a single downtown core altered the look, feel and overall DNA of our modern suburbs. From

"The End of the Suburbs [Time Magazine 7/31/2013]", adapted from THE END OF THE SUBURBS: WHERE THE AMERICAN DREAM IS MOVING by Leigh Gallagher, copyright © 2013 by Leigh Gallagher. Used by permission of Portfolio, an imprint of Penguin Publishing Group, a division of Penguin Random House LLC.

then on, residential communities were built around a different model entirely, one that abandoned the urban grid pattern in favor of a circular, asymmetrical system made of curving subdivisions, looping streets and cul-de-sacs.

But in solving one problem—the severe postwar housing shortage—we unwittingly created some others: isolated, single-class communities. A lack of cultural amenities. Miles and miles of chain stores and Ruby Tuesdays. These are the negative qualities so often highlighted in popular culture, in TV shows like *Desperate Housewives*, *Weeds,* and *Suburgatory,* to name just a few. In 2011, the indie rock band Arcade Fire took home a Grammy for *The Suburbs*, an entire album dedicated to teen angst and isolation inspired by band members' Win and William Butler's upbringing in Houston's master-planned community The Woodlands. Although many still love and defend the suburbs, they have also become the constant target of angst by the likes of Kate Taylor, a stay-at-home mom who lives in a suburb of Charlotte and uses the Twitter name @culdesacked. "If the only invites I get from you are at-home direct sales 'parties,' please lose my number, then choke yourself. #suburbs."

There is still a tremendous amount of appeal in suburban life: space, a yard of one's own, less-crowded schools. I don't have anything against the suburbs personally—although I currently live in Manhattan's West Village, I had a pretty idyllic childhood growing up in Media, Pennsylvania, a suburb twelve miles west of Philadelphia. We are a nation that values privacy and individualism down to our very core, and the suburbs give us that. But somewhere between leafy neighborhoods built around lively railroad villages and the shiny new subdivisions in cornfields on the way to Iowa that bill themselves as suburbs of Chicago, we took our wish for privacy too far. The suburbs overshot their mandate.

> **"The differences between cities and suburbs are diminishing," says Brookings' Metropolitan Policy Program director Bruce Katz, noting that cities and suburbs are also becoming more alike racially, ethnically, and socio-economically.**

Many older suburbs are still going strong, and real estate developers are beginning to build new suburban neighborhoods that are mixed-use and pedestrian-friendly, a movement loosely known as New Urbanism. Even though almost no one walks everywhere in these new communities, residents can drive a mile or two instead of ten or twenty, own one car instead of two. "We are moving from location, location, location in terms of the most important factor to access, access, access," says Shyam Kannan, formerly a principal at real estate consultancy Robert Charles Lesser and now managing director of planning at the Washington Metropolitan Area Transit Authority (WMATA.)

As the country resettles along more urbanized lines, some suggest the future may look more like a patchwork of nodes—mini urban areas all over the country connected to one another with a range of public transit options. It's not unlike the dense settlements of the Northeast already, where city-suburbs like Stamford,

Greenwich, West Hartford and others exist in relatively close proximity. "The differences between cities and suburbs are diminishing," says Brookings' Metropolitan Policy Program director Bruce Katz, noting that cities and suburbs are also becoming more alike racially, ethnically, and socio-economically.

Whatever things look like in ten years—or twenty, or fifty, or more—there's one thing everyone agrees on: there will be more options. The government in the past created one American Dream at the expense of almost all others: the dream of a house, a lawn, a picket fence, two or more children, and a car. But there is no single American Dream anymore; there are multiple American Dreams, and multiple American Dreamers. The good news is that the entrepreneurs, academics, planners, home builders, and thinkers who plan and build the places we live in are hard at work trying to find space for all of them.

Get Out of Town

By Nicholas Lemann
The New Yorker, June 27, 2011

Cities, like children, bear such a heavy load of projection that their real character can be hard to see. Depending on the tenor of the moment, they can appear bleak, filthy, dangerous, and inhumane, or gloriously sophisticated, varied, and exciting. These days, cities so dominate the world that you can use them to demonstrate any truth you choose. What people think about them is usually an expression of what they think about class, work, the way society is organized, money and who gets it, and what's really valuable.

Still, at every moment there is a prevailing consensus. In the United States right now, after a long run of "urban crisis" (punctuated by periodic hopeful reports of revitalization), cities are viewed positively again. The dramatic reduction in violent crime in many big cities has brightened the picture; less obvious, but probably more important, is a change in the way we think about the suburbs, which still lurk in the background of everything said about urban life in America. Cities and suburbs have started to seem less like fundamental opposites, and more like points on a continuum.

It will help to define terms. A metropolitan area is a zone of contiguous settlement—the expanse from the heart of downtown to where open land begins. In the 2000 census, 80 percent of Americans lived in metropolitan areas with populations of more than a hundred thousand, which explains why so much of the country is so lightly populated. (A graphic designer named Shane Keaney recently calculated that if the entire American population was as densely settled as that of Brooklyn it could fit into the state of New Hampshire, leaving the forty-nine other states as open land.) A suburb is the portion of a metropolitan area that lies outside the formal city limits. During the first half of the twentieth century, vast numbers of Americans moved to the cities; during the second half, vast numbers moved to the suburbs. By 2000, the United States had become a majority-suburban nation.

Twenty-five years ago, I moved from Austin, Texas, to New York. Austin hadn't yet achieved its current empyrean, SXSW-hosting status. But it was clearly a city, not a town, even though almost nobody there lived in high-rise apartment buildings and almost everybody drove to work. The city limits stretched outward for miles in every direction, so that even many brand-new subdivisions were, legally, in Austin.

"Get Out of Town" © 2011 by Nicholas Lemann. Used by Permission. All rights reserved.

The people I knew who had consciously rejected city life lived not in suburbs but at the end of rural dirt roads, and even they were often still legally residents of Austin.

New York, on the other hand, was a Manichaean world in which the choice between suburbs and city was seen as life-determining. Demographically, New York as a metropolitan area became majority-suburban long before the country did. But in 1986 the prevailing idea was that the suburbs were for the privileged few and the cities for the poor, the bohemian, and the principled. A few years earlier, the *Post* discovered that Michael Harrington, the author of *The Other America,* had moved to Westchester County, and ran a screaming headline about it: "SOCIALIST LEADER FLEES TO LARCHMONT."

Besides being thought of as rich, the suburbs were seen through resonant mid-century depictions offered by writers of fiction like John Cheever and Richard Yates and by writers of nonfiction like William H. Whyte (*The Organization Man*) and David Riesman (*The Lonely Crowd*). They were conformist, anti-intellectual, homogeneous, antifeminist, alcoholic, and shot through with anomie. Almost all my friends who had grown up in New York's suburbs had, sometime during adolescence, taken a solemn vow to leave as soon as they had the opportunity and never return.

This vision has been worn down over time by a number of factors. Most residents of American cities—including economic and cultural centers such as Austin and Seattle and Minneapolis and Los Angeles—live in a manner that reads to New Yorkers as suburban: single-family detached house with a yard and a garage. So the city-suburb distinction has begun to seem a little artificial. After all, cities in the Northeast and the Midwest have more suburbs than cities in the South and the West because of where jurisdictional lines happen to be drawn. Also, American cities generally, and New York in particular, have more obviously taken on the economic form of European cities like Paris and London: the city is for the rich (and the poor), and the outer boroughs and many of the suburbs are for the ethnic working and middle classes. That complicates the old picture of men in suits and fedoras rushing to make the five-forty express to Scarsdale while the artists and intellectuals stayed behind in Manhattan. Culturally, New York increasingly operates on the farmers'-market model: artists, writers, musicians, and actors can't afford to live in the city center, so they come in only for encounters with the commercial supporters of their work.

Once you start to move beyond the city-suburb culture wars, there's room for other topics, and these days the main one is globalization. "Global city" theorists don't think of American cities in contrast with their agricultural hinterlands (as in *Sister Carrie* or *Native Son*) or with their suburbs (*Revolutionary Road*); they think of them in relation to cities in other countries. People, money, and goods glide frictionlessly around the world, and cities expand or contract based on their marginal attractiveness. Cities are assumed to be places to flee to, not flee from. But with work, community, friendship, and money so unmoored and virtualized today, you might wonder why cities exist at all. Instead of gathering, why don't we scatter to the four winds? What benefit are we meant to harvest by living so close to so many other people?

A striking feature of cities is their theatrical aspect. We all inhabit private realms made up of people of our own ethnicity, class, and belief system, but in cities there are public spaces where a broad range of people can congregate. Sometimes they interact, sometimes they just gawk, but the rules of human display and behavior are different. The veteran sociologist Elijah Anderson's latest book, *The Cosmopolitan Canopy: Race and Civility in Everyday Life*, posits that there are certain venues in cities (Philadelphia is his example), such as public markets, where the races can come together temporarily without conflict. But he cautions against taking too much from this. He offers detailed, occasionally first-person descriptions of how racially charged life can be for an upper-middle-class black man when he ventures outside the cosmopolitan canopy—even if he's a tenured professor at an Ivy League university like Anderson, in a sophisticated city like Philadelphia. A relentless and depressing procession of examples document the "nigger moments" that punctuate the lives of black professionals in restaurants, building lobbies, taxis, and stores. (It's impossible to read *The Cosmopolitan Canopy* without reflecting on how much effort must go into the Obamas' casually post-racial self-presentation.) If the level of public tolerance in cities isn't really so high, though, you might wonder whether the cosmopolitan canopy is an exclusively urban phenomenon. Couldn't it extend to suburban shopping malls? Are cities so different from suburbs as social environments?

Maybe the real benefits are economic. Certainly, a lot of writing about globalization takes economic development to be the ultimate good. Traditional structures and interests in society are regarded as mere impediments, with no useful function. Human activities are to be organized around the goal of "innovation." Good things happen for simple, clear, catchy reasons. There are rules that explain why life proceeds on the course it does. In this kind of writing, which often emanates from business schools and economics departments and is aimed at an audience of people who are on business trips, one often finds easily digestible, anecdotalized theoretical and historical sweep and the exemplary stories of successful entrepreneurs blended with anecdotes about the author's own life.

One person who helped usher in the new era of urban cheer is Richard Florida, who burst out of monographic obscurity in 2002 with a big, ambitious book called *The Rise of the Creative Class*. Florida, who, like many of the leading writers about cities these days, operates a consulting and lecturing business, has published three books since then; the latest, *The Great Reset*, came out [in 2010]. He now directs the Martin Prosperity Institute, at the University of Toronto's business school.

Florida argues that there is an identifiable cluster of occupations (scientist, architect, academic, artist) that, taken together, constitute something called the Super-Creative Core. Adjacent to the Super-Creative Core sits the lesser, but larger part of the Creative Class, made up of managers, lawyers, accountants, and so on. The two groups combined are the Creative Class: thirty-eight million people, making up 30 percent of the labor force. The key factor in determining whether a city

> Most residents of American cities—including economic and cultural centers such as Austin and Seattle and Minneapolis and Los Angeles—live in a manner that reads to New Yorkers as suburban: single-family detached house with a yard and a garage. So the city-suburb distinction has begun to seem a little artificial.

is successful is how significant a cohort of the Creative Class it attracts.

One might argue that Florida's Creative Class isn't all that different from the Bureau of Labor Statistics' less exciting professional, managerial, and technical occupational categories, and that he's really saying that the urban economy is now white-collar rather than industrial. But that would ruin the fun. There is something delightfully counterintuitive about Florida's theory as he chooses to state it: you would have thought it was dull Babbitts who made a city commercially successful, but no—it's kids with scruffy beards and tattoos who have alt-rock bands, script iPhone apps, and wait tables in vegan restaurants.

What's the connection between them and prosperity? (Their parents are probably asking the same question.) They generate an atmosphere of cultural richness and innovation that attracts more obviously productive types, who have lots of choices about where to live and will pick places they find exciting and attractive. (Florida's best-known obiter dictum is that the more gay-friendly a city is the better it will do economically.) So: "Seattle was the home of Jimi Hendrix and later Nirvana and Pearl Jam as well as Microsoft and Amazon. Austin was home to Willie Nelson and its fabulous Sixth Street music scene before Michael Dell ever stepped into his now famous University of Texas fraternity house. New York had Christopher Street and SoHo long before Silicon Alley erupted. All of these places were open, diverse and culturally creative first. *Then* they became technologically creative and subsequently gave rise to new high-tech firms and industries."

Florida's breezy pronouncements are what got him the world's attention, but they have also created the impression that making them is all he does. Especially in *The Rise of the Creative Class*, which is by far the best of his books, he shows himself to be an amiable, unpretentious thinker—not somebody with an arrestingly original mind but a dogged, careful compiler of data and assimilator of material drawn from across a wide range. In the line of descent from Jane Jacobs, he sees cities as the sites of small-scale, unplanned human interactions that, in the aggregate, yield big civilizational rewards.

Florida's theory represents the perspective of someone who (like President Obama) has chosen to live his adult life in urban neighborhoods near universities. He dreams of a world that respects cultural and intellectual life, and the downmarket, ethnically diverse older neighborhoods where it often takes place. It's a sign of the times that the most effective way to promulgate such values is to present them as preconditions of economic development. And people take his argument on its own terms: in Michigan, Governor Jennifer Granholm recently tried to reposition depressed factory towns like Flint and Lansing as "Cool Cities," and in New Mexico the developer Albert Ratner is building a huge suburb in the desert outside Albuquerque called Mesa del Sol, which he says is designed to attract the Creative Class.

"It would be a mistake for cities to think they can survive solely as magnets for the young and hip," the Harvard economist Edward Glaeser writes in his new book, *Triumph of the City*, by way of dismissing Richard Florida. Glaeser is a sterner character than Florida: the genial Florida repeatedly praises Glaeser in his work, but Glaeser doesn't return the favor, and, although he's pro-city, he does think some changes must be made before cities can reach their full soaring potential.

For Glaeser, the key factor that makes cities successful is not the presence of the Creative Class but "proximity," the way they bring people into contact, enabling them to interact in rich, unexpected, productive ways. "In a big city, people can choose peers who share their interests," he writes, "just as Monet and Cézanne found each other in nineteenth-century Paris, or Belushi and Aykroyd found each other in twentieth-century Chicago." Accordingly, Glaeser is an enthusiast for high-rise apartment houses and office skyscrapers, and he wants public policy to favor this kind of development and density. He thinks architectural preservationism is out of hand, likes political autocrats who can get things done (such as Chicago's Richard M. Daley and Singapore's Lee Kuan Yew), and wants us to stop subsidizing the suburbs via tax credits and highway construction.

Although Glaeser confesses that he has recently moved to the suburbs with his wife and young children, he blames this on "the anti-urban public policy trifecta of the Massachusetts Turnpike, the home mortgage interest deduction, and the problems of urban schools." He hopes that "the twentieth-century fling with suburban living will look, just like the brief age of the industrial city, more like an aberration than a trend." He points out that, thanks to the public-health miracles of the past century, cities in the developed world have gone from being pestilential to unusually healthy, and that dense cities like New York have low carbon footprints. If the latter-day admirers of Jane Jacobs—Glaeser isn't one; he thinks Jacobs didn't understand the law of supply and demand—would give up their attachment to small-scale urban neighborhoods and allow more high-rise construction, cities might become affordable again and sprawl might end.

Though Edward Glaeser considers Richard Florida's celebration of cities sentimental and unrigorous compared with his own celebration of cities, the same trump card of hard-hearted rigor could be played against Glaeser. What makes him so sure that sprawl is not a naturally popular and efficient economic form? There are, in fact, theorists who argue that, if you really love the twenty-first-century city, you have to embrace sprawl as an inextricable part of it. Back in 1991, Joel Garreau, then a reporter for the *Washington Post* (and now the head of the Garreau Group, a consulting company), laid out this position in *Edge City*, a perverse celebration of those brand-new, characterless, mega-malled, pedestrian-unfriendly places which have sprung up all over the country, beyond the traditional suburban zone. Edge Cities—Garreau's prime example was Tysons Corner, Virginia, outside Washington, D.C.—violate the ideas that all right-thinking people hold about how metropolitan life should be organized. They house offices as well as residences, so they complicate our conception of commuting without the collateral benefit of reducing traffic and pollution. Recently, they have served as incubators of the world financial crisis, since Edge Cities in the Sun Belt tended to have the highest rates of defaulted mortgages. But, as a matter of what economists call revealed preference, they're a big hit.

An odd, fascinating new book called *Aerotropolis* takes Garreau's idea and brings it to an even stranger place, predicting that, in the future, cities will reorient themselves around enormous airports. The book's strangeness begins with its authorship: it was written by an entity called "John D. Kasarda/Greg Lindsay"—just the names, no "by." Kasarda is a sociologist who teaches at the business school of the University of North Carolina, Chapel Hill, and has become a globe-trotting economic-development guru. Lindsay is a business journalist. The two seem to have struck a deal in which Kasarda would get primary author's credit even though he is really the subject and Lindsay did all the writing. Lindsay is no ghostwriter or collaborator working from a series of long living-room interviews with his partner. He did extensive, lively reporting all over the world, the book is in his voice, and for long stretches Kasarda disappears entirely. Their arrangement certainly demonstrates that Kasarda is a skilled negotiator.

In keeping with its peculiar mode of authorship, *Aerotropolis* often feels like two books trapped inside the same cover. The first lays out Kasarda's theory, mainly through examples drawn from his consulting gigs. Urban strategists have a penchant for magically simple explanations, but Kasarda takes it to an extreme: for him, air freight is the core element of human civilization, and so if a city wants to do well it must build a mega-airport.

Kasarda is right to remind us that the Internet hasn't taken the place of physical goods, and that much information technology is merely an enabling device for shipping. Globalization makes airports all the more important, then, because factories are frequently halfway around the world from their customers, who expect nearly instant delivery. In the past, cities always grew up around transportation hubs, so why not now? Kasarda's theory, at least as presented by Lindsay, is all-powerful and impervious to evidence. Washington, Los Angeles, and Chicago are doomed because they don't have enough runways. (If an aerotropolis fails, like Suvarnabhumi, in Thailand, a Kasarda client, it's only because of poor execution.) The American future belongs to places with big airports, such as Memphis (of FedEx), Louisville (of U.P.S.), and Denver, and maybe in a few years even Detroit, if it proceeds with a long-shot plan to create an aerotropolis between Detroit's airport and a small regional airport west of the city. Abroad, Kasarda's models include Dubai; New Songdo, an aerotropolis being built on a man-made island off the coast of South Korea; and the forthcoming Beijing Airport City. He predicts that people will increasingly want to live in subdivisions near giant airports.

The only obstacle to this alluring future is the way governments are hamstrung by the Lilliputian political interests that often halt progress in older cities. Kasarda is inspired, accordingly, by the fact that Beijing could build a new airport from scratch without debate, and by its plans to build yet another one. Its location is a "state secret," but it "almost doesn't matter, because the government will simply do what it did at the site of the current one, which was to flatten fifteen villages and resettle ten thousand residents without compensation. Kasarda was awed by the ministry's rationale: 'Democracy sacrifices efficiency.'"

The second book contained within the covers of *Aerotropolis* is Lindsay's, and it is an enthralling and only intermittently dogmatic tour of some of the gigantic, no-context sites that globalization has created, such as the all-night flower auction in Amsterdam that gets roses from Kenya to Chicago before they've wilted, the FoxConn factory in China where iPods and iPhones are made, and the megahospital Bumrungrad, in Bangkok, which performs cut-rate major surgery on the uninsured from all over the world. You can get some feeling for the bizarreness of this new world from Lindsay's description of New Songdo: "an English-speaking island stocked with prep schools from Boston, malls from Beverly Hills, and a golf course designed by Jack Nicklaus. . . . New Songdo cherry-picks the signatures of universally beloved cities and recycles them as building blocks. The city trumpets itself as an amalgam of New York, Venice, and Savannah."

Another journalistic visitor to the extremes of urban globalization is Doug Saunders, a reporter for the Toronto *Globe and Mail* and the author of *Arrival City*. Saunders leads us on a brisk world tour of enormous urban-fringe neighborhoods populated by people who have left the countryside, among them Tatary, in west-central Poland; Kibera, in Nairobi; and Petare, in Caracas. All over the world, farms and villages are emptying out, Saunders says, and cities are filling up: "The modern arrival city is the product of the final great human migration. A third of the world's population is on the move this century, from village to city."

That's how London and New York and Chicago became big cities in the nineteenth century—by offering, in succession, an unusually high economic return to newcomers. "Throughout the nineteenth century, North America offered stunning levels of upward mobility," Saunders writes. Middle-class reformers usually look at arrival cities as an urgent problem to be fixed—take a look at Jacob Riis's descriptions of the Lower East Side in *How the Other Half Lives*—but Saunders wants us to think kindly of them. Sometimes they are squalid, but they contain elaborate systems of mutual support that are often invisible to outsiders, and tearing down the slums and dispersing their residents is not necessarily doing them a favor. Perhaps because Saunders is a journalist who isn't selling his advice, his version of the city is unlovelier than the rest—overwhelming, at times—but also more persuasive.

Still, the new urban optimism leaves a lot of questions unanswered. First, why *are* cities so economically successful? Catchy explanations like the Creative Class and big airports are entertaining but surely not sufficient. In Restoration-era Paris, as rendered by Balzac and Flaubert, ambitious young men like Lucien de Rubempre and Frédéric Moreau would come to the city from the stolid provinces and encounter a world of relaxed social convention (not least regarding sex), elaborate public role-playing, and ruinous expense. The costumed afternoon promenade in the Tuileries was quintessentially urban, but it had far more to do with culture and society than with economic progress. Hardly anybody newly urban in nineteenth-century novels seems to make money; were the novelists missing a crucial element of economic enablement in the social tableau? William Whyte, the author of *The Organization Man*, spent his later years, in the 1970s and 1980s, in part trying to demonstrate that big companies that moved their headquarters from Manhattan to suburban campuses were going to hurt themselves economically, by sealing themselves off from varied human interaction. He did this by camping out in midtown with a notebook and a camera, so as to record the random, fruitful collisions of the human molecules. But Silicon Valley is entirely made up of office campuses. Its secret seems to be its proximity to a major university, Stanford, and a dense, fluid concentration of interrelated high-level talent, capital, and technology within easy driving range—not serendipitous pedestrian culture. Is city life productive or merely interesting? That's what we don't know.

I lived in the suburbs—Pelham, in Westchester County—for twenty-one years, after which my family moved to an apartment in New York City. We're all intermittently homesick, especially at this time of year, when suburbia feels like the land of fecundity, as green as a jungle, the streets and sidewalks jammed with children playing. Pelham is devoted to a (long) season of life, parenthood. Most people moved there because they couldn't afford to live decently in the city with children, and, like Frank and April Wheeler in *Revolutionary Road,* they claimed that they stayed there only out of necessity. As time passed, our collective secret became clear. It wasn't just good public schools and one bedroom per child that kept us in Pelham. We actually liked it—liked the houses, the slower pace, the regular unplanned access to each other. And, given the kids, we couldn't have done all the wondrous things you can do only in cities anyway.

This raises a second unresolved question about cities: is there really a huge pent-up demand to move from the suburbs to the city, just waiting to be released by wiser government policies? James S. Russell, the architecture critic for Bloomberg News and the author of a new book called *The Agile City,* uses the term "megaburbs" to describe what cities have become. In much of the world, it seems pretty clear that most people who have the chance do leave dense inner cities, while staying in metropolitan areas. Even "arrival cities," Doug Saunders acknowledges, are often in the suburbs. Can this great tide really be reversed just by raising gas taxes and easing urban building codes, or should we figure that sprawl is here to stay, and focus on managing it better?

Anyway, all these questions about life within metropolitan areas are beginning to seem minor compared with the immensity of a broader phenomenon: the expansion of the metropolitan areas themselves. Urban growth (whether upward or outward) is taking place on a scale that, if we hadn't become so sanguine about it, would be frighteningly large and rapid. Industrial capitalism, in its day, was an unstoppable force, but it generated enormous moderating and countervailing forces, like labor unions, the welfare state, and Communism.

Globalization, for all its velocity and power and relentless mutation, will not simply proceed unimpeded either. Many people are unwilling to participate in a social compact based on perpetual motion. Masters of the new economy, social visionaries, and tongue-studded app developers figure large in the imagination of urban theorists these days, but most people are looking for something pretty mundane: a neighborhood, a patch of ground, a measure of peace and security, a family, status, dignity. In twentieth-century America, some people found those things in tightly packed neighborhoods. Far more found them in the suburbs. They tended their gardens, washed their cars, took their children to Little League games, went to PTA meetings and to religious services. It's one thing to create a vast metropolis. It's another to create a society, with a distinctive order and a set of embedded bargains regarding who gets how much of what. Twenty-first-century cities haven't yet figured out that part.

Baby Boomtowns: The U.S. Cities Attracting the Most Families

By Joel Kotkin
Forbes, September 11, 2014

With the U.S. economy reviving, birth rates may be as well: the number of children born rose in 2013 by 4,700, the first annual increase since 2007. At the same time new household formation, after falling precipitously in the wake of the Great Recession, has begun to recover, up 100,000 this June from a year before.

This impacts the economy strongly in such areas as single-family home construction, the supply of labor and consumer demand.

For cities, being family friendly may become increasingly important as the large millennial generation starts entering their thirties, the primary years for raising children. In order to identify the parts of the country where new families are being formed most rapidly, we turned to demographer Wendell Cox. He crunched the data on the changes in the number of 5- to 14-year-olds since 2000 in the nation's 52 largest metropolitan statistical areas.

We picked this age range because it encompasses when parents often move due to such issues as school quality, the cost of housing and long-term economic security. A toddler can do quite well in a small apartment, but when it's time to go to school, or if the parents decide to have a second or a third child, many parents are forced to make what are often difficult and long-lasting choices about where to live.

Baby Boomtowns

Virtually all the metro areas where there has been the strongest growth in families from 2000 to 2013 are highly suburban, highly affordable and located in the South and Intermountain West. If they also have a strong economy, like top-ranked Raleigh, N.C., they are even more attractive. In concert with strong net in-migration, the number of children in the Raleigh metro area between the ages of 5 and 14 grew by 63,600 from 2000–2013, or 55.7%. That's roughly 10 times the national growth rate of 0.5% for this demographic.

The same combination of affordable housing and economic growth has helped No. 2 Austin, Texas, where there were 86,200 more children in 2013 than in 2000, growth of 49.3%, as well as No. 4 Charlotte, N.C. (+82,100, 32.9%).

From Forbes, September 11 © 2014 Forbes LLC. All rights reserved. Used by permission and protected by the Copyright Laws of the United States. The printing, copying, redistribution, or retransmission of this Content without express written permission is prohibited.

Several of the high-ranked metro areas on our list are housing bubble hot spots that experienced rapid population growth in the first half of the last decade but then stalled out in the Recession. No. 3 Las Vegas posted 35% growth among 5- to 14-year-olds from 2000 to 2010. Since 2010 its child population has expanded at a modest 2.3% rate. A similar pattern can be observed in No. 5 Phoenix.

> There's a steady drumbeat in the media proclaiming that families with children are returning to dense cities and expensive regions. In reality, the numbers don't add up. Among the 10 large metro areas with the lowest percentage of children are New York, Boston and San Francisco–Oakland, where the percentage of 5- to 14-year-olds is 11.5%, the lowest in the nation except for Pittsburgh (10.8%).

In most of the top 10 metro areas on our list kids in the age range we looked at account for over 14% of the total population, compared to a national average of 13%. The city with the largest share of kids is No. 12 Salt Lake City, where 16.2% of the residents are between the ages of 5 and 14.

The Great American Kiddie Desert

The largest declines in the 5 to 14 cohort since 2000 have almost all occurred in the large coastal metropolitan centers, led by Los Angeles, 46th out of the 52 cities on our list, where the child population has dropped by 303,000, or 15.3%, since 2000. In the New York metro area (40th), the number of 5- to 14-year-olds fell by 238,000.

Economics alone does not explain this. Some of these metro areas, notably New York and Boston (38th, -8%), have done fairly well in the aftermath of the Great Recession. Yet they are only doing marginally better in attracting families than the (mostly) hard-hit metro areas at the bottom of our list: Buffalo and Rochester, N.Y., Pittsburgh and Detroit. (New Orleans actually ranked last behind Buffalo, but that's a function of population flight due to Hurricane Katrina.)

So why are otherwise thriving areas losing families? One possible explanation may come from cultural and political factors. As Austrian demographer Wolfgang Lutz has pointed out, an increasingly childless society creates "self reinforcing mechanisms" that make childlessness, singleness and one-child families increasingly predominant. In this process, which is further advanced in Japan, much of East Asia and throughout large parts of Europe, civic priorities often favor adult cultural amenities over things like parks and schools that are more important to families. Many areas that are increasingly child-free also often embrace density-oriented land use policies that lead to less affordable housing.

Of course, there's a steady drumbeat in the media proclaiming that families with children are returning to dense cities and expensive regions. In reality, the numbers don't add up. Among the 10 large metro areas with the lowest percentage of children are New York, Boston and San Francisco–Oakland, where the percentage of 5- to 14-year-olds is 11.5%, the lowest in the nation except for Pittsburgh (10.8%).

All else being equal, high housing prices, particularly for single-family homes, drive people with young children away. Across the country, the biggest decline in child populations found in the 2010 Census took place in the urban core and close-in suburbs of expensive metro areas, while net increases were counted almost exclusively in further out suburbs. In Los Angeles, the central city and older suburbs have had large declines in children while almost all family growth has occurred in suburbs like the Inland Empire, Irvine, the Antelope Valley and Valencia.

A Different Kind of Divide?

Much has been written about the various divides—political, racial, cultural, religious—afflicting the country. The geography of family formation poses yet another. In some parts of the country families appear to be proliferating, notably the Southeast and Intermountain West. In others, mostly in coastal California and the Northeast, they seem to be becoming rarer.

To some extent, this parallels the "red" and "blue" divide, but not entirely. Some bluish regions have enjoyed growth in their 5 to 14 population, most notably No. 2 Austin, although this is helped largely by the booming Texas economy and liberal land regulation, particularly in the burgeoning suburban ring. Only three others slipped into the top 20 of our list: Denver (13th), greater Washington, D.C. (17th), and Portland, Ore. (20th). Washington's government driven job growth is doubtless a factor. Denver and Portland are more than 90% suburban and exurban, and boast housing that is relatively affordable compared to the Bay Area, Los Angeles or New York.

Far more than politics, the interplay of economics and affordability tend to drive family migration. Take San Francisco–Oakland (33rd), which has had a robust economy over the past five years, but high housing prices have slowed the growth of families. Since 2000, the number of 5- to 14-year-olds in the metro area has dropped 2.7%. A recent real estate survey showed a million dollars would buy only 1,500 square feet in San Francisco, 2,000 in Boston, 2,198 in Washington and roughly 2,300 in either New York or Los Angeles. In contrast, that amount of money could purchase over 10,000 square feet in Houston and 8,850 in Raleigh.

Perhaps more important, high housing prices also make moving into a desirable area—particularly one with good schools—very difficult. In some core cities like Los Angeles, generally only the wealthiest areas have reliably decent public schools. In other parts of the country, you can still purchase a nice house for under $250,000 and be close to excellent schools. Unless the more expensive urban areas can expand their educational choices, many families will continue to look elsewhere for the critical combination of affordable housing and decent education for their children.

Ultimately, these metro areas, so favored in the media, will face increased competition from those that can better attract young families. Even most hipsters eventually grow up, start a family, seek to buy a house and aspire to a middle-class life. Places that can attract young families will have several things going for them compared to their increasingly child-free rivals: a growing adult labor force, an expanding consumer market and a spur to the local construction industry. If demography is destiny, nowhere is this more likely the case.

This Is the Most Economically Segregated City in America

By Alan Pyke
ThinkProgress, February 24, 2015

Amid record high economic inequality, America's wealthy aren't just buying rare caviar and Hammacher Schlemmer hoverboats. They're also purchasing physical separation from the rest of us, a new paper from University of Toronto researchers argues, resulting in higher and higher levels of residential segregation in American cities—especially densely populated large and mid-size metro areas where there are relatively few blue-collar jobs.

The rankings that Charlotta Mellander's and Richard Florida's research produced stand out from other oft-discussed rankings of economic reality and quality-of-life in U.S. cities. Lists of the most unaffordable places to live in America, based on median rent and income, are generally topped by the largest cities in the country. But the residential segregation rankings look somewhat different. San Francisco, which typifies the housing affordability crisis and often tops lists like this one, ranks right in the middle of the pack here. Four of the 10 most economically segregated metro areas are in Texas. Midsize culturally liberal college towns like Austin, TX, and Columbus, OH, top the list, outdoing bustling metros like Houston, Los Angeles, and New York, where the cost of living is higher. Those cities are still relatively segregated compared to the country, ranking in the top 10 metro areas out of the 359 that the researchers examined.

The new work looks to advance previous research into economic segregation that was based primarily on income. The researchers combined measures of segregation by income with ones tied to educational level and to the type of job a person has, and created an index of overall economic segregation in hundreds of U.S. metro areas. The resulting rankings and comparisons yield a variety of conclusions, some surprising and some expected, but key among them is this: "the behavior and location choices of more advantaged groups" are driving the rise in economic segregation at least as much as the isolation and ghettoization of poorer families.

The segregation effects pop up along other divisions besides wealth, too. The researchers found that occupation and education—which are correlated to a person's earning power, certainly, but represent a more complex distinction than breaking the population down purely by income—also exhibit the same self-isolating residential patterns. People with higher educational credentials tend to cluster, especially

---

This material was created by ThinkProgress (thinkprogress.org).

People with higher educational credentials tend to cluster, especially in densely populated metro areas, and members of the "creative class" tend to self-segregate into concentrated neighborhoods while people who work in service industries aren't able to do the same and end up scattered.

in densely populated metro areas, and members of the "creative class" tend to self-segregate into concentrated neighborhoods while people who work in service industries aren't able to do the same and end up scattered.

Residential segregation is therefore driven primarily by the choices that wealthier, higher-earning people make about where it would be cool to live—and as the *Washington Post* notes, the pattern amounts to "the well-off choosing to live in places where everyone else is well-off, too."

The larger the share of blue-collar jobs in a local economy, however, the less intense both educational and occupational segregation are. Where it is possible to make a comfortable living from lower-skill jobs, neighborhoods are more diverse. The researchers note that residential segregation wasn't always so intense, and point out that it has spiraling effects in a democracy: Previously, "the people who cut the lawns, cooked and served the meals, and fixed the plumbing [for the wealthy] used to live nearby—close enough to vote for the same councilors, judges, aldermen, and members of the board of education. That is less and less the case today."

Economic segregation is harmful to those born into the resulting high-poverty neighborhoods. Growing up in poverty damages the brain in the same ways that severe trauma or going without sleep do. Even a child born into a family of means will have a harder time rising up the economic ladder if that family lives in a poor zip code. And everyone else in the country suffers too, as economic segregation and concentrated poverty create harder-to-see macroeconomic costs for the whole nation to bear.

Mini-D.C.'s: A Small-City Boom Revitalizes Downtowns Once Left for Dead

By John Woodrow Cox
The Washington Post, October 31, 2014

Drew Murphy stepped out of his law office on a recent Thursday afternoon, walked two blocks south to pick up chicken salad and, four blocks later, entered his brick rowhouse to share lunch with his wife. He seldom drives because he doesn't have to. He can walk in 11 minutes to his favorite upscale restaurant, eight to his favorite wine bar and four to his favorite park to play with their dog, Henry.

Murphy, 31, lives the quintessential life of a young, successful professional in the District—except that he lives nowhere near the District. His walkable world is in downtown Frederick, Md., a thriving city 45 miles from the nation's capital with one-tenth of the population.

Many of the same forces fueling Washington's renaissance are driving a small-city boom regionally and nationally. From the historic cities of Alexandria, Annapolis and Leesburg to the newer Metro-centric communities of Bethesda and Clarendon, the desire to live within walking distance of restaurants, bars, theaters and parks has revitalized once-withering downtowns, according to demographers and real estate experts.

Elsewhere, examples of the boom abound: Evanston outside Chicago, Pasadena outside Los Angeles, West Palm Beach outside Miami, said Christopher B. Leinberger, a George Washington University business professor who has studied the trend for years.

In the Washington region, few places have benefited more from the phenomenon than downtown Frederick, where a flourishing restaurant, bar and art scene has transformed the 18th century county seat into a mini-D.C. In the past five years, the city has added 40 businesses to its eclectic downtown, Frederick officials say, and demand for houses in the most walkable parts of the city has pushed up median home prices.

Still, a mini-D.C. is not D.C.

Big housing complexes, large retailers and especially plentiful job opportunities are often scarce in small cities. The regulations that mandate architectural preservation in historic downtowns can also make development difficult or cost-prohibitive.

From The Washington Post, May 5 © 2015 Washington Post Company. All rights reserved. Used by permission and protected by the Copyright Laws of the United States. The printing, copying, redistribution, or retransmission of this Content without express written permission is prohibited.

The long-term prosperity of downtown Frederick and similar places will likely depend on a steady influx of people just like Murphy and his wife, Meghan, a 27-year-old clinical social worker.

They used to live in the heart of Baltimore, but he grew up in Frederick County and wanted to move back. When a law firm made him an offer last year, she was reluctant. "I'm not ready for cornfields just yet," she told him. So they rented a restored downtown rowhouse.

"We're kind of still keeping what we had in Baltimore," she said, between bites of chicken salad. "Just with a small-town feel."

"It's amazing."

A man with a bushy beard and arms sleeved in tattoos held a folded stack of receipts. Chris Ritchie, 44, had just returned to Frederick after a week of buying antiques for his five-month-old home furnishings store, Smokestack Studios, when a fellow downtown business owner stopped in to say hello. He ticked off the new clients that had recently offered him work: an upscale restaurant, a local nonprofit group, two salons.

"Holy cow," she said.

"Yeah," he told her. "It's amazing."

Ritchie, who has two decades of experience in the furniture industry, searched from North Carolina to Pennsylvania for a spot to open his store. He sells everything from $100 original Swiss Army canvas backpacks to $2,600 high-grade leather sofas designed after Babe Ruth's baseball glove.

"I was literally driving my car through Frederick," he recalled, "and I said, 'This is it.'"

Next door to Ritchie's 4,000-square-foot studio is Brewer's Alley, which is owned by Phil Bowers, whose family in Frederick goes back at least six generations. Bowers, who also operates four other restaurants in town, remembers an age not long ago when Ritchie would have just kept driving.

"You know," Bowers said, "timing is everything."

The history of Frederick's downtown sounds much like that of many others. It served for two centuries as the community's bustling commercial center until cars triggered an exodus to the suburbs. A nearby mall lured away four of the downtown's anchor retailers, while interstates to Washington and Baltimore siphoned off jobs and remaining shopping dollars.

"The very asset that made it successful originally—that it was walkable—became a disadvantage in the late 20th century when everybody wanted to drive everywhere," Leinberger said. "Now that very asset is what's bringing it back."

In Alexandria, the small-city boom has been underway for years and continues to transform a downtown brimming with historic buildings, bars, restaurants and retail shops that are a short drive or Metro ride from Washington.

Between 2000 and 2012, rent rates in the Old Town area nearly doubled, and median home prices rose to almost $700,000. In the next three to five years, according to the Alexandria Economic Development Partnership, about 5,700 new housing units (mostly rentals) will be built within walking distance of the downtown area.

Though easy access to Washington is a huge asset, a number of small downtowns are still prospering without it.

Gwen Pangle owns a real estate company 40 miles from the District in downtown Leesburg and has lived in Loudoun County since the late 1970s.

"I can remember a time actually when IHOP was the only restaurant Leesburg would support," she said. "Everything else that came here would close."

The downtown—where President John Quincy Adams and former president James Monroe once escorted the Marquis de Lafayette during his grand tour of the United States—now hosts more than two dozen eateries. Homes sell for more than twice what they did in the late 1990s.

A 2013 poll by the Urban Land Institute helps illustrate why. Millennials—who along with empty-nesters are leading the movement back to cities large and small—place a premium on walkability and distance to work and school. The survey of 1,200 adults also found a shift in taste across all generations, with more than half saying they would prefer to live near a mix of shops, restaurants and offices.

> Millennials—who along with empty-nesters are leading the movement back to cities large and small—place a premium on walkability and distance to work and school. The survey of 1,200 adults also found a shift in taste across all generations, with more than half saying they would prefer to live near a mix of shops, restaurants and offices.

But that doesn't mean everyone wants to move to big cities, said David Versel, senior research associate at the George Mason University Center for Regional Analysis. Many people prefer smaller downtowns, where they can remain close to family and avoid big-city housing prices, congestion, crime and sometimes troubled public schools.

Liz Sizemore, 26, so enjoys living in downtown Fredericksburg, Va., that she takes a 90-minute train ride to and from Washington four days a week to her job as a gift shop manager.

"I love D.C., but I thrive in smaller towns," she said. "It's worth it."

"[M]ore job opportunities"

By day, Frederick's downtown streets are neither big-city loud nor sleepy-town quiet. Slow-shuffling tourists take photos on the bridges over Carroll Creek as coffee-carrying millennials maneuver past sidewalk signs that advertise lunch specials and spa treatments, tattoos and yoga.

By night, available street-side parking is sparse, especially on performance nights at the Weinberg Center for the Arts. At Volt, the Tasting Room and Firestone's

Culinary Tavern, tables are packed and bottles are emptied. The bars crowd with drinkers.

"It's the best of D.C. or Baltimore or New York without the hassle," said Valerie Hartman, who moved here with her husband, John, after raising their three children in a larger suburban house.

With demand strong, downtown homes that used to stay on the market for three months now typically go in one, said Sue Collins, who has been selling real estate in Frederick since 2001. In that time, she has also seen the city's population grow by more than 25 percent to 67,000. Her daughter, Sarah, 26, who also sells real estate, just returned to Frederick—and rented an apartment downtown—after living in Baltimore and Phoenix.

But even its biggest boosters acknowledge that Frederick faces challenges. It lacks a grocery store or much new housing. In all cities, large and small, it remains unclear whether millennials will stick around to raise their children. Some in Frederick are trying, but many others won't, including downtown devotees Drew and Meghan Murphy, who recently broke ground on a suburban home that they think will better suit a family.

And then there's jobs.

Just 6,500 people work downtown, though that's 1,500 more than a decade ago. City officials hope the area's first hotel and conference center, tentatively scheduled to open in 2017, will provide an additional boost.

"Over time, we're going to have the types of jobs that people are looking for," said Richard Griffin, director of economic development. "It just doesn't happen immediately."

Alyssa Molina and Gloria Majchrzak, both 22, emerged from a Mexican restaurant near the creek on a recent evening. They both grew up in the area and said they have long imagined living and working in downtown Frederick.

Molina has even picked out a dream home near Baker Park. It has a garden and a white exterior and Victorian architecture. Majchrzak, a manager at a Target 40 miles away, pointed to a second-floor apartment above a now-closed deli: "I would love to have that."

"Now that we've revitalized downtown," Molina said, "there needs to be more job opportunities."

Instead, she plans to start her career in New York City. Majchrzak intends to move to downtown Baltimore.

How Suburban Are Big American Cities?

By Jed Kolko
FiveThirtyEight, May 21, 2015

What, exactly, is a city? Technically, cities are legal designations that, under state laws, have specific public powers and functions. But many of the largest American cities—especially in the South and West—don't feel like cities, at least not in the high-rise-and-subways, "Sesame Street" sense. Large swaths of many big cities are residential neighborhoods of single-family homes, as car-dependent as any suburb.

Cities like Austin and Fort Worth in Texas and Charlotte, North Carolina, are big and growing quickly, but largely suburban. According to Census Bureau data released [in May 2015], the population of the country's biggest cities (the 34 with at least 500,000 residents) grew 0.99 percent in 2014—versus 0.88 percent for all metropolitan areas and 0.75 percent for the U.S. overall. But city growth isn't the same as urban growth. Three cities of the largest 10 are more suburban than urban, based on our analysis of how people describe the neighborhoods where they live.

Official government data obscures how suburban America really is. There's no definition of "suburb" or "suburban" in the census's otherwise exhaustive list of geographic terms and concepts. The census definition of urban areas amounts to the 81 percent of the U.S. population that is not rural, but this definition, as we'll see below, lumps together urban and suburban neighborhoods.

Researchers and official data sources sometimes treat the portion of a metropolitan area outside its largest city or cities as the suburbs, but this gets many neighborhoods wrong in both directions. Just as big cities contain neighborhoods that feel suburban, some areas outside big-city boundaries—such as Hoboken, New Jersey, and West Hollywood, California—feel more urban than parts of their neighboring big cities.

To develop a standard definition of suburban that reflects what residents experience, the online real estate site Trulia, where I am the chief economist, surveyed 2,008 adults from across the U.S. We asked them to describe where they live as urban, suburban or rural, and we purposely did not define these terms for them.[1] We also had each respondent's ZIP code, which we used to identify his or her city, metropolitan area and state of residence. For this research, we treated ZIP codes as neighborhoods even though many ZIP codes encompass more area than what people may think of as a neighborhood.

Reprinted with permission.

It turns out that many cities' legal boundaries line up poorly with what local residents perceive as urban. Nationally, 26 percent of Americans described where they live as urban, 53 percent said suburban and 21 percent said rural. (This comes close to the census estimate that 81 percent of the population is urban if "urban" is understood to include suburban areas.) Within "principal cities" of metropolitan areas (the census designates one or more cities in each metro as "principal"), respondents split 47 percent urban, 46 percent suburban and 7 percent rural, though those percentages include people in many small cities and metro areas. Looking only at respondents in the larger principal cities (those with a population greater than 100,000) of larger metropolitan areas (those with a population greater than 500,000), the breakdown was 56 percent urban, 42 percent suburban and 2 percent rural. That means close to half of people who live within city limits describe where they live as suburban.

Our analysis showed that the single best predictor of whether someone said his or her area was urban, suburban or rural was ZIP code density. Residents of ZIP codes with more than 2,213 households per square mile typically described their area as urban. Residents of neighborhoods with 102 to 2,213 households per square mile typically called their area suburban. In ZIP codes with fewer than 102 households per square mile, residents typically said they lived in a rural area.[2] The density cutoff we found between urban and suburban—2,213 households per square mile—is roughly equal to the density of ZIP codes 22046 (Falls Church in Northern Virginia); 91367 (Woodland Hills in California's San Fernando Valley); and 07666 (Teaneck, New Jersey).

Other factors played minor roles in predicting how respondents described where they live. Residents of very small cities and towns rarely said they lived in an urban area, even if their neighborhood was quite dense. Residents of lower-income neighborhoods with older housing stock often said they lived in an urban area, even if it was lower-density. Residents of lower-density ZIP codes with lots of businesses sometimes called their neighborhoods urban; so did residents of lower-density, higher-income ZIP codes that are next to higher-density ZIP codes. But, in general, ZIP code density alone gets us most of the way to predicting whether people say they live in an urban, suburban or rural area.

> **When we're looking to understand the economic, social and demographic issues facing urban and suburban America, city boundaries can mislead. Looking instead at neighborhoods, classified by their characteristics into urban, suburban and rural, shows more clearly how suburban America—including many of its largest cities—actually is.**

Because we surveyed only about 2,000 people, we had no respondents in the vast majority of the more than 30,000 U.S. residential ZIP codes. So we can't conclude anything directly about how residents describe a particular ZIP code. However, using these cutoffs for density and other predictors from our model, and census data on density and other ZIP code characteristics, we were able to classify nearly all U.S. ZIP codes as urban, suburban or rural. Then, for every city, we calculated the share of households who live in ZIP codes that our model, based on survey responses, classified as urban as opposed to suburban or rural.[3] Of course the model might classify some neighborhoods differently from how their residents perceive them.

By this measure, many large cities are overwhelmingly urban. Among the 10 largest cities, New York, Chicago and Philadelphia are at least 95 percent urban. Outside the largest 10, San Francisco, Detroit, Seattle, D.C., Baltimore and Boston are also entirely urban or nearly so. Los Angeles—despite its reputation for sprawl—is 87 percent urban. But three of the 10 largest cities are mostly suburban, including San Diego (49 percent urban), San Antonio (35 percent urban) and Phoenix (30 percent urban).

Furthermore, the new census population data shows that the fastest-growing large cities tend to be more suburban. Among the 10 fastest-growing cities with more than 500,000 people, five— Austin, Fort Worth, Charlotte, San Antonio and Phoenix—are majority suburban, and a sixth, Las Vegas, is only 50 percent urban. Only one of the 10 fastest-growing, Seattle, is at least 90 percent urban.

Among all cities with at least 100,000 residents, the correlation between population growth in the past year and urban share is −0.29. That's statistically significant, but it indicates that there are plenty of exceptions to the general pattern of suburban cities growing faster—there are both fast-growing urban cities (such as Seattle) and slow-growing suburban cities (such as Albuquerque, New Mexico, and Louisville, Kentucky).

City growth, therefore, does not necessarily mean more urban living. In order to understand policing, schools, property taxes and other typical responsibilities of city governments, we need to look at cities as defined by their legal boundaries. But when we're looking to understand the economic, social and demographic issues facing urban and suburban America, city boundaries can mislead. Looking instead at neighborhoods, classified by their characteristics into urban, suburban and rural, shows more clearly how suburban America—including many of its largest cities— actually is.

Notes

1. The survey was conducted online in November 2014.
2. We used decision trees to find the cutoffs for density and other characteristics that best aligned with how respondents described where they lived.
3. Technically we used ZIP Code Tabulation Areas (ZCTAs), a census approximation of ZIP codes.

Foreclosures Fuel Detroit Blight, Cost City $500 Million

By Christine MacDonald and Joel Kurth
The Detroit News, June 3, 2015

Subprime lending and bargain-basement sales of foreclosed homes by banks and other mortgage lenders have helped create miles of blight in Detroit and a half-billion dollar liability for the city.

The Detroit News scoured thousands of property records to catalog the conditions of 65,000 mortgage foreclosures since 2005. The investigation shows for the first time the extent of damage to neighborhoods and the bill Detroit inherited when foreclosed homes were left open to destruction.

The toll is massive: 56 percent of mortgage foreclosures are now blighted or abandoned. Of those 36,400 homes, at least 13,000 are slated for demolition at a projected cost of $195 million, *The News* found. The city lost another $300 million in tax payments from foreclosed homes that Wayne County seized for nonpayment of taxes.

There's plenty of blame, from homeowners who signed loans they couldn't repay, to investors who failed to secure properties.

In cities such as Baltimore and Memphis, Tennessee, banks and other lenders were successfully sued over the condition of their properties. In Detroit, few efforts were made to hold institutions accountable for damage after those lenders blanketed city residents with risky loans, and then sold homes for as little as $1 after they were foreclosed on.

"There's an ironclad correlation between subprime lending and abandoned, blighted and in-need-of-demolition houses in Detroit," said Steve Tobocman, former co-director of the Michigan Foreclosure Task Force that was formed in 2007 to respond to the crisis.

"We had an opportunity to move forward on some of those homes and abuses, and we didn't take that opportunity."

Mortgage industry officials said they are easy scapegoats and worked to prevent foreclosures and maintain properties.

"Once we sell the property, it is someone else's property," said Brad German, a spokesman for Freddie Mac, a government-controlled mortgage company that according to *The News* analysis also had 56 percent of its foreclosed properties

Reprinted with permission.

considered blighted and tax delinquent as of last year. "It would be the same if I sold you a house and you walked away from it.

"There isn't a post-sale responsibility."

The News investigation comes as Detroit emerges from bankruptcy and Mayor Mike Duggan is searching for more federal funds to continue a blitz that demolished 3,500 buildings last year at a cost of about $15,000 per home. Tens of thousands remain.

The News based its findings by comparing data from real estate tracking companies RealtyTrac and CoreLogic with a 2014 survey of all city parcels by the Detroit Blight Task Force.

The News found:

- Detroit had one of the highest rates of subprime lending in the country: 68 percent of all city mortgages in 2005, compared to 27 percent statewide and 24 percent nationwide, according to federal records.
- Designed for those with damaged credit, the loans have higher interest rates than traditional mortgages and were at least four times more likely to default, according to federal records. Nearly $4 billion of the high-cost loans were written in Detroit in the four years before the 2008 real estate crash.
- Blight followed: Up to 78 percent of foreclosed homes financed through subprime lenders are now in poor condition or tax foreclosed.
- Foreclosed homes were sold for a quarter of what city assessors said they were worth. The cheap prices made it less likely for buyers to maintain properties or pay taxes.
- When tax foreclosures are included, more than 1 in 3 city properties have been foreclosed in the past 10 years.

Experts said that was like adding gas to the fire in a city whose neighborhoods had suffered decades of abandonment. In one triangle-shaped area between Grand River, Dexter and Joy, 80 percent of 200 mortgage foreclosures from 2005–2013 are blighted or have been seized by the county for unpaid taxes.

"People making bad decisions"

Alfred Pointer is surrounded by empty shells of what were once stately brick homes in his Virginia Park neighborhood north of New Center.

In the 3000 block of Carter, 27 of 49 homes have been foreclosed because of defaulted loans or back taxes. Pointer maintains an abandoned mortgage foreclosure next door, but two more are across the street, including one that looks as though it could collapse in a strong breeze.

It was sold by Freddie Mac to an investor for $1,500 in 2008, three months after subprime lender Washington Mutual foreclosed over an $84,000 debt. Three years later, Wayne County seized the home for nonpayment of taxes.

Financial firms got more than $200 billion from the federal government as part of the bailout to keep the economy afloat after the real estate crash. Pointer said Detroit neighborhoods were left with the mess.

"The banks walked away and left us high and dry," Pointer said. "We all got juked."

Lenders blanketed Pointer's neighborhood in the mid-2000s: Nearly 80 percent of mortgages to homeowners there were written at subprime rates.

His neighborhood is one of eight in Detroit that were among the top 20 census tracts nationwide with the highest rates of subprime lending in 2005, according to *The News'* analysis of federal loan data. Others were in enclaves of St. Louis; Houston; Memphis, Tennessee; Jacksonville, Florida; and Jackson, Mississippi. All are overwhelmingly African-American neighborhoods, data show.

Until the collapse, the loans were lucrative: Monthly payments on a $100,000 loan at 9 percent are $200 more a month than those at a 6 percent rate, or $73,000 over a 30-year mortgage.

"The stage was set with gross irresponsibility by the banking industry, and I still think that they ought to be made to pay cities that are left to clean up the mess," said Frank Ford, a senior policy adviser for the Thriving Communities Institute, a nonprofit land protection group based in Cleveland that has studied vacant land and foreclosures in northern Ohio. "This was done by people making bad decisions, repeatedly, in some cases knowingly."

In Detroit, subprime lenders left a string of problem properties: 78 percent of the Long Beach Mortgage Co.'s foreclosed loans are on homes that are now blighted or abandoned, while the rate is 67 percent of those by New Century Financial Corp. and 70 percent for Ameriquest and Argent.

Those companies, along with many others that dealt primarily with subprime loans, are out of business. Other subprime lenders such as Ameriquest were accused of inflating appraisals, failing to verify income of borrowers and deceiving them about terms of loans.

"Tried to do our best"

When loans failed, financial firms practically gave away some homes in Detroit.

Warren landlord Alan Thorne said he bought 50 homes for $1 apiece in 2007 from subprime lending giant Ocwen Financial Corp. of Georgia.

A year later, his company paid $9,600 for 10 foreclosed homes from Novastar Financial, a Kansas City–based subprime lender, records show.

Since then, all but one of the properties have been foreclosed on by the county for nonpayment of taxes.

"I just don't see how the city can charge you $3,000 per year in taxes for a house you paid $1 for," Thorne said. "If you're getting $600 a month in rent and paying $3,000 in taxes, the math doesn't add up."

Thorne blamed renters and scrappers for blight at his former properties, saying "you always have to worry that everything will be stolen overnight."

The mortgage industry divides roles among financial institutions, with some owning loans, others accepting payment and still others holding title for several investors. The system wasn't established to handle widespread foreclosures and couldn't handle the volume in Detroit and elsewhere, said Guy D. Cecala, CEO and publisher of "Inside Mortgage Finance" that tracks the industry.

Citywide, lenders sold foreclosed homes for $10,500 on average, nearly $30,000 less than city assessors believed they were worth, according to city data from 2012 and 2013. The average foreclosed home in Detroit had an $83,000 mortgage, according to RealtyTrac data from 2006 to 2014.

"There comes a point in time. . . the bank will just say, 'We have to get these toxic loans off the books,'" said Harry J. Glanz, co-founder of Capital Mortgage Funding in Southfield.

John Llewellyn, a spokesman for the Lansing-based Michigan Bankers Association, said member banks maintain properties, provide neighborhood groups with contacts to call if there are problems and donate properties to nonprofits. But when banks try to sell to qualified buyers, few are interested, driving down prices, he said.

> "I don't think anybody did enough to hold banks responsible. There should be a lot more (bankers) out there doing hard time who are out living in mansions."

Dan Gilbert, founder of Quicken Loans and a co-chairman of the Detroit Blight Removal Task Force, said there's not enough data to conclude mortgage foreclosures caused blight in Detroit. He blamed high taxes and other factors.

"Existing blight causes other blight. Poor city services. All of it together," Gilbert said.

All told, 52 percent of Quicken mortgages that ended in foreclosure from 2005-2014 are now blighted. Gilbert said his company made good loans to qualified borrowers and sold mortgages soon after writing them, and isn't responsible for foreclosed homes' current condition.

"A look at the past"

The arguments don't make life any easier for Edda Dickerson, a retired school teacher, or her neighbors on Birwood Street in Northwest Detroit that was decimated by foreclosures.

"I don't think anybody did enough to hold banks responsible," Dickerson said. "There should be a lot more (bankers) out there doing hard time who are out living in mansions."

Her former neighbor of 20 years, Ronda Morrison, visited her foreclosed home for the first time this year at the request of *The News*.

The home she once adored was now full of dirty clothes, rubbish and ashes.

It was foreclosed in 2012, after negotiations failed for a short sale to sell it for less than she owed. For months before, Morrison said she tried to work with Bank of America to reduce the $64,000 debt on the home appraised at $28,000. She said the bank wouldn't budge unless her mortgage was in default.

"I need help. That's what I said. I didn't want to leave," said Morrison, 52, who owns a nearby shoe repair shop. "Let's renegotiate to what the house is worth. . . . I am not going to be 90 years old paying a mortgage on Birwood."

Fannie Mae owned the loan and is controlled by a government group, Federal Housing Finance Agency, that opposes reducing homeowners' debt. Bank of America, which serviced the loan, said Morrison only reached out when she attempted a short sale.

A year after the foreclosure, Fannie Mae sold the home to an international investor for $13,500. It will cost more than that for the city to tear it down.

"If we could have sold that property for a higher price, we absolutely would have. . . . It is [a] very, very difficult circumstance that we are doing everything we can to address," said Andrew Wilson, a Fannie Mae spokesman.

Fannie Mae paid $4,700 of the city tax bill for Morrison's home and spent $1,500 in repairs before selling it, Wilson said. When it was empty, scrappers plundered the home and it was set on fire.

Now, it's scheduled to be demolished, as tires and debris cover the mint she planted around her cedar wood deck. A room she used to meditate in is now damaged by fire. And the kitchen sink is gone.

"This is becoming too much for my stomach," said Morrison in tears. "I used to have such a life here."

3
Economy and Industry

© Richard Nowitz/National Geographic Creative/Corbis

Pittsburgh's central business district, photographed from Point State Park on September 29, 2014. After years of blight following the decline of the steel industry, Pittsburgh is experiencing an economic revival, particularly in the educational, medical, and technology industries.

Jobs, Opportunity, and Innovation in Urban Environments

After many years of economic loss and stagnation, American urban environments have seen a recent resurgence in vitality and popularity. More and more modern consumers, residents, executives, and entrepreneurs are gravitating towards the unique aesthetic, amenities, and cultural environment of downtown urban areas. As businesses and city governments adjust to these changes, there has been a subsequent spread in both economic and residential development, revitalizing not only the larger cities but also smaller cities and nearby suburbs surrounding the major metropolitan areas. Though the future of current trends remains unclear, the changing tastes of both consumers and companies is helping to redefine urban work and living.

Three Generations of Economic Exodus

The economic environment of modern cities has been affected by the long-term phenomenon of settlement and expansion called suburbanization, which began in the 1920s with the establishment of the first peripheral communities where individuals who worked in the cities could purchase single-family detached homes in smaller, planned communities outside those cities. This lifestyle became especially appealing to a large number of young white families after World War II, leading to the birth of modern suburban development, and accelerated with the establishment of the highway system in the late 1950s, essentially allowing more and more Americans to live outside the city, while still working in downtown urban areas. This process continued into the 1990s, draining urban areas of population and creating a new center for residential and commercial communities.[1]

The first generation of Americans to live in the suburbs in the 1950s still commuted into the city for work. In a 1993 article in the *Journal of Economic Perspectives*, the authors cite research indicating that 70 percent of all employment opportunities were located in cities in the 1950s. By 1960, only 63 percent of jobs were in cities, and the percentage of jobs in the city continued to decline with progressive suburban growth, reaching 55 percent in 1970, 50 percent in 1980. By 1990, 55 percent of all employment opportunities were located outside urban areas.[2] In some of the largest metropolitan areas, the loss of jobs was severe by the 1970s. For instance, in 1970 New York City, 78 percent of jobs were in the suburbs.[3]

The economic exodus from U.S. urban areas followed the exodus of the population from downtown areas. The first businesses to move to the suburbs were service businesses, like gas stations, restaurants, and grocery stores. These essential businesses moved out to suburbs to take advantage of growing suburban customer populations. Essentially, as suburbs become more and more independent, suburban developments attracted more and more community businesses, like medical/dental offices, schools and educational institutions, banking and financial services, and consumer goods retailers. One example of this trend is in the establishment of "shopping centers" and "strip malls," which became a standard feature of the suburban environment. There were only eight shopping centers in America at the end of World War II, but the number increased to 3,840 in 1960.[4]

In the 1960s and 1970s, inflation and the rising cost of urban property helped to accelerate the loss of jobs in American cities. One of the early pioneers of this trend was Birmingham, Alabama, natives Ervin Jackson and Newman H. Waters, who established a new commercial building movement in 1955 with the nation's first "office park," a low-rise building with space to accommodate a variety of office environments and surrounded by planted green space. The office park innovation took off, with thousands emerging over subsequent decades as it became normal for urban residents to commute out to the counties for work, shopping, and other essential business.[5] Similarly, for expanding industrial businesses, cities offer little in terms of room for expansion without expensive property development. Urban areas also had extensive regulations and limitations on industrial development as a result of congestion and the need to accommodate residential and commercial interests in relatively small areas. It therefore became more and more common for large commercial businesses to build new factories, office centers, and expanded facilities outside cities.

The loss of population, followed by a loss of jobs, created blight and decay in many of America's urban environments. Buildings and homes that were abandoned were often left empty as there were fewer new businesses or residents looking to move into downtown areas. In Philadelphia, Pennsylvania, for instance, a 2013 study indicated that the downtown area had more than 40,000 abandoned houses, lots, and commercial buildings.[6] Similar patterns of urban decay occurred around the nation as the center of economic and population growth shifted to the suburban centers outside the cities. Three generations of Americans, the postwar generation, their children the "baby boomers," and the children of the baby boomers, often called Generation X, have favored suburban work and life over the cities. The millennial generation might reverse the trend, but might also follow earlier generations as more and more millennials begin raising families.

A Decade of Renewal?

To combat decay, city and state governments, cooperating with developers, real estate specialists, and economists have attempted to stimulate "urban renewal" by making downtown areas more attractive to consumers and businesses. Urban renewal programs have been in place since suburbanization, but in most cases, renewal programs have been ineffective in combating the outward movement of economic and population resources. There has been considerable speculation, among sociologists and historians, that the millennial generation (also known as Generation Y; individuals born in the 1980s and 1990s) might be the first generation of

Americans to return to urban environments in large numbers. This has led to a resurgence in renewal programs, though most continue to have limited results. For instance, between 2000 and 2010, jobs within 3 miles of city centers fell from 24.5 percent of jobs to 22.9 percent of all available positions. Meanwhile, growth of "outer suburbs," more than 15 miles from city centers, continued to accelerate with a growth of 40.9 to 43.1 percent of jobs between 2000 and 2010.[7]

To encourage business growth in the cities, city and state governments offer tax breaks for corporations who remain in or move to urban areas. Tax abatement and tax break programs have helped to encourage corporate involvement in urban areas. Despite the continuing slow growth of urban economies, there has been a resurgence of residential interest in downtown areas inspired by millennial preferences. Between 2013 and 2014, 2.3 million more residents moved into metro areas around the country, and the loss of population also slowed, with the majority of the nation's 381 cities recording rising or stable population levels between 2012 and 2014.[8]

Cities have long been the primary location for immigration, and city economies depend on the influx of both workers and entrepreneurs. In Los Angeles, immigrant labor accounts for more than a third of the city's economic output. Immigrants have long played an important role in economic growth in large cities, but Census Bureau data shows that the influence of immigrant labor and entrepreneurship has spread to smaller cities and suburbs as well, for instance, in Nashville, Tennessee, where the immigrant population doubled between 2000 and 2014. Reviews of the Nashville economy indicate that immigrants are twice as likely as natives to start businesses and have taken up a significant role in "local" industry, including construction, health care, and hotels. While immigration remains one of the nation's more controversial issues, many cities court immigration precisely because city administrators realize that the immigrant labor force plays an important role in growth.[9]

A wave of population growth in urban areas has been accompanied by an emerging trend of businesses returning to cities. For instance, the Motorola Company left Libertyville, Illinois, in 2013 to return to a new business space in downtown Chicago, a move prompted in part by changing preferences among executives who would rather work in cities than in office parks and suburban communities. Studies found commercial vacancy rates in central business districts falling in many of the nation's urban areas faster than vacancies in equivalent suburban centers. The businesses have essentially followed the preferences of consumers and executives. A 2010 study found, for instance, that 43 percent of Americans with bachelor's degrees were choosing to remain in cities for work, thus providing increased incentive for businesses to remain as well.[10] The resurgence of American cities has been notable in cities like Cleveland, Ohio, and Pittsburgh, Pennsylvania, that were once heavily focused on industrial manufacturing but lost as much as 50 percent of their peak populations due to a loss of core industries in the 1970s and 1980s. Younger generations seeking a lower cost of living and opportunities for entrepreneurship began looking towards the underutilized rust belt cities in the 1990s, and modest growth has continued into the 2010s. In 2015, former industrial rust belt cities have begun to make small gains in immigration, which is further stimulating growth and diversity in these areas.[11]

The stability of the recent trend toward renewal remains in question. While some studies clearly show a resurgence of interest in urban living and urban business, current trends are far too recent to draw lasting conclusions. Over the next five to ten years, millennials could increasingly move to suburban areas, as their parents did, to raise their families and thus reverse the recent influx of businesses into cities.

The Urban Tech Revolution

Despite the growth of the suburban office parks, there are some amenities offered by downtown real estate that cannot be easily reproduced in suburban environments. Chiefly, companies that prefer downtown spaces gain prominence and access to the amenities of downtown districts, including food, shopping, mass transit, and other downtown services and businesses. As more and more Americans embrace mass transit, bicycling, pedestrian commuting, and the vibrant social/commercial diversity of urban areas, urban commercial real estate becomes more attractive.

For many decades, the downtown skyscrapers present in most urban central business districts were home to banking and financial institutions. For instance, the 52-story office building at 555 California Street in San Francisco has hosted Bank of America, Goldman Sachs, and Morgan Stanley. The building caters to big business residents by offering a variety of built-in amenities, like first floor shops and businesses, 24/7 security, and a variety of other "upscale" features. However, banking and financial businesses have increasingly moved out to the suburbs, while tech businesses, the fastest growing and most vibrant sector of the modern business world, have been increasingly moving into downtown real estate. Companies like Microsoft and LinkedIn have a younger population of executives. Occupying downtown buildings in San Francisco, New York, and other cities attracts young talent, as do the night life and recreational options of the city and the opportunity to eschew commuting to the suburbs for work. From 2010 to 2013 at least a dozen tech companies moved from the office parks of the suburban Silicon Valley to downtown headquarters in San Francisco.[12]

This trend was mirrored on the East Coast in the nation's most expensive city, New York, where a variety of tech startups have relocated since 2010. By 2014, New York City, after decades of stagnant growth, had become the number two location for tech startups in the nation. Between 2003 and 2010, New York City saw a 60 percent increase in tech jobs in the city and between 2010 and 2011 alone, real estate for tech companies expanded from 3.8 million square feet to more than 6 million.[13]

Web businesses Tumblr and Kickstarter have headquarters in Manhattan while Google also has a New York satellite office in the Port Authority building on Eighth Avenue. A number of CEOs whose companies have relocated to cities have also expressed interest in the process of building or revitalizing urban environments through their involvement, essentially creating a new resource for urban businesses and services by opting for urban corporate centers. In addition, some executives have expressed interest in the idea that the closer spaces of urban environments encourage both competition and collaboration to a greater extent than the isolated corporate oases of suburban office parks.[14]

The urban tech boom of the 2010s, like many other features of the broader trends in urban revitalization, may turn out to be a transient phenomenon. Tech companies, especially virtual service companies like Tumblr, Facebook, and LinkedIn, are especially vulnerable to rapidly changing consumer preferences. For instance, though Facebook remains the world's most popular social network in 2015, analysis suggests that usage of the media giant has peaked, and Facebook suffered a 12 percent decline in users in 2014 while alternative social media companies like Twitter and Instagram gained traction with young users. Downtown urban environments tend to cater to large businesses with sufficient resources to afford high property and rent expenditures. It remains to be seen, therefore, whether the current generation of urban tech companies can remain profitable enough to afford the amenities and costs of urban corporate centers. The future of urban tech is complicated also by the increasing tendency for executives to telecommute and similar trends that have reduced the importance of physical office spaces. It also remains unclear how these trends will affect demand for urban property in the future.

Small Cities for Big Business

There are a number of drawbacks to establishing a business in America's larger urban environments. For one, many cities have limited space available for small businesses and charge exorbitantly high rents for available space due to increasing demand. Much of the available business spaces in cities consist of former factories or large office buildings abandoned during the height of suburbanization but unaffordable or inappropriate for many types of new businesses. The increasing preference of young executives and professionals for urban environments, coupled with the need for affordable real estate have created an emerging trend toward the expansion in America's smaller cities.

For instance, in 2015 Lafayette, Indiana, ranked second on *Forbes* magazine's list of the best places for startup businesses and career building. Low cost of living, coupled with affordable property and commercial space, propelled the small city forward in the 2010s with the expansion of the local Subaru Automotive plant and a variety of development projects through Purdue University. Small cities with universities, like Lafayette, Indiana, and Lawrence, Kansas, have been especially fast to grow with new businesses and population, thanks to the attractive social and cultural benefits brought about by the proximity of the university coupled with affordability.[15]

Small cities may have become the new "middle ground" between the expensive, competitive environments of larger urban business districts and the spread out, culturally impoverished and isolated environments of suburban developments. The fastest growing cities in the United States in 2015 were smaller like Raleigh, North Carolina; Austin, Texas; and San Jose, California.[16] As small cities have grown, American suburbs have also adjusted to changing consumer demands by becoming more "urban," with walkable commercial areas, more public transit options, and other city style amenities. Economic growth is always a compromise between affordability and desirability and, as populations continue to grow, and millennials take over as heads of businesses, economic growth is spreading into previously unexplored areas. If trends continue, America's smaller cities could become more important cultural centers in coming years, and the urbanization of suburbs could result in what is essentially a new era of growth in American cities, expanding through satellite communities.

Micah L. Issitt

Notes

1. Jackson, *Crabgrass Frontier.*
2. Mieszkowski and Mills, "The Causes of Metropolitan Surburbanization."
3. Van Horn and Schaffner, *Work in America*, 530.
4. "The Postwar Economy: 1945–1960," Rutgers University.
5. Scribner, *Renewing Birmingham*, 75-76.
6. Hurdle, "Philadelphia Raises Stakes with Plan to Reverse Blight."
7. Hargreaves, "America's Jobs Are Moving to the Suburbs,"
8. Westcott, "More Americans Moving to Cities, Reversing the Suburban Exodus."
9. Hesson, "Why American Cities Are Fighting to Attract Immigrants."
10. Weber, "Companies Say Goodbye to the 'Burbs."
11. Kotkin, "The Rustbelt Roars Back from the Dead."
12. Roose, "The Tech Sector's New, Urban Aesthetic."
13. Bowles and Giles, "New Tech City."
14. Florida, "The Joys of Urban Tech."
15. Badenhausen, "The Best Small Cities for Business and Careers 2015."
16. Carlyle, "America's 20 Fastest-Growing Cities."

The Nation's Future Depends on Its Cities, Not on Washington

By Michael Hirsh
National Journal, August 31, 2013

The residents of Minneapolis-St. Paul suffer, collectively, from a serious insecurity complex. They're always talking about how no one knows anything about their "twin" cities on the upper Mississippi River. Young professionals never want to live there, complains local author Jay Walljasper, who did a study of where those sought-after Gen X-ers and Y-ers want to go. "They all had aspirations for Toronto, Chicago, Pittsburgh, Washington, Montreal. I kept waiting for them to mention Minneapolis-St. Paul," he says. "But we were not on the radar."

To the extent that anybody pays attention at all, people tend to make fun of "MSP" (the preferred abbreviation; the cities' collective name is as ungainly as its reputation)—even homeys such as Garrison Keillor, who's made a career out of Minnesotan self-deprecation. Some "Twin Citians" (many hate that nickname, too) grimly joke that the last thing that brought them national attention was *The Mary Tyler Moore Show,* the 1970s sitcom about a thirtysomething TV reporter based there. As if to drive home just how deep the insecurity runs, the middle of downtown Minneapolis features a slightly ridiculous bronze statue of the actress throwing her "tam," as in the opening credits of her long-ago show.

And yet in an odd way, the Twin Cities' identity crisis has also proven to be one of their greatest economic strengths. One can't quite put one's finger on exactly what's there because, well, there's an awful lot there. Diversity, in a word, is the secret sauce that creates urban success. Though once known as a grain-milling capital, MSP lost that title to Buffalo in the 1930s, and now a slew of Fortune 500–sized companies with a vast variety of businesses are headquartered in the region, including Cargill, General Mills, 3M, Target, and U.S. Bancorp. And driven by all that ambition to put themselves on the map, Twin Citians display a civic pride that has prompted constant reinvention and inspired regional cooperation. As a result, MSP today enjoys the lowest unemployment rate (5.1 percent) of any major metropolitan area in the nation, and its population is surpassing Detroit as the second largest in the Midwest, after Chicago. Minneapolis-St. Paul has also enjoyed more economic stability since World War II—with fewer ups and downs, and steadier growth—than most other American cities. "We don't know what we are," says former *Minneapolis Star Tribune* columnist Steve Berg. "But it's still a great place to live."

Copyrighted 2015. National Journal Group. 119105:0815RR

Detroit, of course, never suffered an identity crisis. Everyone always knew what the Motor City stood for: the Big Three automakers. So much so that "Detroit" has been as much a synonym for America's chronically ailing auto industry as "Washington" is for the federal government. And that, in sum—a lack of diversity—was one of Detroit's biggest problems, contributing to last month's largest-ever bankruptcy filing by a city in U.S. history. The city's entire socioeconomic system was built around autos, with an "industrial middle class" nurtured by the United Auto Workers. When the auto industry fell on hard times, everything went with it. The blue-collar working class—non-college-educated, trained only to build and service cars—drifted into poverty with no recourse. For cities, economic diversity is as important as maintaining a broad portfolio of stocks is for investors.

What also sank Detroit was that its leaders failed to connect with the sprawl around it and turn the suburbs into part of a unified economic base. That is another feature of Minneapolis-St. Paul's success: It established a tax-sharing plan with scores of suburban communities. In the Detroit area, by contrast, the city and suburbs became virtual enemies. A similar dynamic led to other failed cities, such as Newark, N.J., once the haven (and inspiration) of a large Jewish population, including Philip Roth, who fled to the suburbs and never looked back. There was, on one hand, a desperate inner city that led to "white flight," and on the other an affluent, largely Caucasian suburbia that did everything but put up walls against the city that engendered it. In today's world, that is a recipe for ruin.

"Detroit was dealt a fairly bad hand, at least in recent years. The decline of manufacturing and real hourly wages in the United States had made it a tough 40 or 50 years for the demographic that Detroit depends on," says Mark Funkhouser, the former mayor of Kansas City, Mo., and an urban consultant based in Washington. "On the other hand, they played that hand fairly badly. The thing to do in a really harsh economic environment is to enhance competitiveness and compete for a larger tax base. Detroit did the opposite. Under Coleman Young [Detroit's first black mayor, who served from 1974 to 1994], everything was done for political reasons. Every time another white family left Detroit he lost some opposition votes. So he had no interest in reaching out to suburban communities. He benefited from white flight." Detroit went from being more than 80 percent white in 1950 to more than 80 percent African-American today.

This is also the great negative lesson for cities and regions that want to avoid Detroit's fate, because to a great extent the future belongs to successful cities and, even more, to the metropolitan areas for which they serve as hubs.

Ironically, given the nature of our high-tech, super-connected age, the future will look more and more like the city-states that ruled the world for millennia, from the days of Athens, Sparta, Carthage, and Rome, and that were last dominant 500 years ago, in such places as Venice and Florence, before the formation of most modern nation-states. Today, the shining example is Singapore, the city-state of 5.2 million people that, all by itself, has become an Asian tiger. The city-state of the future will not be sovereign, of course, but instead will act largely independently. "What we are experiencing is a metro-centered driving force of change. This is the center of the economic universe," says James Brooks, program director of the National League of Cities. "The United States is not one national economy but a series of smaller metropolitan economies."

The future, in other words, is going medieval.

Why Cities Work

The rise of the city-state has been a long-term trend, but it's gaining speed. Today, the 388 metro areas in the United States make up 84 percent of the nation's population and an astonishing 91 percent of gross domestic product. The top 100 metro areas alone total two-thirds of the U.S. population and three-quarters of GDP. And the world is catching up. "Today's roughly 50 percent urban population will climb to nearly 60 percent, or 4.9 billion people, in 2030. Africa will gradually replace Asia as the region with the highest urbanization growth rate," according to a recent report by the government's National Intelligence Council. Urban centers are estimated to generate 80 percent of economic growth in the world, and the percentage may be growing because of the way well-built urban areas with good infrastructure—including state-of-the-art Internet and telecom pipelines—can better apply resources and make more efficient use of tight public funds.

Thinking Regionally

The 100 largest metropolitan areas by population make up 72 percent of the nation's gross domestic product, and 65 percent of its population. The 10 largest metros by GDP account for a third of national GDP, and anchor urban "mega-regions."

Metropolitan area	GDP as a percentage of U.S. GDP (top 10)	Population (millions)
New York City	8.2%	19.0
Los Angeles	4.8	12.9
Chicago	3.5	9.5
Washington	2.8	5.7
Houston	2.7	6.0
Dallas	2.5	6.5
Philadelphia	2.3	5.9
San Francisco	2.2	4.3
Boston	2.1	4.5
Atlanta	1.8	5.3

Sources: U.S. Census Bureau; Bureau of Economic Analysis; Tim Gulden/George Mason University, Richard Florida

Perhaps that's why, in his new book *Antifragile: Things That Gain From Disorder*, the trader-turned-philosopher Nassim Nicholas Taleb writes that the city-state is more adaptable and therefore more durable than the nation-state. Consider the political paralysis at the national level in the United States and Europe—in part the result of governments that are just too huge, sclerotic, and cumbersome—and the potential fracturing of states in the Middle East even as cities such as Baghdad or Damascus will likely remain intact. For multinational companies, thriving metropolitan regions are increasingly the basic macroeconomic unit. "A city is too small, and a country is too big," Funkhouser says. "Countries are too blunt an instrument in which to compete."

Critically, the politics works better at the metro level as well: Republican and Democratic mayors in metropolitan areas tend to cooperate more than their counterparts at the national level, says Scott Smith, the Republican mayor of Mesa, Ariz., and president of the U.S. Conference of Mayors. Why? "Because they have to solve problems. In Washington they don't sense this need," Smith told *National Journal*. "I still have to pick up the garbage on Thursday. When someone dials 911, I have to make sure the police show up." Smith adds: "There is no such thing as national economies anymore. That's why you see the big business deals done not so much between commerce secretaries any more as between mayors, like the mayor of Shanghai and the mayor of Los Angeles."

The smartest city leaders have long since recognized these trends. Consider the story of Mike Bell, the mayor of Toledo, Ohio, a seemingly typical Midwestern Rust Belt city. Because the fate of Toledo, like that of Detroit, was linked to the auto industry, as soon as he was elected in 2010, Bell began carefully studying his much larger sister city's ailments. And he acted to prevent Toledo from suffering the same fate: Since 2010, Toledo has gone from a $48 million budget deficit to a $5 million surplus, without raising taxes or laying off cityworkers. How? One key to his success, Bell says, was to realize that his role as both mayor and salesman-in-chief isn't limited to Toledo proper; he needed to pitch his subregion as far away as China. "I'm a regional mayor, and I'm also a global mayor," Bell explained in an interview.

When talking to potential foreign investors, he would draw a circle around Toledo showing that if you moved out from the city 500 miles in every direction, you could reach 60 percent of the entire Midwestern population. "A picture is worth a thousand words," Bell says. He took that putatively ancient Chinese wisdom directly to investors in Shenzhen, winning a surprising amount of investment in businesses as diverse as restaurants and sheet metal. All of his missions have included other mayors and Port Authority officials from the region. In the end, according to a study by the McKinsey Global Institute, Bell has given Toledo an outsized reputation considering that it ranked only 182nd in Forbes' "2012 Best Places for Business and Careers."

Funkhouser says officials such as Bell have it right. "When I was mayor, I told my officials that the Kansas City region competes against the Denver region—but also the Shanghai region. That's really the way the economy works now. If you are a fragmented dysfunctional region, if the center city doesn't get along with the suburbs, then you lose the critical mass you need." Detroit, once again, provides a doleful counterexample where growth was ungoverned and not underpinned by effective mass transit or infrastructure. "The level of job sprawl in Detroit is staggering," says Bruce Katz, an urban expert at the Brookings Institution. "About 80 percent of the jobs are located more than 10 miles away from the central business district. The average for the country is about 40 percent."

The Information Age characterized by hyper-connectedness and competition among centers of innovative activity has, ironically, tended "to reward those places where innovation happens in closed spaces," Katz says. The more integrated and "thicker" the economy—the more densely layered it is with an agglomeration of companies and researchers—the greater the rewards. Just last week, the National Science Foundation published a report concluding that a quarter of all America's scientists and engineers live in just five metropolitan areas in California, New York, and Texas.

Interestingly, the new metro age once again puts the U.S. at a competitive advantage with the world, Katz says. "In part, our success is that we are the quintessential metropolitan nation--more metropolitan than Europe or rising countries like China or Brazil. Even in Europe, it's a smaller portion of the population that lives in cities, though they are urbanizing now."

Global Urbanization

By 2025, almost 60 percent of the world's population—or 4.6 billion people—will live in urban areas. About 630 million of them will live in one of 37 megacities, those with populations greater than 10 million.

Population living in urban areas in 2025

North America	85%
Latin America	83
Europe	76
Oceania	71
World	58
Asia	53
Africa	45

-United Nations, Department of Economic and Social Affairs, Population Division

Heeding Dolly Parton

Urban experts say it's important for city planners to get the proper blend of investment and resources for each particular city and metro area, because each has a unique profile. "Dolly Parton, a great economist, once said, 'Find out who you are, and do it on purpose,'" Katz jokes. That applies to cities as well, which are constantly overreaching in their efforts to reinvent themselves—and grow fast. Everyone, it seems, wants to be the next Silicon Valley, and that won't work. The rush to build cluster-like industrial or research parks can misfire if the right combination of investments isn't achieved. "Sixty to 70 percent of clusters fail; even if you do build them, it can take 20 years to find out," says Jonathan Woetzel of the McKinsey Global Institute, who recently coauthored a report called "How to Make a City Great."

One admonitory tale is the rise and relative decline of Research Triangle Park, the vast complex that lies between Raleigh, Durham, and Chapel Hill in North Carolina. Considered state-of-the-art thinking when it was built in 1959, the park helped to bring North Carolina into the Internet age. But its visionaries failed to keep pace with the new cachet of cities. IBM sold its computer business, and jobs moved out. Worst of all, it became uncool. "The current generation of tech workers doesn't want to toil in the soulless Office Space complexes surrounded by moats of parking that dot Research Triangle Park's sprawling vastness," wrote Lydia Depillis in *The New Republic* last year. Now the park is trying to give itself a new "urban living" image in an attempt to achieve more "density."

"Over the past couple of decades, what we saw were a lot of cities that were copycatting, essentially," Katz says. "They were particularly focused on the consumption economy: stadium building, convention-center expansion. You'd go from one city to another and see pretty much the same thing. What they weren't focused on was the portion of their economy that drives everything else. What goods do you make? What do you trade, who do you trade with, both domestically and globally?"

Stadiums and big-league teams add allure, but the more sustainable need is for "economic gardening" for grassroots growth, Woetzel says. Let the private sector make most of the decisions, and don't succumb to the temptation to overplan. Above all, don't stray too far from your city's raison d'etre. "In Kansas City, the city fathers and mothers are embarrassed about the image of a cow town, and they run away from it, which is absolutely absurd," Funkhouser says. "The reason for Kansas City's existence is that it was as far north as you went to put cattle into cars to go to Chicago," where they were slaughtered. As a result, today Kansas City is a logistical hub, with the second-largest freight-rail system in the country after Chicago. And that, Funkhouser says, is also the source of its future viability. "Instead of running around trying to create entertainment districts and things like that, the livestock, agribusiness stuff ought to be what they focus on. On one hand, you want diversity. On the other hand, you don't want to do a whole lot of 'me-toos.' What is your natural strength? One of the criticisms of Michael Bloomberg in New York was how much he embraced Wall Street. Well, hell, that is the main driver of New York City's economy."

Mayor Smith of Mesa says city planners must resist the temptation to simply follow the most glamorous trend. "There was a time when biomed was popular," he says. "If Mesa went after biomed, that would be a fool's errand because we don't have biomed." Instead, Smith set about figuring out what his city's organic growth centers were and came up with a bumper sticker: HEAT, which stands for health care, education, aerospace, and tourism and technology. He decided his city should try to attract small liberal-arts colleges of the kind that are still too rare in the Southwest.

Healthy growth should also be well paced. Growth that happens too fast can lead to problems such as Beijing's horrific air pollution or to the kind of ungoverned sprawl that outpaces infrastructure or mass transit. That eventually fragments urban areas, as happened in Detroit. Portland, Ore., considered by many to be a model of how to take an old city into a new era, has even controversially laid down a "regional growth boundary." True, Portland had the luck of being situated between the Silicon Valley and Seattle—and the legacy of headquartering Intel and Tektronics—but it also developed a vision for sustainable development and export strategies with Asia.

Brooks says the obstacles holding back growth can sometimes be as simple as getting the city charter right. "The Detroit city charter is very different from other charters. It's very specific about what is required by the city government and what can't be done," he says. "For example, it's very difficult to contract out its services. The charter doesn't allow that. That constrained the flexibility of the city government. Governments have to be nimble."

> Interestingly, the new metro age once again puts the U.S. at a competitive advantage with the world, Katz says. "In part, our success is that we are the quintessential metropolitan nation—more metropolitan than Europe or rising countries like China or Brazil.

The Secrets of Success

The National League of Cities' Brooks and other urban experts point to four ingredients essential to metropolitan success.

Consistent vision. Because successful city planning can take decades to pan out, patience and steadiness are required. Consider Chattanooga, Tenn., where its leaders are still putting in place a 45-year plan that has transformed the city from one of the most polluted in America to a highly livable and sought-after place, attracting huge amounts of foreign investment. Today beleaguered cities such as Cleveland, once derided as "the mistake on the lake," are pursuing new strategies. For Cleveland, it is to become the "green city on a blue lake," as its "Sustainable Cleveland 2019" strategy puts it.

Leadership. Hand in hand with vision comes leadership that is consistent and public-minded. Above all, as in the case of Chattanooga and Portland, a city must have a strong culture that promotes such leaders in the private and public sectors. New York has avoided the image of a has-been city and remained the most competitive because its mayors are constantly reinventing it, as Rudy Giuliani did with his tough anticrime agenda and Michael Bloomberg has done by investing in R&D and "green" innovation.

Public-private partnerships. Business, civic, and government leaders must act as a team. In Pittsburgh, for example, philanthropic efforts by the Carnegies and the Mellons helped the city enormously in making the transition from Rust Belt steel city to educational and medical hub.

Regional thinking. This is the new sine qua non for cities. In the future, none will succeed without it. Like Toledo's Bell, Colorado Gov. John Hickenlooper, when he was mayor of Denver, created a "caucus" of more than 30 area mayors who met regularly and helped jointly develop a regional light-rail system. Officials behind the Greater Houston partnership have made similar efforts. "You can develop regional collaboration in lots of ways," Funkhouser says. "Tax-base sharing, shared-services agreements. But, primarily, it really starts with the relationship between elected leaders. They have to be on the same page. Cities and metro areas are governed essentially as a regime."

All these factors can breed a critical survival trait for successful cities and their metro areas: resilience. Consider the contrasting examples of Stockton, Calif., and Charlotte, N.C. Stockton filed for Chapter 9 bankruptcy a year before Detroit did, a victim of too much dependence on one industry—construction—that collapsed in a matter of months after the subprime-mortgage-generated financial crash in 2008. In Stockton, descendants of California's agricultural workers flocked to home-construction jobs, building houses for middle-class families who worked an hour or two away in the San Francisco Bay Area. The city boomed. But that industry disappeared virtually overnight, and Stockton had nothing to replace it. Today it is a nightmare of boarded-up downtown buildings and rampant crime.

As the home to two major banks—Bank of America and Wachovia—that made disastrous choices during the subprime bubble, Charlotte was also hard-hit. But the city has come out of it strongly. Like Minneapolis-St. Paul, Charlotte is a far more economically diverse city than Detroit, with a lot of civic support from its citizens, and its government has invested heavily in infrastructure (former Mayor Anthony Foxx just became President Obama's Transportation secretary). Ultimately, despite its travails, Charlotte was selected over several other finalists (including Minneapolis-St. Paul) to host the 2012 Democratic convention.

There is always room for improvement, as all those self-conscious, self-doubting Twin Citians know all too well. Minneapolis-St. Paul still has many problems, some of them caused by the exodus from Detroit. It suffers an unusually high "achievement gap," for example, between its black and white populations. On this point, the Taleb thesis on fragility will be sorely tested in MSP: How will a metro area that was once largely Scandinavian and Western European in ethnic character handle a large influx of Hispanics and blacks?

But cities are hardy creatures. There may even be hope for Detroit, if it survives its bankruptcy. Thanks to the city's economic plight, rental rates in Detroit's downtown core are super low, and that is already fostering a boomlet of entrepreneurial businesses. A renewal of civic pride, and a new regional approach begun by former Mayor Dennis Archer—leading to the construction of a bridge across the Detroit River to Canada—is helping as well. "Detroit is like an undervalued stock," says Brookings' Katz. "I think the core is going to come back a lot faster than people think."

Yet in the end, if a new Detroit is to rise, it will have to embrace a very different future. It will have to go medieval.

Can Tax Breaks for Big Corporations Turn Around One of America's Most Dangerous Cities?

By Lidia DePillis
The Washington Post, December 15, 2014

Carlos Merced has lived in Camden, N.J., for 30 of his 34 years. He has worked a lot of jobs in that time, but only one of them—a short stint as a teaching assistant right after he graduated from high school—was actually *in* Camden.

Everything else—working at warehouses, mostly—has been in the surrounding suburbs. He just started a new job working the graveyard shift as a temp at an Amazon warehouse in Hightstown, an hour's drive away. That was after working for a Dunkin' Donuts warehouse in Westampton and a cleaning company in Pennington.

He takes what work he can find to support his 3-year-old daughter, but eventually, he'd like to find a job in the city he lives in—and something to help ease the city's 16 percent unemployment rate, 10 percentage points above the national average.

"Even a Walmart out here," he says. "Something that people can actually come to and apply for and get a job. Some people don't have the money to travel outside Camden to get a job. Some people don't have cars. Some people can't do it."

A huge effort is now underway to try to fix that problem: $614 million in tax breaks promised over the past two years to bring big employers to Camden. So far, the state's Economic Development Authority has made deals with Lockheed Martin, the Philadelphia 76ers, a hospital and a manufacturer of nuclear reactor components. And last week, it approved $117.8 million for Subaru, which is moving its headquarters out of neighboring Cherry Hill and into an old building just outside the city's rundown core.

The incentives aren't all the state has offered corporations. In the 2010s, it has handed out more than $4 billion in tax breaks, as competition for jobs has heated up in the Northeast corridor. That amount is dramatically larger than it was in previous decades, according to calculations by the left-leaning think tank New Jersey Policy Perspective (NJPP)—the cost of a job created by each deal has more than doubled. The subsidies started getting even more generous last year, when the legislature passed a measure that consolidated the state's incentive programs and targeted them toward particularly distressed areas.

From The Washington Post, December 15 © 2014 Washington Post Company. All rights reserved. Used by permission and protected by the Copyright Laws of the United States. The printing, copying, redistribution, or retransmission of this Content without express written permission is prohibited.

The increase, however, flies in the face of economics. Evidence has been piling up in recent years that such subsidies usually don't work—and if they do attract companies to a place where they wouldn't have ended up anyway, the return on investment often isn't as high as promised.

Firms ultimately make location decisions based on factors such as proximity to transportation infrastructure, the availability of skilled workers, and the overall cost of doing business—tax incentives, as the chief financial officer of Panasonic in North America said after accepting $102 million to move from Secaucus to Newark in 2011, are just "icing on the cake." Over time, they undermine the state's tax base, which means citizens and other businesses must make up the difference—even though politicians get to take credit for ribbon cuttings before anyone notices.

"Their fingerprints are erased by the time the cost of these incentives will be realized," says NJPP President Gordon MacInnes. "Nobody will be held account-able for that. It's a politically painless way to make it look that we're bringing our economy out of the great recession."

But is Camden a special case? The state's economic development officials have made a bet that recruiting a critical mass of large corporations to a depressed area will generate enough investment to turn it around—and are offering more for com-panies to move there than anywhere else, in a kind of massive Camden stimulus.

If they pull it off, they'll have bucked economic orthodoxy, and won.

***

Merced remembers when Camden wasn't a pit of crime and poverty. In the 1990s, even, it had multiple grocery stores—it now has one, as of recently, up from zero—and work for most anyone who wanted it. His father worked for the Board of Educa-tion, and his mother was a daycare teacher.

"It was nice, it was nice," Merced says. "There was good jobs out here. And then they just started closing up."

But by the end of the 1990s, suburbanization had taken its toll on Camden, with both jobs and residents fleeing to the smaller towns with their sprawling office parks. The rest of the state was adding jobs fast as it shifted from manufacturing to information processing, hosting the back offices of corporations headquartered in New York and across the world.

Many of those jobs, however, were rendered obsolete by technology in the 2000s. New Jersey's job growth leveled off, and took a sharp dive through the recession. It never rebounded with the vigor that New York and Pennsylvania did, in part because of the impact of Hurricane Sandy, and the federal government's slow response.

Now, it's set to lose 10,000 more jobs with the near collapse of the Atlantic City casino economy. After the building boom of the 1980s and 1990s, New Jersey has a vast overhang of aging suburban office space that has fallen out of fashion with the young and upwardly mobile. And on top of that, the Tax Foundation rated its business climate 49th out of the 50 states, with high tax rates for individuals and businesses.

So, why not improve that climate by lowering taxes for everyone, rather than picking and choosing who gets a free pass? James Hughes, dean of the School of Planning and Public Policy at Rutgers University, says overhauling the state's business-unfriendly tax code is harder than it sounds.

"To change that would be a monumental political feat, both sides coming together, and those who are getting special treatment now will fight it to the death," Hughes says. "What the state has been forced to do has been to compensate for that."

Meanwhile, New Jersey's neighbors have been just as aggressive in offering tax breaks of their own—New York State, which ranks just below New Jersey on the Tax Foundation's list, handed out $709 million just last week. That cycle is almost impossible to break (just one place, bifurcated Kansas City, Mo., has really tried).

"It's led to a Darwinian tooth-and-nail struggle for economic development between New Jersey and New York and Pennsylvania and New Jersey and everywhere else," says Joseph Seneca, a professor at Rutgers' School of Planning and Public Policy who used to chair the state's Council of Economic Advisors. "The economics profession is pretty united that money would be better directed to do broader things. The logic of no state doing it is pretty compelling, but the states have been doing it since we became a nation."

What strikes Seneca as really concerning, however, is the idea of awarding incentives not just for new jobs recruited to the state—but also "retained" jobs, which the company says would go to some other state were it not for a tax break.

> **"Now it seems you can't get anything done in New Jersey because everybody expects someone to come in with a wheelbarrow full of money."**

For example: despite the dubious wisdom of tax breaks for individual companies generally, few have complained about the state abating $82 million in taxes for the Philadelphia 76ers, which agreed to move their headquarters and a practice facility across the river from Philadelphia to Camden, bringing 250 jobs. But more people raised eyebrows at the idea of awarding $117.8 million to Subaru, for shifting jobs four miles from Cherry Hill into Camden, or $107 million for Lockheed Martin, which is moving 250 employees from Moorestown. Now, what's to stop other corporations from threatening to leave, just so they can extract a tax break to stay?

"To me, the EDA is supposed to be a group that helps bring businesses from out of state to our state," says Jeff Land, head of the Cherry Hill Republicans, which protested the subsidy for Subaru. "Now it seems you can't get anything done in New Jersey because everybody expects someone to come in with a wheelbarrow full of money."

* * *

Of course, there are better and worse ways to offer incentives for companies to create jobs in a given place. Some states have gotten burned by providing grants up front and scrambling to fill a budget hole when the company goes bankrupt. Many more simply fail to regularly and accurately assess whether companies were creating as much value as they'd promised.

Because at the end of the day, tax incentives are just cost-benefit analyses. You add up the gains from having the company around, subtract what you're refunding in taxes, and if you've got money left over, the deal pencils.

> **"The entire trickle-down assumption is people going to buy sandwiches at lunch, and that's not going to have a big impact on the city."**

That's why New Jersey argues that it's not actually *giving* money away at all. The Economic Opportunity Act has a formula that adds up factors such as whether the company plans to locate near transit and how much it's expected to invest in a new facility, and assigns a dollar value to each job created. In the end, the economic value of the company's presence must exceed 110 percent of the subsidies granted over 35 years (except in Camden, the bar is lower; the state just has to break even). If the company doesn't hold up its end of the deal each year—does not hire as many people as it promised, for example—it pays full freight.

That works, however, only if it's clear that the company was going to leave the state without intervention. So how does the state decide whether that's true?

Let's take the example of Subaru.

The company had expanded to several buildings in and around Cherry Hill, and wanted to consolidate into a single new headquarters. So it hired a real estate firm to shop around, and ended up seriously considering Philadelphia's Navy Yard, to which the city and the state had attracted the corporate offices of Glaxo Smith Kline and Urban Outfitters. Subaru determined that Navy Yard would've been cheaper than the location Camden offered—an old building owned by Campbells Soup—and provided the analysis to New Jersey, which then signed off on $117.8 million in incentives over 10 years, in exchange for a promise that the company would keep the 500 jobs it has and add 100 on top of that.

Now, despite the overall argument that tax incentives for individual companies are economically inefficient in a macro sense—because they can sway companies to locate to places where they're not as productive, and because they weaken a jurisdiction's focus on fundamentals such as education and transportation—it's possible that focusing a lot of firepower on one place could actually make a difference where all else has failed.

If you live or own a business in Camden, for example, there's no reason not to be encouraged by the influx of corporate behemoths. It's not costing *you* anything, at least in the near term. There will be some initial construction activity, and as New Jersey Economic Development Authority President and Chief Operating Officer Tim Lizura argues, having large businesses in town raises the profile of the city in a way that might attract other investment.

"There are tangible and intangible benefits," Lizura says. Plus, big corporations sometimes give back to their communities, sponsoring Little League teams and food banks and the like. "You all of a sudden have a nucleus of leaders who are ambassadors of the city, stewards of the city."

Clarence Fullard, head of the Rutgers-Camden Small Business Development Center, thinks the reputation thing matters for franchises thinking about whether to open a branch in the city. Fast-food restaurants, hotels and other kinds of service chains consider the presence of other big businesses when making location decisions. "I envision a lot of small businesses coming in around the first of the year, saying, 'I'm looking to expand a second location,'" Fullard says.

But if you were someone without a college degree looking for a job, like Carlos Merced, you might wonder what kind of opportunities these new businesses will bring. The 100 people Subaru will hire, and even the 400 people Holtec will need to manufacture nuclear reactor components, are likely to require specialized skills. There's no binding commitment to hire from the local community to do the work.

"There is a level of concern that the jobs that are being created through these incentives aren't matching people who are already here," says Raymond Lamboy, president of the Camden-based Latin American Economic Development Association. There's also a sense that small businesses aren't getting the same kind of help—his family owns a furniture store, which hasn't received millions of dollars in assistance. "Where's my tax abatement?" Lamboy asks. (Camden is covered by one of the state's Urban Enterprise Zones, which carries some benefits for existing businesses, but nowhere near the special deals for companies relocating to the city.)

In response to the tax break for the Philadelphia 76ers, a coalition of churches and community groups mounted a petition drive to measure the success of incentives by the number of well-paying, long-term jobs they generate. That's not something that just happens: It's easy to build a corporate campus that people drive to from the suburbs and then leave. In fact, another attempt to infuse the city with cash for large projects already failed in the 2000s when the state took over the city, a *Philadelphia Inquirer* investigation found in 2009, leaving Camden's neighborhoods just as poor and plagued with crime as before.

"A lot of these jobs are going to be fly-in, fly-out-type jobs," says NJPP Deputy Director Jon Whiten, noting that Subaru's staffers won't need to move to Camden to work there (only one percent of Campbell's Soup's 1,200 employees live in the city). "The entire trickle-down assumption is people going to buy sandwiches at lunch, and that's not going to have a big impact on the city."

These days, the announcements of new employers and the construction of a few housing projects—plus the proclamations of a relentlessly optimistic mayor—have the headlines shading positive in Camden. It might take a while, though, before the city's longtime residents really feel a difference.

"Invest in *me*," Merced says. "Me as in I mean everyone in Camden city—then think about it, the people in Camden city can actually invest in the community. If we had jobs, then Camden would flourish again."

Merced, for example, has a criminal record, which can be a barrier to employment. What he needs, and what thousands of unemployed residents want, is an entry-level job—or the training to do something higher level. So far, Camden's newest corporate citizens have promised neither.

How American Sports Franchises Are Selling Their Cities Short

By David Uberti
The Guardian, September 22, 2014

This place is sacred ground. At least it is for Tom Derry, who visits the fenced-off shrine in Detroit's Corktown neighborhood every week, in memory of the demigods who once walked here. He also cuts the grass. A star-spangled banner dangles above him from a 125-foot flagpole, standing guard over the 10-acre field.

Across the field, another man repairs flood damage recently suffered at home plate, the altar of this former cathedral of American sport. A father and his young son, careful not to step on his handiwork, play catch nearby.

"People who come here today have memories of coming here with their parents, who came here with their parents, who came here with their parents," Derry tells me when we meet in the now-empty plot one recent morning. West of downtown, his beloved Detroit Tigers baseball team played here for most of the last century, from 1912 to 1999.

When the privately built venue was bought and renovated by the city in 1977, the Tigers remained as tenants. But the lease deal saddled the city with maintenance costs and ultimately, following the team's departure, demolition expenses. For the past five years, Derry has toiled here with a small band of volunteers — true believers in the church of baseball—to preserve what's left of the original playing field.

In 2000, the Tigers settled into another publicly owned ballpark in the northern reaches of downtown Detroit. Local officials, wary that the Tigers could follow Detroit's American football and basketball teams outside the city limits, pledged $115 million (£70m) in public money toward the new, $300 million Comerica Park. Derry, for one, opposed spending public money this way, in a city with deteriorating schools and crumbling infrastructure. The lifelong Tigers fan refused to attend a game in Comerica Park for eight years.

"I didn't believe the public should have paid for that new stadium costing millions of dollars when we have a perfectly fine one right here," he says. The Detroit native and longtime postman looks down at the freshly cut grass of old Tiger Stadium for a moment, adding, "If [owners] don't get their way, they threaten to leave. And unfortunately, we tend to give in to them."

Copyright Guardian News & Media Ltd 2015

Derry's point is underlined by what happened next in Detroit. With business and political leaders trumpeting a downtown renaissance, voters subsequently backed a publicly owned American football stadium next door to Comerica Park for the Detroit Lions. City and county bodies together contributed about $125m to the project, roughly a quarter of its total cost. Two years later, 65,000-seat Ford Field opened across the street from 42,000-seat Comerica Park. Ford Field hosts around 10 American football games a year, along with various other entertainment.

When Tigers owner Mike Ilitch's stadium deal was struck in 1995, he said it would "really get the city moving." The following year, a Detroit Lions official called their new football venue "part of the rebirth of the city." Nearly two decades later, the palatial structures indeed dominate the north end of downtown Detroit, an area that has since seen a modest revitalization. Bars and restaurants are sprinkled throughout the modern stadium district, which sits across Woodward Avenue from the elegant Fox Theatre, also owned by Ilitch.

But it would be an overstatement to say the publicly backed stadiums jumpstarted an urban boom. They're nestled beside a handful of parking lots, court buildings and highways that cut through the city core—remnants of mid-century visions of urban renewal. Residential areas north of the district are still marred by abandonment. And for most of the year, the hulking structures stand vacant.

***

The story in Detroit has played out in almost every American metropolis, at least those that crave to be a "major-league" city. For decades, sports franchises have leveraged hometown pride and promises of economic spin-offs to garner billions in government handouts for stadium construction. Such megaprojects typically produce far fewer tangible benefits than advertised. And they siphon public funds away from other programs. Still, extraordinarily wealthy franchise owners—a tiny group of athletic oligarchs—continue to bend American cities to their will.

Most stadiums today are built with a mix of public and private money. Cities trying to keep teams in place—or others attempting to lure them away—routinely promise hundreds of millions to sway owners one way or another. In the past few years, such princely sums have been promised to teams in Atlanta, New York, Seattle, Dallas, Indianapolis, Phoenix, Sacramento, and many others. The estimated bill for two venues in Cincinnati alone surpassed $1 billion, and Minnesota has pledged a cool half-billion more for a new football stadium downtown.

"It's not going to end unless something really major happens," says Neil deMause, co-author of *Field of Schemes*, a book examining stadium construction across the US. "It's the backbone of the sports industry now. That's how you make money. If you can get someone to build you a free stadium that generates revenue—which you usually keep 100% of—you have an incredibly powerful incentive to maintain the status quo."

"It's like the defense industry and the Pentagon," he adds. "That's their bread and butter."

There are 122 teams in the four major North American sports leagues—football, baseball, basketball and hockey—attracting a combined attendance of 125 million last year. The independently owned clubs operate as regional franchises, sanctioned to play in the top-level professional leagues. More than 50 venues have been built across the US for them since 1999. While a handful of projects—such as the $1.6 billion MetLife football stadium in New Jersey—were entirely privately financed, many still received tax breaks, public infrastructure improvements or cheap land sales.

Cumulative construction and maintenance costs can be hard to track. But some estimates for public contributions have reached tens of billions of dollars. Municipalities typically finance such investments through tax-free bond sales, depriving the federal treasury of billions in revenue and punting costs toward the back end of deals. In Miami, for example, where county officials sold about $500 million in bonds to finance a new baseball stadium, steep interest rates could multiply costs nearly five-fold by 2048. Residents often end up footing such bills through increased tourism, sin or sales taxes. The National Football League and National Hockey League, on the other hand, are tax-exempt.

> For decades, sports franchises have leveraged hometown pride and promises of economic spin-offs to garner billions in government handouts for stadium construction. Such megaprojects typically produce far fewer tangible benefits than advertised. And they siphon public funds away from other programs. Still, extraordinarily wealthy franchise owners—a tiny group of athletic oligarchs—continue to bend American cities to their will.

Franchises, and in turn many politicians and media, have for decades billed such projects as engines of development, economic "grand slams." But researchers overwhelmingly pan those claims. Victor Matheson, a sports economist at College of the Holy Cross in Massachusetts, says spin-off activity has historically been 20% or less of what franchise- or public-commissioned economic impact studies forecast. While new stadiums might provide a jolt to a very concentrated area of town, that often comes at the expense of consumer spending elsewhere in the region—what economists call the substitution effect. It leaves the lion's share of venues providing negligible economic effects.

"Teams aren't in the business of making sure to generate a lot of money for the local bar across the street," Matheson says by phone. "They're in the business of selling you the $11 beer to you once you're inside the stadium."

Today's athletic amphitheatres last just a few decades before being thrown away for more lustrous replacements. And despite a long history of multipurpose venues in the US, contemporary stadiums are usually used for just one sport. The huge complexes, sprawling grounds and expansive parking lots are effectively deserted for most of the year—occasional concerts or wrestling matches notwithstanding. Teams in the NFL play just eight regular season home games each season.

To be sure, a number of sports venues have indeed helped revitalize surrounding neighborhoods—take Progressive Field and Quicken Loans Arena in Cleveland, Coors Field in Denver, or Petco Park in San Diego, all of them squeezed into dense, walkable areas. Just as housing and shopping culture have shifted back toward American downtowns, sporting culture is beginning to follow suit.

Still, a large body of research suggests governments typically pay top-shelf prices for bottom-shelf benefits. Franchises increasingly make money from luxury seating, cable deals, venue naming rights, seat-licensing fees and other new revenue streams. So most money spent inside lavish stadiums flows to the pockets of players and owners, more often than not millionaires and billionaires, respectively.

As more cities have been burned, of course, Americans have grown increasingly skeptical of stadiums as tools for urban growth. But public funding became engrained in the sports business model long ago, so teams still have every reason to convince their fans to believe.

Publicly financed stadiums were the norm after the Second World War, as officials offered up huge sums to entice major league clubs to relocate to their districts, often in suburbs. Milwaukee began the trend in 1953, building the $5 million Milwaukee County Stadium to attract the Boston Braves to the Midwest. Four years later, writer Douglas S. Powell penned in *American City & County* magazine that the American pastime was "rapidly becoming a municipal pastime." The same would eventually hold true for football and—to a lesser degree—basketball and hockey. At the national level, meanwhile, Congress granted the NFL and MLB antitrust exemptions that allowed them to sometimes behave as monopolies.

Though entirely publicly financed stadiums are rare nowadays, owners still garner hundreds of millions in public funds to pad their private investments. Franchises typically have the upper hand in such negotiations, especially in small- or mid-sized markets that crave the "major league" label. Their outsized bargaining power stems largely from an artificially low supply.

Each of the four major leagues has limited itself to about 30 franchises, even though there are growing number of metropolitan areas that want teams. Los Angeles, for example, hasn't had a professional football squad in 20 years.

The imbalance allows leagues to play communities against one another for the juiciest packages of development aid. Owners and league officials frequently voice threats of leaving town—some empty, others not—to garner the sweetest deals, says Robert Trumpbour, a professor at Penn State Altoona and author of *The New Cathedrals: Politics and Media in the History of Stadium Construction*.

"The owners have gotten much better at hardballing the negotiations," Trumpbour says. "And politicians don't like to be blamed that a team leaves. . . . It's amazing how the threats are played out [in the news media]."

Local media, too, are gears in the urban growth machine. Sports draw a large share of audiences to metro newspapers and newscasts, so stadium construction speculation is given a disproportionate amount of column inches and airtime.

Though the question they face is fundamentally political—should government subsidise a local business?—the media has a history of implicitly cheering for the home team, putting even more pressure on elected officials to deliver.

Of course, the public's calculation of whether to back a sports franchise goes beyond mere dollars and sense. Teams represent not only a slice of a metropolitan economy, but also a cornerstone of its collective identity. The value of such an intangible benefit remains impossible to measure. Nevertheless, it provides owners with yet another point of leverage over even the stingiest of politicians, for letting a team leave is unpopular indeed.

In Buffalo, home of the Bills football team, the late owner Ralph Wilson Jr. threatened in 1971 to move his franchise to Seattle unless a new stadium was built nearby. A "stunned silence fell over the chambers of the [Erie] County legislature when informed of Wilson's threat," one news report said. Then–New York governor Nelson Rockefeller stepped in soon after, saying "the state will continue to do everything it can to help Erie County and the city resolve its stadium problem." Two years and $22 million in public spending later—$118 million today—Rich Stadium held its first Bills game.

Now known as Ralph Wilson Stadium, the 74,000-seat venue stands in Orchard Park, a wealthy suburb about 10 miles southeast of downtown Buffalo. The Bills will only play eight regular season games there this season, leaving its 10,000-spot parking lot bare most days. The stadium lies in a primarily residential area, and a community college and shopping mall are the only major developments nearby.

"The current stadium has basically zero to negative economic impact to the area," says Jamie Moses, editor of Buffalo's weekly *Artvoice* newspaper. The publication recently devoted a cover story to advocate for a new stadium downtown. "Most people go there, they sit in the parking lot, they drink, they go to the game and they drive home drunk. It means nothing to the city."

Many observers in Buffalo endorse the national trend toward urban stadiums, an about-face from the postwar boom that drew many franchises to fledgling suburbs. Moses believes a new downtown venue could help reverse 50 years or more of commercial flight.

"We made a whole lot of mistakes that were big mistakes," Moses says of Buffalo. But he later adds: "There's a big movement to that area. It's not just the stadium. The stadium would just be one piece of it. There are a lot of developers and entrepreneurs who want to do business downtown, in that core."

Though the Bills have fallen on hard times on the field recently, the team still boasts some of football's most vociferous fans. That conviction, coupled with the fact Buffalo is the second-smallest market in the NFL, has only increased the league's bargaining power. In 2012, the state and county committed $226 million to the team in a new lease deal. While diffuse, the cost would cover renovations—now finished at a price tag of $94 million—and up to a decade's worth of operating subsidies and capital payments—starting at $11.5 million a year. The Bills promised $44 million of their own money for the project, which top brass said in 2012 would keep the team near Buffalo "for many decades to come." The agreement also included a promise by the state to form an advisory group exploring the potential for a new stadium in the future.

"The Bills, the state and the county have done a great job of continuing to make improvements to the stadium to keep it competitive," NFL commissioner Roger Goodell said at the time. "But you have to continue that."

Indeed. Two years later, renovations on Ralph Wilson Stadium have been completed, and its namesake, the franchise's longtime owner, has passed away. Local energy billionaire Terry Pegula agreed to purchase the franchise for $1.4 billion this month, assuaging fears that the Bills would skip town for a gleaming venue elsewhere.

Goodell ginned up that speculation in May, saying the Bills would need a new stadium to remain economically viable. The claim is hard to verify, as privately owned NFL franchises don't open their books to the public that subsidizes them. But last year alone, the league's 32 franchises shared about $6 billion of national revenue, most of it culled from lucrative TV deals. That comes in addition to income from tickets or concessions sales. In New York, local and national media have reported the Bills earned at least $30 million in net profits last season.

Goodell added: "The intention is that whoever buys the team will make the team work in western New York." Though governor Andrew Cuomo has said he's "not convinced" of the need for a new stadium, he followed Goodell's comments by assuring fans: "We will do what we have to do to keep the Bills in western New York." It's unclear how much a new stadium would cost—or how much the public could contribute to it. But the past three NFL stadiums to open have all eclipsed $1 billion.

It's an election year in both New York and Michigan, where ground will be broken on Thursday for a publicly backed, $450 million ice hockey arena for the Mike Ilitch–owned Detroit Red Wings. The downtown stadium plan has sparked familiar talk of an urban revival among the region's business, political and chattering classes. The former heart of American industry needs its heroes, of course, and Detroiters can't help thinking of the city that could be—living their mantra, hoping for better things.

"This is part of investing in Detroit's future," Michigan governor Rick Snyder, a Republican, told reporters of adding a new hockey arena downtown. "Detroit moves from a place where people might have had a negative impression—although there are great things already going on—to being a place that will be recognized across the world as a place of great value and a place to invest."

The Red Wings will continue playing in the ugly, publicly owned Joe Louis Arena until 2017. The construction of that facility 35 years ago was financed with $30 million in municipal bonds, and its coming demolition will likewise fall on the public dime. The hockey team's new home will sit in what's now a blighted corridor across Woodward Avenue from Comerica Park and Ford Field.

The Ilitch family pledged another $200 million to improve infrastructure around the new hockey arena and develop a five-neighbourhood entertainment district with restaurants, office buildings and shops. "The vision thrills," wrote Stephen

Henderson, a Pulitzer Prize–winning scribe for the *Detroit Free Press*. Stadium backers argue that the plan will push Detroit past the tipping point it's tried to reach for so long, creating a critical mass of activity and physical and economic links between the city core and trendy Midtown.

"This arena is an anchor for much more real estate development," says Mark Rosentraub, a University of Michigan professor and Ilitch consultant. "That changes the story of Detroit. And that creates the opportunity for other investors because people start taking the city seriously again."

Local-born Ilitch, an 85-year-old pizza baron whose family is worth more than $3 billion, has been credited over the years for moving his company's business operations downtown and keeping his sports teams—he also owns the Tigers—within city limits. But he's had every reason to do so.

Just a week after the City of Detroit filed for bankruptcy protection in July 2013, a state board approved $284 million in public money for the hockey venue. Most of the funds—$262 million—will come from property taxes levied through a construct called tax increment financing. It allows the city's quasi-public Downtown Development Authority to earmark tax revenue from a 615-acre area for certain projects. The City Council, meanwhile, sold more than three dozen parcels of publicly owned land where the arena will be built—all for $1. The Ilitch organization will pay no rent to play in the city-owned stadium and pocket 100% of the revenue it generates.

Critics contend that such huge public sums should be funnelled away from billionaires and toward more pressing—though admittedly less exciting—improvements to schools, public safety and the like. And these sceptics need look only 25 miles northwest along Woodward Avenue to see the ugly aftermath of stadiums past.

The publicly financed Pontiac Silverdome was home to the Detroit Lions football team from 1975 to 2001. Built for $55 million—about a quarter of a billion dollars today—the suburban stadium has sat mostly vacant and increasingly derelict since the football team returned downtown. The indoor venue was sold to Toronto-based investors for a paltry $583,000 five years ago. Since the new owners' plans for an indoor soccer team fell through, they have been pawning off Silverdome relics at auction. Pontiac has continued its quiet deterioration around the empty monument.

Back in Corktown, Joe Michnuk kicks dirt on the pitcher's mound in what's left of old Tiger Stadium. The 55-year-old worked as a locker room security guard in the venue in 1984, the last time the baseball team won the World Series. "It was the best year of my life," says Michnuk, 25 at the time and now a member of the Tom Derry–led grounds crew. "It was a dream."

Michnuk, who grew up in Detroit and now lives in bordering Dearborn, has seen stadiums come and go. "You can't prevent it," he says, calling himself a realist. And he's doubtful a new ice hockey arena will catalyze a downtown revival. "So it's a new arena—big deal. It's another sweetheart deal for the owner."

Michnuk points toward Corktown businesses within eyeshot. The neighborhood, devastated by the disinvestment and population decline that ravaged Detroit for 60 years, has seen new causes for optimism more recently. The area is far from vibrant. But a smattering of bars and restaurants has sprouted up along Michigan Avenue, and nearby residential developments are approaching full occupancy. Just a block away, a few hundred paying spectators watch souped-up cars weave through the grounds of the towering, abandoned Michigan Central Station. "This is what jumpstarts an area—small businesses, grassroots stuff," Michnuk says above the roaring engines.

Yet the baseball romantic intimately understands the way sports teams tug at a city's heartstrings, how they become an integral part of urban lore. "I've had some great times at Comerica Park. It's nice," he says, wearing a Tigers hat and leaning on a rake. "But it'll never be Tiger Stadium. I love this place as much as I did when there were 54,000 people in the stands."

He turns back toward centerfield, pointing at the red, white and blue banner waving in the clear summer light. "Look at that flag," he says. "That flag's been there for 102 years."

Why Millennials Still Move to Cities

By Kevin Maney
Newsweek, April 10, 2015

Technology has failed to make the world flat after all. Every ounce of logic says technology should have whipped geography by now—flattening the world, in Thomas Friedman's lexicon, by allowing people to live anywhere and still engage in the global economy. If technology was living up to its promise, more and more people should be moving out of cities to tele-work from charming small towns and lakeside cottages.

Instead, we're streaming to cities like ants to a dropped Popsicle. For the first time, more people globally now live in cities than outside of them. And this is not driven by retirees moving back to get their party on. The best jobs are increasingly in the most dynamic cities and not anywhere else. And people seem to want to work at such jobs, believe it or not, in person. Technology could let us work remotely, yet we are choosing to fight traffic, pay extravagant housing costs and put up with lots of people we don't like. How come?

It seems that in an innovation-driven economy, more innovation happens when smart people are swirled together with a ton of other smart people. Innovation needs an ecosystem, argues economist Enrico Moretti in *The New Geography of Jobs,* which details the shift of work to hotbed cities such as San Francisco, New York, Boston and Seattle. "A growing body of research suggests that cities are not just a collection of individuals but complex, interrelated environments that foster the generation of new ideas and new ways of doing business," Moretti writes. "By clustering near each other, innovators foster each other's creative spirit and become more successful."

A study by think tank City Observatory found that since 2007, cities had a 0.5 percent per year growth in jobs, while suburbs suffered a 0.1 percent drop. Millennials—the adults under 30, the biggest generation in U.S. history—are leading that population shift. A U.S. Census study shows that millennials are not heading for the suburbs the way past generations did.

The trend is palpable in Northern California. Silicon Valley, which is really a sprawling suburb, reigned as technology's hot spot for decades. Now the region's office-park campuses are starting to seem as tired as old Sears-anchored shopping malls, while the new superstar tech companies move into urban clusters in San Francisco.

From Newsweek, March 30 © 2015 IBT Media. All rights reserved. Used by permission and protected by the Copyright Laws of the United States. The printing, copying, redistribution, or retransmission of this Content without express written permission is prohibited.

The crazy thing is that technology seems to make centralized city offices less necessary now than ever. Just 20 years ago, at the birth of the web, remote work was barely possible. If you owned a PC, you still had to bleep and buzz through a modem just to get some crappy version of email. Today, you can get your entire work experience delivered to a phone in your pocket. I recently met with Citrix Chief Executive Mark Templeton, who showed me his company's latest offering, which he dubs the "software-defined workplace." Technology can now be the workplace. A physical office could just be an adjunct to a company that otherwise lives in cyberspace.

Technology could also let us live remotely better than ever. We can see our cloud friends on Facebook, shop at online stores, stream movies, attend Harvard classes online. If you want to start a company in Tuscaloosa or Saskatoon, you don't need to kowtow in person to those Sand Hill Road VCs with their Teslas and Apple Watches. Just go on Kickstarter and get funded, no matter where you are.

So basically, the only reason to clump together in cities is, well, the people. As Moretti explains, in our old manufacturing-driven economy, we moved where the factories were, which often was near necessary resources (furniture factories near forests; steel plants near coal mines, and so on). In an innovation economy, we move to what are essentially idea factories: cities full of people.

Moretti's findings dovetail with Steven Johnson's observations in his book *Where Good Ideas Come From*. Breakthrough ideas come from connections between people and their ideas, and more connections create exponentially more ideas. That leads to cities.

Quoting historical studies, Johnson writes, "A city that was 10 times larger than its neighbor wasn't 10 times more innovative; it was 17 times more innovative. A metropolis fifty times bigger than a town was 150 times more innovative."

This helps explain why Yahoo CEO Marissa Mayer famously ordered her teleworking employees back to the office. It's why Hillary Clinton, onstage at last year's Dreamforce conference, said she doesn't just Skype with world leaders. "Technology has put an even higher premium on face-to-face," she said. Recent management trends—in particular, Agile development—thrive on intense, collaborative, in-person group work.

For all these reasons, Moretti argues that the migration to high-innovation cities has staying power. As long as innovation is the surest path to wealth and success, smart people will gravitate to whatever is the most effective way to innovate. Right now, that means going to cities.

A couple of things could change that in another decade or so. One is the huge demographic pull of the millennials. The generation has largely put off marriage and kids, so they are largely single. . . and on Tinder. So of course they want to be in cities. Who'd want to live in rural Iowa, swipe on Tinder and find out the nearest eligible female is a dairy cow? Only when that huge generation breaks down and finally starts to have families will suburbs start to look appealing.

Maybe by then technology will be good enough to let people move out of cities yet maintain the contact that's so important to innovation. The software-defined workplace is only going to get better. Virtual reality glasses, now the bailiwick of the rich and dorky, will go mainstream and allow you to sit in a home office yet feel as if you're in a conference room with a half-dozen colleagues.

That combination of family and technology might finally finish the world-flattening job. Millennials could then drain out of cities like water from a punctured bucket, heading off to do their virtual innovating from greener surroundings.

And that will be just fine for boomers like me, who are just waiting for them to leave so we can move back in.

Why Are There So Many Shuttered Storefronts in the West Village?

By Tim Wu
The New Yorker, May 24, 2015

At the end of this month, the House of Cards & Curiosities, on Eighth Avenue, just south of Jane Street, in the West Village, will close its doors after more than twenty years in business. It was, admittedly, not a store whose economic logic was readily apparent. Along with artistic greeting cards, it sold things like small animal skeletons, stuffed piranhas (which were hanging from the ceiling), and tiny ceramic skulls. Nonetheless, it did good business for many years, or so its owner, James Waits, told me. Its closing leaves four shuttered storefronts on just one block. With their papered-up windows and fading paint, the failed businesses are a depressing sight in an otherwise vibrant neighborhood. Each represents a broken dream of one kind or another.

The fate of the House of Cards & Curiosities is just one example of something odd that's happening in some of New York's richest and best-known neighborhoods—a surge in closings and shuttered shops. Consider, in particular, the West Village, the place that Jane Jacobs once described as a model for a healthy neighborhood, in her classic book *The Death and Life of Great American Cities*. The average per-capita income there is now more than a hundred and ten thousand dollars per year, and it retains its jazz clubs and fancy restaurants. It is both rich and vibrant, yet also now blighted with shuttered stores in various states of decay.

Abandoned storefronts have long been a hallmark of economic depression and high crime rates, but the West Village doesn't have either of those. Instead, what it has are extremely high commercial rents, which cause an effect that is not dissimilar. "High-rent blight" happens when rising property values, usually understood as a sign of prosperity, start to inflict damage on the city economics that Jane Jacobs wrote about.

In the West Village, rent spikes are nearly universally reported as the reason so many storefronts have closed over the past few years. Cafe Angelique reportedly closed when its sixteen-thousand-dollar rent increased to forty-two thousand dollars. A Gray's Papaya on Eighth Street closed after its owner reported a rent increase of twenty thousand dollars per month. "We are witnessing our destruction," Nicky Perry, the outspoken owner of the neighborhood restaurant Tea & Sympathy, said. She called the situation "insane."

Compounding the problem is the fact that the closed storefronts often stay that way, sometimes for years, in an apparent contradiction of the law of supply and demand. If a storefront remains empty for a long time. . . basic economics suggest that the price being charged is too high. So why doesn't the owner lower the rents?

There are potentially some tax benefits for the owners of empty storefronts. But the more likely explanation is that landlords are willing to lose a tenant and leave a storefront empty as a form of speculation. They'll trade a short-term loss for the chance eventually to land a much richer tenant, like a bank branch or national retail chain, which might pay a different magnitude of rent. If you're a landlord, why would you keep renting to a local café or restaurant at five thousand or ten thousand dollars a month when you might get twenty thousand or even forty thousand dollars a month from Chase? In addition, if a landlord owns multiple properties, dropping the price on one may bring down the price for others. That suggests waiting for Marc Jacobs instead of renting to Jane Jacobs.

As for Jane Jacobs, she famously argued that cities were explosive drivers of economic growth, based on a theory of intra-city trade. She highlighted, among other things, the ease with which local businesses trade goods and services with each other, and eventually make the city into a net exporter of desirable goods and services. But high commercial rents can threaten that basic dynamic. If national businesses, not local ones, come to fill a neighborhood, the area may become merely an importer of goods and services supplied by CVS or Dunkin' Donuts. Local wealth isn't created, and the economy of the area begins to match the less-inspiring examples of suburbia. In addition, high rents, like high taxes, can damage business generally, whether local or not. Consider that even Starbucks, despite fourteen billion dollars in revenue, has begun to shutter some of its New York locations because the rent is just too high.

In the longer term, high commercial rents also damage what made neighborhoods like the West Village attractive and appealing to buyers and renters in the first place. One usually pays for distinction, and there is nothing distinct about a neighborhood where new businesses are national chains or safe, high-margin operations. The preservationist Jeremiah Moss, the author of the Vanishing New York blog, points out that Greenwich Village has been a bohemian center since the eighteen-fifties, but, since the rise in rents, it "no longer drives the culture," and instead is becoming what James Howard Kunstler termed "a geography of nowhere." It is possible that entire classes of stores may disappear from some neighborhoods, like mid-range restaurants, antique stores, curiosity shops, bookstores, and anything too experimental. Brooklyn has emerged as a cultural center in the past two decades in part because it has lower rents and thus more interesting businesses. But, as Brooklyn's property values rise, it might expect some of the same problems that parts of Manhattan have.

If high-rent blight hurts New York's municipal economy, what, if anything, might be done? Because the problem is tied almost inextricably to the value of New York real estate generally, there are no simple fixes. The #SaveNYC movement and the Small Business Congress NYC advocate the regulation of lease renewal. They support a bill written by the small-business advocate Steve Null that tries to limit rent spikes by making commercial-lease-renewal disputes subject to mandatory mediation and arbitration, like some baseball salaries. Gale Brewer, the Manhattan borough president, supports a different regulation of lease renewals, coupled with zoning rules, that encourages landlords to quit waiting for the jackpot and to start renting. Some, like Moss,

> **At some point high property values may begin to destroy local economic activity. The West Village once served as a model for what a healthy neighborhood economy looks like. Its ongoing story marks a new chapter in the life and death of the great American City.**

want to fine landlords who leave storefronts abandoned, in the hope that they'll then rent to smaller, quirkier companies instead of Chipotle. There may also be other original solutions to the specific problem of high-rent blight, such as, perhaps, finding ways to let pop-up stores use abandoned spaces on a seasonal basis.

Waits, the owner of the House of Cards & Curiosities, doesn't endorse any particular solution, and he admitted that the doubling of his rent wasn't the only thing that hurt his business. (The closing of a local hospital and the drop in the euro, he said, also took their toll; European tourists apparently have a taste for skeletons and other oddities). But, he said, the tax increases passed on by his landlord have pushed individual businesses like his to the "bursting point." Waits has no plans to reopen elsewhere, meaning that we will have to live without what was probably the only place on Earth where you could shop for tarantulas and Mother's Day greeting cards at the same time.

The fate of small businesses in the West Village may be a local issue, but it is one with large implications. For one thing, cities remain major drivers of economic growth, and small businesses continue to form a larger part of G.N.P. than their larger cousins. But there is a deeper issue as well. Since the nineteen-sixties, when Americans faced an extreme wave of urban blight, they have understood rising property values as a reliable measure of recovery. But everything can go too far, and at some point high property values may begin to destroy local economic activity. The West Village once served as a model for what a healthy neighborhood economy looks like. Its ongoing story marks a new chapter in the life and death of the great American city. "I recently walked by Jane Jacobs' old house on Hudson Street," Jeremiah Moss wrote me in an e-mail. "It's now a real-estate brokerage."

Why American Cities Are Fighting to Attract Immigrants

By Ted Hesson
The Atlantic, July 21, 2015

Immigrants take our jobs. They don't pay taxes. They're a drain on the economy. They make America less. . . American.

You've probably heard all of these arguments, especially with the country recovering from a financial disaster. Indeed, they've been heard for a century or two, as successive waves of immigrants to this nation of immigrants have first been vilified, then grudgingly tolerated, and ultimately venerated for their contributions.

This time, too, there is ample evidence that immigrants are creating businesses and revitalizing the U.S. workforce. From 2006 to 2012, more than two-fifths of the start-up tech companies in Silicon Valley had at least one foreign-born founder, according to the Kauffman Foundation. A report by the Partnership for a New American Economy, which advocates for immigrants in the U.S. workforce, found that they accounted for 28 percent of all new small businesses in 2011.

Immigrants also hold a third of the internationally valid patents issued to U.S. residents, according to University of California (Davis) economist Giovanni Peri. In a 2012 article published by the Cato Institute, the libertarian (and pro-immigration) think tank, Peri concluded that immigrants boost economic productivity and don't have a notable impact—either positive or negative—on net job growth for U.S.-born workers. One reason: Immigrants and native-born workers gravitate toward different jobs.

Immigration isn't without its negative effects, especially on Americans who lack a high school diploma, according to George Borjas, a professor of economics and social policy at Harvard's John F. Kennedy School of Government. In a 2013 report published by the immigration-restrictionist Center for Immigration Studies, Borjas calculated that immigrants might have depressed the wages of native-born high school dropouts by 6 percent between 1990 and 2010, mainly due to foreigners who'd arrived illegally.

But immigration, on the whole, bolsters the workforce and adds to the nation's overall economic activity. Look at the impact on cities that attract the most foreign-born residents. New York, Los Angeles, Chicago, and Houston are all major immigrant destinations and also economic powerhouses, accounting for roughly one-fifth of the country's gross domestic product. In New York, immigrants made up 44

© 2015 The Atlantic Media Co., as first published in The Atlantic Magazine. All rights reserved. Distributed by Tribune Content Agency, LLC

percent of the city's workforce in 2011; in and around Los Angeles, they accounted for a third of the economic output in 2007.

Immigrants tend to contribute more to the economy once they've learned English and become citizens. A few cities—notably, New York—have a long history of ushering immigrants into the mainstream society and economy. Other parts of the country have less experience with newcomers but are learning to adapt.

Take Nashville, for instance. As recently as 2009, immigrants living in the Tennessee capital had reason to worry. A conservative city council member proposed amending the municipality's charter to require that all government business be conducted in English, allegedly to save money. This raised hackles. "Would the health department be allowed to speak Arabic to a patient?" or so *The Tennessean,* Nashville's leading newspaper, wondered. "Could a city-contracted counselor offer services in Spanish?"

The voters apparently wondered, too, for they soundly defeated the English-only amendment, which had earned the enmity of businesses, religious organizations, and advocacy groups. "A significant moment in the city's history when it comes to immigration," recalls Nashville's mayor, Karl Dean, a Democrat who had recently taken office. "Since that moment, the city really hasn't looked back."

The foreign-born population in the Nashville metropolitan area has more than doubled since 2000; immigrants accounted for three-fifths of the city's population growth between 2000 and 2012, and now constitute an eighth of all Nashville residents. When President Obama delivered a speech on immigration last December, he did it in Nashville. The city famed as the nation's country music capital now boasts the largest U.S. enclave of Kurds, along with increasing numbers of immigrants from Myanmar and Somalia.

They've been drawn to Nashville's booming economy, which has ranked among the fastest-growing in the nation in recent years. But they're not only benefiting from the local prosperity—they're contributing to it. Immigrants are twice as likely as native-born Nashville residents to start their own small businesses, according to data compiled by the Partnership for a New American Economy. They also play an outsized role in important local industries, including construction, health care, and hotels.

Nashville has welcomed these immigrants with open arms, in ways that other municipalities around the country are trying to emulate. In the forefront is a non-profit organization called Welcoming Tennessee, started in 2005 to highlight immigrants' contributions and potential role in Nashville's future. It put up billboards around Nashville—"Welcome the immigrant you once were," and the like—in hopes of defanging the political debate. The current race to elect a new mayor next month has drawn questions at campaign forums indicative of the new political tone, about how candidates would handle a diverse school system and assure that city services are available to all immigrants, legal or otherwise.

The "welcoming" movement that started in Tennessee has evolved into "Welcoming America," a national network of organizations that preach the economic upside of immigration and help people adjust to life in the United States. Since 2009, 57 cities and counties, from San Francisco and Philadelphia to Dodge City, Kansas, have taken "welcoming" pledges, meaning that the local governments committed themselves to a plan to help immigrants assimilate.

> **In a 2012 article published by the Cato Institute. . . Peri concluded that immigrants boost economic productivity and don't have a notable impact—either positive or negative—on net job growth for U.S.-born workers.**

The private sector, too, has shown an interest in bringing immigrants into the mainstream of American life. Citigroup is promoting citizenship efforts in Maryland, while another big bank, BB&T, has been holding educational forums across the Southeast to explain a federal program that issues work permits to young undocumented immigrants. Retailers such as American Apparel go out of their way to help foreign-born employees learn English and apply for citizenship. Beyond motives of altruism lay considerations of the bottom line. Foreign-born residents now make up 13 percent of the U.S. population, a not-to-be-ignored share of the consumer market. The next generation is more lucrative still: One in four American residents younger than 18 has an immigrant parent.

Local governments, mindful of their pressing economic needs, have taken the lead. Many cities have created offices devoted to serving "new Americans" locally. Dayton, Ohio, has intensified its efforts to redevelop a neighborhood with a growing Turkish community. Nashville runs a program called MyCity Academy, which teaches leaders from immigrant communities about local government.

Not every community that dubs itself a "welcoming city" will be able to replicate Nashville's success. But Cecilia Muñoz, the director of the White House Domestic Policy Council, suggests some guidelines. Teaching immigrants how to speak English is "sort of foundational," she says, "but it's helpful if the conversation doesn't stop there," by also including how immigrants can thrive economically and gain access to health care. Muñoz endorses programs to connect ethnic leaders with local movers and shakers, to show the public that helping immigrants assimilate is "about all of us, as opposed to an 'us and them' kind of thing."

The biggest obstacle to welcoming immigrants may be the usual one: a lack of resources. "Every area, you could probably be putting money into," says Nashville Mayor Dean. Even so, he's pleased that another potential obstacle—community opposition—has faded. "I'm sure there's people who are concerned," he says, "but they're quiet about it."

He adds, with more than a trace of civic pride: "I call it the happy moment here, how well the city has adjusted to being more diverse. . . It's a good story, and you've got to be encouraged by it."

4
Crime and Policing

© Nyc Labretš/Demotix/Corbis

In spite of a hypermilitarized police and National Guard presence, the mood was festive on May Day in Baltimore following the arrests of six police officers for the murder of Freddie Gray. Photographed May 1, 2015.

Law and Disorder

After decades of rising crime rates, the 2010s have seen falling crime rates across the nation. Despite overall reductions in crime, social scientists argue that American society has significant problems to address in terms of crime and punishment, including racism, bias in police and judicial policies, and a deepening economic divide across the country that exacerbates criminal behavior. In the new era of urban renewal, police, politicians, and the citizenry are engaged in passionate debates about the effectiveness of current strategies and the changes needed to bring about peaceful cities in the future.

The Age of Mass Incarceration

Though the United States accounts for only 5 percent of the global population, U.S. prisons house 25 percent of the world's prison population, a population that has risen by more than 700 percent since 1970.[1] The United States is the world's largest jailer, leading to what some social analysts have called the "age of incarceration," and with the rising cost of imprisonment and prison overpopulation, reducing prison populations has become an important issue.

During the Civil Rights era in the 1960s, predominantly white citizen lobbies and federal legislators were concerned that civil unrest, especially among poor minority populations, would lead to mass violence. Though violent crime had seen a ten-year decline in 1965, President Johnson assuaged public fear by promising that his administration would conduct a "war on crime" to keep the streets and cities safe. Johnson's administration then created the Law Enforcement Assistance Administration (LEAA) and a system by which federal funding and equipment could be distributed to state and local police based on "arrest rates."[2] In addition, federal and state judicial authorities increasingly adopted longer sentences and more punitive policies in imprisonment designed to increase the effectiveness of prison as a deterrent.

These policies continued with the "war on drugs," started in 1971 under President Richard Nixon, with a rapid proliferation in possession and drug use arrests and convictions and longer prison sentences for drug crimes, collectively intended to discourage drug use and related crime. Though social scientists and medical professionals argued that drug addiction should be treated as a mental disorder or disease, the prevailing policy through the 2000s was to increase penalties for all drug offenses, including minor charges. The war on drugs cost U.S. taxpayers an estimated $1 trillion between 1970 and 2010 and resulted in no measurable reduction in drug use, the import of illegal narcotics, or drug addiction and overdoses among groups targeted for anti-drug campaigns.[3] The larger "war on crime," also had dismal results as the violent crime rate rose from 200.2 per 100,000 U.S. citizens to 684.6 per 100,000 during the same period.[4]

Race and Poverty in the Incarceration Age

Linking funding to arrest rates created a phenomenon in which police focus on areas in which arrests and convictions will be easier to achieve. For instance, while it is estimated that drug dealers and drug users are approximately 5 times more likely to be white than black, 38 percent of those arrested for drug use or sales are African Americans. In addition, 59 percent of all individuals imprisoned for drug offenses are African American.[5] Essentially, police focus drug control activities on poor urban communities where drug use is more "apparent" due to poverty, homelessness, and other factors, and where arrests and convictions are more likely, thus increasing funding through the apparent "success" of policing policies.[6]

Reviews of criminal justice statistics from 70 police departments indicate that African Americans are arrested at nearly 10 times the rate of white offenders and are more than 6 times more likely to be incarcerated than a white offender accused of a similar crime.[7] Police and court officials engage in racial and social profiling in making arrests and determining sentences. Stereotypes that associate poor populations and minorities (especially young minority males) with violence and drug crimes influence the attitudes of police, judges, and members of criminal juries. Complicating this trend is the fact that members of poor communities cannot afford the same level of representation and may be less effective in their own defense as a result of educational disparities.

Many of the poor, minority neighborhoods in U.S. cities developed after the "white middle class" exodus to the suburbs that began in the 1950s. In many suburbs, minority families were discouraged and, at times, prohibited from settlement. Dwindling population and tax revenues diminished the quality of inner-city schools and reduced the availability of jobs, thus furthering blight and poverty. As members of low-income urban communities are arrested, convicted, and incarcerated, the situation worsens. Children of incarcerated individuals are essentially orphaned, and released convicts have fewer prospects for advancement and reintegration. Essentially, impoverishment drives crime, and incarceration creates conditions that encourage crime. Local and state agencies continue to focus on arrests and imprisonment, with far less emphasis on preventing crime by improving the prospects for residents of poor communities or released convicts.

In a 2014 article in *The Atlantic*, Heather Ann Thompson argues that higher levels of violence in poor neighborhoods are linked to the competition for resources in the drug trade, which has become "hyper violent" in part *because* of police efforts to engage in a militant "war" against dealers and users.[8] The war on drugs effectively created the underground drug market as it exists in 2015. The cost and value of narcotics increased as a result of police pressure, thereby transforming minor criminal markets into billion dollar industries and thus providing incentive for more and more individuals to enter the trade. Meanwhile, as police and drug trade workers fight in the streets, social scientists and criminologists continue to argue that the drug use and abuse should be treated as a public health concern and a legitimate "disease," rather than as simply a genre of crime.[9]

War on the Home Front

Another consequence of the war on crime was the increasing militarization of local police forces. The ACLU investigation "War Comes Home," for instance, found that SWAT teams, which were originally created for use in case of "state emergencies," are now regularly deployed in drug raids. The increasing militarization of police forces has been linked to programs that provide used military weaponry and equipment to police departments, effectively making civil police departments part of the larger military complex.[10]

The militarization of police came to the forefront of the public debate in 2015, largely as a result of widely publicized public protests against police brutality and violence aimed at young African Americans. This movement, popularized through social media activist campaigns like "BlackLivesMatter," transformed into national protests after the death of Michael Brown in Ferguson, Missouri, and the "chokehold" death of Eric Garner on Long Island, New York. In both incidents, protestors argued that police had used excessive force and unnecessary violence and that the deaths of Brown and Garner represented a much deeper pattern of abuse in which aggressive, predominantly white police, target, persecute, and commit violence against young African Americans.[11]

Studies indicate that aggressive confrontational police policies are not very effective. For instance, a study of 4.4 million New York City "stop-and-frisk" incidents in which police detained and searched individuals to find illegal firearms, indicated that only 1 percent of such searches were successful. Opponents of the policy argued that the success rate indicates that police lack appropriate guidelines for identifying suspects while the "stop-and-frisk" policy effectively heightens tension and conflict, encouraging the perception that all citizens are under scrutiny and may be subject to random searches based on age, economic status, and race.[12]

The long-standing police policy in New York known as "broken window" policing holds that aggressively addressing minor crimes will stem a pattern of criminal behavior that ultimately leads to more serious crimes. The policy results in a vast increase in fines, arrests, detentions, and incarceration among poor communities for crimes like drinking in public, jaywalking, and similar "minor offenses." Though supporters point to lower crime rates in New York as proof that "broken windows" has been effective, a number of criminologists disagree, arguing that there are no substantive links between the aggressive focus on misdemeanors and overall decreases in crime rates.[13]

In May 2015, President Obama instituted a new federal policy in which police departments will no longer receive military equipment except in cases where the police department submits to new and more stringent oversight. In press statements, President Obama argued that the mere presence of military equipment can isolate, intimidate, and alienate residents, creating a situation in which citizens view police with fear and suspicion rather than seeing police as members of their communities.

Militarization is part of a broader series of public debates that also involve the controversial use of invasive digital surveillance systems in the wake of the nation's latest "war," the war on terror.[14]

The Goal of a Peaceful City

While crime rates rose rapidly from the 1960s to the 1990s, from the late 1990s to the 2010s, crime rates have decreased across the nation. For instance, the Federal Bureau of Investigation found that there was an 8 percent reduction in robbery and a 17 percent reduction in auto-theft in 2009, even as the "great recession" was driving unemployment and poverty rates across the nation.[15] The reason for this decline has not been determined. Supporters of aggressive incarceration, "broken windows" policing, police militarization, and the overall "war on crime" approach have embraced reduced crime rates as an indicator of success. Studies, however, indicate that war on crime policies have had little to no effectiveness. A variety of other factors are also in play, including an increase in the effectiveness of antidepression medication, a reduced reliance on cash, and an overall demographic shift that has reduced the size of the younger population most likely to commit certain types of crimes.[16] Sociologists currently believe that the reduction in crime is the result of many coinciding factors.

Is the United States a nation perpetually at war? The "wars" on crime, drugs, and terror are political campaigns, designed to appeal to individuals who believe that the best way to address society's ills and problems is to "crack down" or "get tough" on the issue. Meanwhile, social scientists and criminological studies have repeatedly indicated that addressing crime requires addressing underlying economic and sociological issues. Supporters of this more holistic approach argue that crime is not a military tactic, but more often represent acts of desperation by individuals whose motivations are complex and cannot be easily represented by notions of good and evil or right and wrong. Creating the peaceful cities desired by all urbanites may require moving away from the warfare mind-set and toward a more nuanced and complex attitude that promotes understanding, rehabilitation, and community-based efforts to promote the common good.

Micah L. Issitt

Notes

1. "The Prison Crisis," ACLU.
2. Hinton, "Why We Should Reconsider the War on Crime."
3. Mendoza, "U.S. Drug War Has Met None of Its Goals."
4. Branson, "War on Drugs a Trillion-Dollar Failure."
5. "Criminal Justice Fact Sheet," NAACP.
6. Ingraham, "White People Are More Likely to Deal Drugs, but Black People Are More Likely to Get Arrested for It."
7. Heath, "Racial Gap in U.S. Arrest Rates: 'Staggering.'"

8. Thompson, "Inner-City Violence in the Age of Mass Incarceration."

9. Pager, "Marked: Race, Crime, and Finding Work in an Era of Mass Incarceration," pg 1–6.

10. "War Comes Home," ACLU

11. "Eric Garner, Michael Brown Cases Spark 'Legitimate Concerns' about US Policing—UN Experts."

12. Gearty and Siemaszko, "NYPD Stop-and-Frisk Policy Yielded 4.4 Million Detentions but Few Results."

13. "With Baltimore Unrest, More Debate over 'Broken Windows' Policing," NPR.

14. Johnson, "Obama: U.S. Cracking Down on 'Militarization' of Local Police." NBC News. NBC. May 18, 2015. Web. Aug 7, 2015.

15. Wilson, "Hard Times, Fewer Crimes."

16. Lind and Lopes, "16 Theories for Why Crime Plummeted in the US."

Inner-City Violence in the Age of Mass Incarceration

By Heather Ann Thompson
The Atlantic, October 30, 2014

Over the summer, media outlets across the country fixated on the mounting death toll of young people in inner cities across America. "11 shot, including 3-year-old boy, as Chicago gun violence worsens," read the large headline of one major U.S. newspaper, while another, the *Chicago Tribune*, published a painfully graphic photo essay that chronicled the degree to which gun violence in particular had shocked and destabilized entire neighborhoods in 2014.

This fall, television reporters still stand nightly outside of dimly-lit apartment buildings and row houses, telling yet more stories of children felled by bullets and showing new heartbreaking scenes of mothers wracked by sobs. And yet, other headlines suggest that this nation is far safer and much less violent than it used to be. They note that gun violence has plummeted a startling 49 percent since 1993 and, aside from some brief spikes and dips in the last few years, most policymakers seem to feel quite good about America's overall crime rate, which is also at a noticeable low.

Why is it then that some American neighborhoods, from the south side of Chicago to the north side of Philadelphia to all sides of Detroit, still endure so much collective distress? Might there be something about these *particular* neighborhoods, pundits wonder, that make them more prone to violence?

According to one well-respected scholar, "high rates of black crime" continue to exist despite declining crime rates nationally because African Americans live in highly segregated and deeply impoverished neighborhoods. Not only does his work suggest that both segregation and poverty breed violence but, more disturbingly, that the ways in which poor blacks decide collectively and individually to protect themselves seems only to "fuel the violence," and gives it "a self-perpetuating character."

Segregation and poverty are indeed serious problems today, and too many of America's poorest all-black and all-brown communities also suffer a level of violence that, if one disregards the horrific killing sprees in places like Columbine, Seattle, or Sandy Hook, is largely unknown in whiter, more affluent neighborhoods. Whereas the violent crime rate in the mostly black city of Detroit was 21.23 per 1,000 (15,011 violent crimes) in 2012, that same year the virtually all-white

© 2014 The Atlantic Media Co., as first published in The Atlantic Magazine. All rights reserved. Distributed by Tribune Content Agency, LLC

city of Grosse Point, Michigan, nearby reported a rate of only 1.12 per 1,000 (6 violent crimes).

Notwithstanding such seemingly damning statistics, though, we have all seriously misunderstood the origins of the almost-paralyzing violence that our most racially-segregated communities now experience and, as troublingly, we have seriously mischaracterized the nature of so much of the violence that the residents of these communities suffer.

To start, locating today's concentrated levels of gun violence in hyper-segregation and highly concentrated poverty is quite ahistorical. As any careful look at the past makes clear, neither of these social ills is new and, therefore, neither can adequately explain why it is only recently that so many children of color are being shot or killed in their own communities.

Indeed, throughout the twentieth century, racially-segregated communities have been the norm. Everything from restrictive covenants to discriminatory federal housing policies ensured that throughout the postwar period, neighborhoods in cities such as Detroit or Chicago would be either all white or all non-white and, until now, none of these segregated spaces experienced sustained rates of violence so completely out of step with national trends.

To suggest, as both scholars and the media have, that the violence experienced by all-black or all-brown neighborhoods today stems in large part from their residential isolation is problematic for other reasons as well. It leads some to suspect that if people of color simply spent more time with white people, lived next to them, and went to school with them, they would be less violent—they would perhaps learn better ways to resolve disputes and deal with stress and anger. Again, though, history belies this logic.

White Americans also have a long history of violence—not only when asked to share residential space with African Americans or even to treat them as equals in schools or on the job, but also when nary a person of color is near. From the lynching of blacks in the Jim Crow era to the crimes committed against African Americans every time they tried to move onto a white block after World War I and World War II, ugly incidents of white violence were both regular and unremarkable. Even among those who look just like them, whites historically have engaged in a

> **Notably, the national policy embrace of targeted and more aggressive policing as well as highly punitive laws and sentences—the so-called "War on Crime" that led eventually to such catastrophic rates of imprisonment—*predated* the remarkable levels of violence that now impact poor communities of color so disproportionately.**

variety of violent behaviors that would make many shudder—from their propensity to engage in brutal duels and to "eye gouge" their fellow whites in the decades before the Civil War, to their involvement in mass shootings in more recent years.

Just as hyper-segregation doesn't explain the violence that so many have to endure today in America's inner city communities while still raising children, attending church, and trying to make ends meet, neither does highly-concentrated poverty.
Because of their exclusion from virtually every program and policy that helped eventually to build an American middle class, non-whites have always had far less wealth
than whites. From the ability to maintain land ownership after the Civil War, to the
virtual guarantee of welfare benefits such as Social Security and FHA loans during
the New Deal, to preferential access to employment and housing in the postwar
period, white communities have always had considerably more economic advantage
than communities of color. And yet, no matter how poor they were, America's most
impoverished communities have never been plagued by the level of violence they
are today.

But if neither racial segregation nor the racial poverty gap can account for the
degree to which poor communities of color are traumatized today, then what does?
What is altogether new is the extent to which these communities are devastated by
the working of our nation's criminal justice system in general and by mass incarceration in particular.

Today's rates of incarceration in America's poorest, blackest, and brownest neighborhoods are historically unprecedented. By 2001, one in six black men had been
incarcerated and, by the close of 2013, black and Latino inmates comprised almost 60 percent of the nation's federal and state prison population. The numbers
of incarcerated black women are also stark. According to the Bureau of Justice
Statistics, young black women ages 18 to 19 were almost five times more likely to be
imprisoned than white women of the same age in 2010.

When President Lyndon B. Johnson passed the Law Enforcement Assistance
Act in 1965—legislation which, in turn, made possible the most aggressive war on
crime this nation ever waged—he was reacting not to remarkable crime rates but
to the civil rights upheaval that had erupted nationwide just the year before. This
activism, he and other politicians believed, represented not participatory democracy
in action, but instead a criminal element that would only grow more dangerous if
not checked.

Notably, the national policy embrace of targeted and more aggressive policing as
well as highly punitive laws and sentences—the so-called "War on Crime" that led
eventually to such catastrophic rates of imprisonment—*predated* the remarkable
levels of violence that now impact poor communities of color so disproportionately.

In fact, the U.S. homicide rate in 1965 was significantly lower than it had been
in several previous moments in American history: 5.5 per 100,000 U.S. residents as
compared, for example, with 9.7 per 100,000 in 1933. Importantly, though, whereas
the violent crime rate was 200.2 per 100,000 U.S. residents in 1965, it more than
tripled to a horrifying 684.6 per 100,000 by 1995. Though mass incarceration did
not originate in extraordinarily high rates of violence, mass incarceration created the
conditions in which violence would surely fester.

The quadrupling of the incarceration rate in America since 1970 has had devastating collateral consequences. Already economically-fragile communities sank into

depths of poverty unknown for generations, simply because anyone with a criminal record is forever "marked" as dangerous and thus rendered all but permanently unemployable. Also, with blacks incarcerated at six times and Latinos at three times the rate of whites by 2010, millions of children living in communities of color have effectively been orphaned. Worse yet, these kids often experience high rates of post-traumatic shock from having witnessed the often-brutal arrests of their parents and having been suddenly ripped from them.

De-industrialization and suburbanization surely did their part to erode our nation's black and brown neighborhoods, but staggering rates of incarceration is what literally emptied them out. The overwhelmingly-black east side of the Motor City has been ravaged by the effects of targeted policing and mass incarceration in recent years with one in twenty-two adults there under some form of correctional control. In some neighborhoods, the rate is as high as one in 16.

Such concentrated levels of imprisonment have torn at the social fabric of inner-city neighborhoods in ways that even people who live there find hard to comprehend, let alone outsiders. As the research of criminologist Todd Clear makes clear, extraordinary levels of incarceration *create* the conditions for extraordinary levels of violence. But even mass incarceration does not, in itself, explain the particularly brutal nature of the violence that erupts today in, for example, the south side of Chicago. To explain that, we must look again carefully and critically at our nation's criminal justice system.

The level of gun violence in today's inner cities is the direct product of our criminal-justice policies—specifically, the decision to wage a brutal War on Drugs. When federal and state politicians such as New York Governor Nelson Rockefeller opted to criminalize addiction by passing unprecedentedly punitive possession laws rather than to treat it as a public health crisis, unwittingly or not, a high level of violence in poor communities of color was not only assured but was guaranteed to be particularly ugly. This new drug war created a brand-new market for illegal drugs—an underground marketplace that would be inherently dangerous and would necessarily be regulated by both guns and violence.

Indeed, without the War on Drugs, the level of gun violence that plagues so many poor inner-city neighborhoods today simply would not exist. The last time we saw so much violence from the use of firearms was, notably, during Prohibition. "[As] underground profit margins surged, gang rivalries emerged, and criminal activity mounted [during Prohibition]," writes historian Abigail Perkiss, "the homicide rate across the nation rose 78 percent. . . [and] in Chicago alone, there were more than 400 gang-related murders a year."

As important as it is to rethink the origins of the violence that poor inner-city residents still endure, we must also be careful even when using the term "violence," particularly when seeking to explain "what seems to be wrong" with America's most disadvantaged communities. A level of state violence is also employed daily in these communities that rarely gets mentioned and yet it is as brutal, and perhaps even more devastating, than the violence that is so often experienced as a result of the informal economy in now-illegal drugs.

This is a violence that comes in the form of police harassment, surveillance, profiling, and even killings—the ugly realities of how law enforcement wages America's War on Drugs. Today, young black men today are 21 times more likely than their white peers to be killed by the police and, according to a recent ProPublica report, black children have fared just as badly. Since 1980, a full 67 percent of the 151 teenagers and 66 percent of the 41 kids under 14 who have been killed by police were African American. Between 2010 and 2012 alone, police officers shot and killed fifteen teens running away from them; all but one of them black.

This is the violence that undergirded the 4.4 million stop-and-frisks in New York City between 2004 and 2014. This is the violence that led to the deaths of black men and boys such as Kimani Gray, Amadou Diallo, Sean Bell, Oscar Grant, and Michael Brown. This is the violence that led to the deaths of black women and girls such as Rekia Boyd, Yvette Smith, and 7-year-old Aiyana Stanley-Jones. And this is the violence that has touched off months of protests in Ferguson, Missouri, just as it also touched off nearly a decade of urban rebellions after 1964.

A close look at the violence that today haunts America's most impoverished and most segregated cities, in fact, fundamentally challenges conventional assumptions about perpetrators and victims. America's black and brown people not only don't have a monopoly on violence, but, in fact, a great deal of the violence being waged in their communities is perpetrated by those who are at least officially charged with protecting, not harming, them. As residents of Ferguson well know, for example, in the same month that Michael Brown was shot to death by a police officer, four other unarmed black men were also killed by members of law enforcement.

Indeed, the true origins of today's high rates of violence in America's most highly segregated, most deeply impoverished, and blackest and brownest neighborhoods—whoever perpetrates it—are located well outside of these same communities. Simply put, America's poorest people of color had no seat [at] the policy table where mass incarceration was made. But though they did not create the policies that led to so much community and state violence in inner cities today, they nevertheless now suffer from them in unimaginable ways.

Two Architects of Broken Windows Policing Go On the Defensive

By Eric Jaffe
Citylab, December 29, 2014

Few city-related topics have generated as much debate in 2014 as broken windows policing. New York has played host to this discussion, especially in the aftermath of the over-aggressive arrest that led to Eric Garner's terrible death, but the whole country has taken part. Critics suggest the broken windows approach—which holds that stopping petty crimes ultimately deters big ones—is broken itself: unfairly targeting minorities, destroying community trust in police, and arguably doing more harm to the city than good.

Two architects of broken windows policy come to its defense in the Winter 2015 issue of *City Journal*, a quarterly from the Manhattan Institute. NYPD Commissioner William Bratton, who's been using a broken windows strategy in major U.S. cities for decades, and criminal justice scholar George Kelling, who (along with James Q. Wilson) popularized the concept in a 1982 issue of *The Atlantic*, counter their critics point by point. In hopes of a sharper public discourse, we summarize some of their key arguments below, then raise additional challenges.

- **Broken windows is not stop-and-frisk.** Bratton and Kelling argue that these two policing approaches have been wrongly conflated in the public mind. Stop-and-frisk—the widely condemned practice that New York has dialed back significantly—is based on a "reasonable suspicion" of criminal activity, leaving lots of room for officer interpretation, and thus abuse. In contrast, they say, broken windows policing directly addresses illegal behavior in action.

- **Most people want to stop minor offenses.** Bratton and Kelling also argue, based on their experience in "countless" public meetings, that locals consider it extremely important to stop the types of small-scale disorderly conduct at the heart of broken windows policing (from graffiti to litter to public drug use). They point to an August 2014 poll, conducted in the wake of Garner's death, which found that a majority of New York voters want police to enforce quality-of-life offenses. That support was true not only of whites (61–33) but also blacks (56–37) and Hispanics (64–34).

- **The statistics suggest broken windows works.** Broken windows went into full effect in New York circa 1994, when Bratton was commissioner

© 2014 The Atlantic Media Co., as first published in Citylab. All rights reserved. Distributed by Tribune Content Agency, LLC

under then-Mayor Rudy Giuliani. At that time the city's murder rate was 26.5 per 100,000 people, and New York accounted for about 8 percent of all U.S. homicides, Bratton and Kelling report. Today the city's murder rate is 4 per 100,000—lower than the national rate of 4.5—and the share of U.S. homicides is 2.4 percent.

- **So does the science.** In response to the charge that there's no evidence broken windows works, Bratton and Kelling point to recent controlled experiments showing it does. In one study conducted in real cities (Jersey City, New Jersey, and Lowell, Massachusetts), crime declined at a greater rate in areas randomly assigned to receive broken windows policing, compared to those that received routine policing. Another field study, published in *Science,* found similar results: people stole an envelope of cash placed near a mailbox significantly more often when it was surrounded by litter and graffiti than when it wasn't.

- **Broken windows doesn't lead to over-incarceration or excessive force.** Here Bratton and Kelling bring several trends to their side. They note that the New York City jail population has declined 45 percent since 1992, and that fewer than 10 percent of misdemeanor arrestees receive jail sentences. They also note that force was used less than 2 percent of the time during misdemeanor arrests in the first half of 2014, and that it wasn't used at all during this period in the 321 arrests for untaxed cigarettes—which was Garner's offense.

- **Disorder is not a victimless crime.** Broken windows critics often contend that public disorder doesn't harm anyone, and therefore should be left alone. Bratton and Kelling disagree. Subway fare evasion is a minor offense, for instance, but it erodes the city's ability to provide strong mobility and job access—and besides, they argue, three of four evaders are issued summonses rather than arrested. So even if quality-of-life crimes don't have a clear victim, they have a serious impact on "the way people feel about their homes, their safety, and their general well-being."

●   ●   ●

Bratton and Kelling are as expert as it gets on the subject of broken windows policing, and many of their points in its defense are very well taken. But they do themselves a disservice by taking a dismissive tone; at one point they huff at "ivory-tower studies. . . treated with reverence by the media," a rather odd shot coming from a think tank journal. And their conclusion that broken windows policing is directly responsible for the high quality of life in New York City today also feels like a stretch in light of all the evidence:

> "It's not clear whether declines in city (and New York City) crime are the result of broken windows policing, or whether order and civility were restored by other broad social trends."

Crime has been plummeting for two decades. . . .Tourism is booming. Public spaces are safe. Property values have escalated. It's a good place to live and work. Lawlessness no longer characterizes the subway system. These conditions didn't just happen. They resulted from thousands of police interventions on the street, which restored order and civility across the five boroughs.

Of course, reduced crime is very high among the reasons why New York City is a great place today. But the specific role played by broken windows in that reduction remains in question.

For one thing, crime has fallen everywhere in recent years. A 2004 study on policing by the National Academy of Sciences failed to find strong evidence that "enforcement strategies (primarily arrest) applied broadly against offenders committing minor offenses lead to reductions in serious crime." Even in New York the case isn't cut and dry; one recent study, done by New York University sociologist David Greenberg, re-analyzed city crime numbers from 1988 to 2001 and found a clear downward trend that began well before 1994.

In other words, it's not clear whether declines in city (and New York City) crime are the result of broken windows policing, or whether order and civility were restored by other broad social trends. (Popular alternative explanations include the waning urban crack epidemic, or decreased toxic lead exposure, or more community-based police tactics.) And many of the other points made by Bratton and Kelling require additional scrutiny or context.

Stop-and-frisk may be distinct from (and more pernicious than) broken windows policing, for instance, but it remains a logical extension. Most New Yorkers may approve of public order (who wouldn't?), but they also disapprove of the type of aggression that led to Eric Garner's death, with 68 percent of those polled in August saying there was no excuse for police behavior in that case. Broken windows policing may not always lead to excessive force, but the fact that it has done so at all—in several recent instances aside from Garner—shows something about the policy itself is, at the very least, fractured.

And even assuming broken windows does work—again, a leap beyond much of the evidence—any benefits must be weighed against the policy's divisiveness. Justin Peters recently argued in *Slate* that broken windows is rooted in racism, noting that Kelling and Wilson initially offered no answer to the question of how police using the approach can avoid being "agents of neighborhood bigotry." Writing today in the *Boston Globe*, columnist Derrick Jackson suggests that black people *themselves* have become the broken windows that a neighborhood must clean up, the very color of their skin a "primary offense."

So if broken windows policing is sound in theory, or even if it's effective at times in practice, plenty of questions remain as to how it's being applied on city streets. That's not the same as calling for broken windows to end—and for sure, it's not much help to criticize an existing approach without offering ideas for a new one (though these ideas do exist). But it does suggest something has to change for the police to "strengthen their relationships with citizens, civic organizations, and communities," as Bratton and Kelling say the NYPD must.

Because such a bond should seem very far off the way things stand now. To critics and honest supporters alike.

The Militarization of U.S. Police: Finally Dragged into the Light by the Horrors of Ferguson

By Glenn Greenwald
The Intercept, August 14, 2014

The intensive militarization of America's police forces is a serious menace about which a small number of people have been loudly warning for years, with little attention or traction. In a 2007 paper on "the blurring distinctions between the police and military institutions and between war and law enforcement," the criminal justice professor Peter Kraska defined "police militarization" as "the process whereby civilian police increasingly draw from, and pattern themselves around, the tenets of militarism and the military model."

The harrowing events of the last week in Ferguson, Missouri—the fatal police shooting of an unarmed African-American teenager, Mike Brown, and the blatantly excessive and thuggish response to ensuing community protests from a police force that resembles an occupying army—have shocked the U.S. media class and millions of Americans. But none of this is aberrational.

It is the destructive by-product of several decades of deliberate militarization of American policing, a trend that received a sustained (and ongoing) steroid injection in the form of a still-flowing, post-9/11 federal funding bonanza, all justified in the name of "homeland security." This has resulted in a domestic police force that looks, thinks, and acts more like an invading and occupying military than a community-based force to protect the public.

As is true for most issues of excessive and abusive policing, police militarization is overwhelmingly and disproportionately directed at minorities and poor communities, ensuring that the problem largely festers in the dark. Americans are now so accustomed to seeing police officers decked in camouflage and Robocop-style costumes, riding in armored vehicles and carrying automatic weapons first introduced during the U.S. occupation of Baghdad, that it has become normalized. But those who bear the brunt of this transformation are those who lack loud megaphones; their complaints of the inevitable and severe abuse that results have largely been met with indifference.

Originally published by The Intercept, August 14, 2014; copyright First Look Media, Inc.

If anything positive can come from the Ferguson travesties, it is that the completely out-of-control orgy of domestic police militarization receives long-overdue attention and reining in.

Last night, two reporters, *The Washington Post*'s Wesley Lowery and *The Huffington Post*'s Ryan Reilly, were arrested and assaulted while working from a McDonald's in Ferguson. The arrests were arbitrary and abusive, and received substantial attention—only because of their prominent platforms, not, as they both quickly pointed out upon being released, because there was anything unusual about this police behavior.

Reilly, on Facebook, recounted how he was arrested by "a Saint Louis County police officer in full riot gear, who refused to identify himself despite my repeated requests, purposefully banged my head against the window on the way out and sarcastically apologized." He wrote: "I'm fine. But if this is the way these officers treat a white reporter working on a laptop who moved a little too slowly for their liking, I can't imagine how horribly they treat others." He added: "And if anyone thinks that the militarization of our police force isn't a huge issue in this country, I've got a story to tell you."

Lowery, who is African-American, tweeted a summary of an interview he gave on MSNBC: "If I didn't work for the *Washington Post* and were just another Black man in Ferguson, I'd still be in a cell now." He added: "I knew I was going to be fine. But the thing is, so many people here in Ferguson don't have as many Twitter followers as I have and don't have Jeff Bezos or whoever to call and bail them out of jail."

The best and most comprehensive account of the dangers of police militarization is the 2013 book by the libertarian *Washington Post* journalist Radley Balko, entitled *Rise of the Warrior Cops: The Militarization of America's Police Forces*. Balko, who has devoted his career to documenting and battling the worst abuses of the U.S. criminal justice system, traces the history and underlying mentality that has given rise to all of this: the "law-and-order" obsessions that grew out of the social instability of the 1960s, the War on Drugs that has made law enforcement agencies view Americans as an enemy population, the Reagan-era "War on Poverty" (which was more aptly described as a war on America's poor), the aggressive Clinton-era expansions of domestic policing, all topped off by the massively funded, rights-destroying, post-9/11 security state of the Bush and Obama years. All of this, he documents, has infused America's police forces with "a creeping battlefield mentality."

I read Balko's book prior to publication in order to blurb it, and after I was done, immediately wrote what struck me most about it: "There is no vital trend in American society *more overlooked* than the militarization of our domestic police forces." *The Huffington Post*'s Ryan Grim, in the outlet's official statement about Reilly's arrest, made the same point: *"Police militarization has been among the most consequential and unnoticed developments of our time."*

In June, the ACLU published a crucial 96-page report on this problem, entitled "War Comes Home: The Excessive Militarization of American Policing." Its central point: "the United States today has become excessively militarized, mainly through federal programs that create incentives for state and local police to use unnecessarily aggressive weapons and tactics designed for the battlefield."

The report documents how the Drug War and (Clinton/Biden) 1990s crime bills laid the groundwork for police militarization, but the virtually unlimited flow of "homeland security" money after 9/11 all but forced police departments to purchase battlefield equipment and other military paraphernalia whether they wanted them or not. Unsurprisingly, like the War on Drugs and police abuse generally, "the use of paramilitary weapons and tactics primarily impacted people of color."

Some police departments eagerly militarize, but many recognize the dangers. Salt Lake City police chief Chris Burbank is quoted in the ACLU report: "We're not the military. Nor should we look like an invading force coming in." A 2011 *Los Angeles Times* article, noting that "federal and state governments are spending about $75 billion a year on domestic security," described how local police departments receive so much homeland security money from the U.S. government that they end up forced to buy battlefield equipment they know they do not need: from armored vehicles to Zodiac boats with side-scan sonar.

The trend long pre-dates 9/11, as [a] 1997 *Christian Science Monitor* article by Jonathan Landay about growing police militarization and its resulting abuses ("Police Tap High-Tech Tools of Military to Fight Crime") makes clear. Landay, in that 17-year-old article, described "an infrared scanner mounted on [a police officer's] car [that] is the same one used by US troops to hunt Iraqi forces in the Gulf war," and wrote: "it is symbolic of an increasing use by police of some of the advanced technologies that make the US military the world's mightiest."

> Much of the war-like weaponry now seen in Ferguson comes from American laws, such as the so-called "Program 1033," specifically designed to re-direct excessive Pentagon property—no longer needed as foreign wars wind down—into American cities.

But the *security-über-alles* fixation of the 9/11 era is now the driving force. A June [2014] article in the *New York Times* by Matt Apuzzo ("War Gear Flows to Police Departments") reported that "during the Obama administration, according to Pentagon data, police departments have received tens of thousands of machine guns; nearly 200,000 ammunition magazines; thousands of pieces of camouflage and night-vision equipment; and hundreds of silencers, armored cars and aircraft." He added: "The equipment has been added to the armories of police departments that already look and act like military units."

All of this has become such big business, and is grounded in such politically entrenched bureaucratic power, that it is difficult to imagine how it can be uprooted. As the *LA Times* explained:

> An entire industry has sprung up to sell an array of products, including high-tech motion sensors and fully outfitted emergency operations trailers. The market is expected to grow to $31 billion by 2014.

Like the military-industrial complex that became a permanent and powerful part of the American landscape during the Cold War, the vast network of Homeland Security spyware, concrete barricades and high-tech identity screening is here to stay. The Department of Homeland Security, a collection of agencies ranging from border control to airport security sewn quickly together after Sept. 11, is the third-largest Cabinet department and—with almost no lawmaker willing to render the U.S. less prepared for a terrorist attack—one of those least [likely] to fall victim to budget cuts.

The dangers of domestic militarization are both numerous and manifest. To begin with, as the nation is seeing in Ferguson, it degrades the mentality of police forces in virtually every negative way and subjects their targeted communities to rampant brutality and unaccountable abuse. The ACLU report summarized: "excessive militarism in policing, particularly through the use of paramilitary policing teams, escalates the risk of violence, threatens individual liberties, and unfairly impacts people of color."

Police militarization also poses grave and direct dangers to basic political liberties, including rights of free speech, press and assembly. The first time I wrote about this issue was back in 2008 when I covered the protests outside the GOP national convention in St. Paul for *Salon,* and was truly amazed by the war-zone atmosphere deliberately created by the police:

St. Paul was the most militarized I have ever seen an American city be, even more so than Manhattan in the week of 9/11—with troops of federal, state and local law enforcement agents marching around with riot gear, machine guns, and tear gas canisters, shouting military chants and marching in military formations. Humvees and law enforcement officers with rifles were posted on various buildings and balconies. Numerous protesters and observers were tear gassed and injured.

The same thing happened during the Occupy Wall Street protests of 2011: the police response was so excessive, and so clearly modeled after battlefield tactics, that there was no doubt that deterring domestic dissent is one of the primary aims of police militarization. About that police response, I wrote at the time:

Law enforcement officials and policy-makers in America know full well that serious protests — and more — are inevitable given the economic tumult and suffering the U.S. has seen over the last three years (and will continue to see for the foreseeable future). . . .

The reason the U.S. has para-militarized its police forces is precisely to control this type of domestic unrest, and it's simply impossible to imagine its not being deployed in full against a growing protest movement aimed at grossly and corruptly unequal resource distribution. As Madeleine Albright said when arguing for U.S. military intervention in the Balkans: "What's the point of having this superb military you're always talking about if we can't use it?" That's obviously how governors, big-city Mayors and Police Chiefs feel about the stockpiles of assault rifles, SWAT gear, hi-tech helicopters, and the coming-soon drone technology lavished on them in the wake of the post/9-11 Security State explosion, to say nothing of the enormous federal law enforcement apparatus that, more than anything else, resembles a standing army which is increasingly directed inward.

Most of this militarization has been justified by invoking Scary Foreign Threats—primarily the Terrorist—but its prime purpose is domestic.

Police militarization is increasingly aimed at stifling journalism as well. Like the arrests of Lowery and Reilly last night, *Democracy Now*'s Amy Goodman and two of her colleagues were arrested while covering the 2008 St. Paul protests. As Trevor Timm of the Freedom of the Press Foundation (on whose board I sit) explained yesterday, militarization tactics "don't just affect protesters, but also affect those who cover the protest. It creates an environment where police think they can disregard the law and tell reporters to stop filming, despite their legal right to do so, or fire tear gas directly at them to prevent them from doing their job. And if the rights of journalists are being trampled on, you can almost guarantee it's even worse for those who don't have such a platform to protect themselves."

Ultimately, police militarization is part of a broader and truly dangerous trend: the importation of War on Terror tactics from foreign war zones onto American soil. American surveillance drones went from Yemen, Pakistan and Somalia into American cities, and it's impossible to imagine that they won't be followed by weaponized ones. The inhumane and oppressive conditions that prevailed at Guantanamo are matched, or exceeded, by the super-max hellholes and "Communications Management Units" now in the American prison system. And the "collect-it-all" mentality that drives NSA domestic surveillance was pioneered by Gen. Keith Alexander in Baghdad and by other generals in Afghanistan, aimed at enemy war populations.

Indeed, much of the war-like weaponry now seen in Ferguson comes from American laws, such as the so-called "Program 1033," specifically designed to re-direct excessive Pentagon property—no longer needed as foreign wars wind down—into American cities. As the Missouri Department of Public Safety proudly explains on its website, "the 1033 Program provides surplus DoD military equipment to state and local civilian law enforcement agencies for use in counter-narcotics and counter-terrorism operations, and to enhance officer safety."

One government newsletter—from "the Law Enforcement Support Office (LESO), a little known federal agency that equips police departments with surplus military gear"—boasted that "Fiscal Year 2011 was a record year in property transfers from the US military's stockpiles to police departments around the nation." The ACLU report notes: "the Department of Defense operates the 1033 Program through the Defense Logistics Agency's (DLA) Law Enforcement Support Office (LESO), whose motto is 'from warfighter to crimefighter.'" The Justice Department has an entire program devoted to "supporting military veterans and the law enforcement agencies that hire them as our veterans seek to transition into careers as law enforcement officers."

As part of America's posture of Endless War, Americans have been trained to believe that everything is justified on the "battlefield" (now defined to mean "the whole world"): imprisonment without charges, kidnapping, torture, even assassination of

U.S. citizens without trials. It is not hard to predict the results of importing this battlefield mentality onto American soil, aimed at American citizens: "From Warfighter to Crimefighter." The results have been clear for those who have looked—or those who have been subject to this—for years. The events in Ferguson are, finally, forcing all Americans to watch the outcome of this process.

City Life

By Jelani Cobb
The New Yorker, May 11, 2015

Somewhere between the ball game played to an empty stadium and the arrest of six police officers on charges including manslaughter and murder, somewhere around the time that a leaked document suggested that a man who suffered a catastrophic spinal injury while in police custody had died of a self-inflicted wound, events in Baltimore slipped into the realm of the surreal. It was not a particularly unfamiliar journey. For a long time, our domestic affairs, or at least the portion of them most explicitly tied to race, have resembled a nightmare doomed to be repeated until the underlying conflict is resolved. President Obama addressed that recurrence in a press conference at the White House last Tuesday, when he spoke about the death of Freddie Gray and what has euphemistically been called the "unrest" in Baltimore:

> Since Ferguson, and the task force that we put together, we have seen too many in-stances of what appears to be police officers interacting with individuals—primarily African American, often poor—in ways that have raised troubling questions. And it comes up, it seems like, once a week now, or once every couple of weeks. . . . What I'd say is this has been a slow-rolling crisis. This has been going on for a long time. This is not new, and we shouldn't pretend that it's new.

It is true that we have grown adroit at feigning astonishment at the episodic convulsions of violence in American cities, but that doesn't make them any less predictable or their roots any less apparent. With the exception of the riots that followed the assassination of Martin Luther King, Jr., every major riot by the black community of an American city since the Second World War has been ignited by a single issue: police tactics. (The explosion in Baltimore occurred in the same week as the twenty-third anniversary of the Rodney King riots, in Los Angeles.) Police departments point to the high rates of crime and violence that prevailed in previous years, and argue that aggressive police tactics to reduce them are therefore a hallmark of civic concern, not signs of callous disregard. The former Maryland governor Martin O'Malley, who is a potential Presidential contender, echoed that sentiment after last Monday night's riot in Baltimore. As the city's mayor from 1999 to 2007, he had introduced zero-tolerance policing, and he told CNN that it was likely responsible for a thousand Baltimoreans being alive, rather than dead, as victims of homicide. Violent-crime and homicide rates in the city did decline, but the numbers today reveal a profane truth. Last year in Baltimore, there were two hundred and eleven homicides; a hundred and eighty-nine of the victims were black males. Those numbers are categorical: Baltimore doesn't have a homicide problem; it has a black-male-death problem.

Talk to people in Baltimore—or Ferguson or Staten Island—and invariably you hear criticism of the police not as the police but as a symbol of an entire web of failed social policies, on education, employment, health, and housing. The real question is not one of police tactics: whether the use of body cameras can reduce civilian complaints or whether police-brutality cases should be handled by independent prosecutors. The real question is what life in an American city should be. The issues extend far beyond the parameters of race, but race is the narrative most easily seized upon. (It's worth noting our tendency to think of declining, mostly white Rust Belt cities elegiacally, and of largely black ones moralistically.)

Midway through the twentieth century, cities—especially those, like Baltimore, which were sustained by ports—connoted a kind of American swagger. Today, the population of Baltimore is six hundred and twenty-three thousand; in 1950, it was nine hundred and fifty thousand. The Second World War diminished ethnic rivalries among white Americans and, with them, the tribal allotments of urban neighborhoods, but that process was accelerated by the fact that those areas were already becoming less appealing. When, in 1910, a black attorney bought a house on a white block in Baltimore, the *Sun* reported that the presence of blacks would drive down property values. That helped bring about a city ordinance—the first of its kind—establishing block-by-block segregation. It is generally assumed that white flight was a product of the political tumult and the spiking crime that afflicted American cities in the nineteen-sixties, but it may well have been the other way around. Baltimore, three-quarters white in 1950, is now two-thirds black. As the surrounding suburbs became increasingly white, transportation networks that once connected the city and the outlying county crumbled. Industry and employment relocated to the surrounding areas. By the late sixties, the city was marked by poverty, a persistent lack of opportunity, and violent crime.

> Talk to people in Baltimore—or Ferguson or Staten Island—and invariably you hear criticism of the police not as the police but as a symbol of an entire web of failed social policies, on education, employment, health, and housing.

Conservative commentators have pointed to Baltimore as a kind of anti-Ferguson, a city where, for decades, blacks have had a secure grasp on political leadership, including the mayor's office; a significant representation in the police force, including, now, the commissioner; and an African-American chief prosecutor, who announced the charges in Gray's death. Yet Baltimore witnessed the same volatile dynamics that we saw in Missouri last year. The implication is that the problem is not racialized policing but the intractable, fraught nature of securing poor, crime-prone communities. That doesn't quite square. As the Department of Justice's report on Ferguson suggests, black representation may diminish but by no means resolve policing practices that disproportionately target African-Americans. And the differences in leadership in the two cities belie their conflicts' common historical roots in segregation. Housing discrimination, of the sort intended by the Baltimore ordinance, was outlawed by a 1948 Supreme Court case, *Shelley v. Kraemer*, which originated in St. Louis, just a few miles from Ferguson.

Between 1980 and 2010, the population of Ferguson flipped from 85 percent white to 69 percent black. At some point soon, Ferguson, like Baltimore, may have more proportional black representation, but the socioeconomic trends in that city won't automatically change. Gray died twenty-eight years after Baltimore's first black mayor took office, yet the statistical realities at the time of his death—a 24 percent poverty rate, 37 percent unemployment among young black men—show how complicated and durable the dynamics of race and racism can be.

Last week, the cover of *Time* featured an image of Baltimore aflame, with the year 1968 crossed out and 2015 penciled in. On social media, split-screen images of the riot that followed King's death and the one that followed Gray's proliferated. The temptation is to believe that nothing has changed, but something has: Baltimore is blacker and poorer than it was then. It was not difficult to see who set buildings on fire there last week. The more salient concern is how cities become kindling in the first place.

The Myth of Police Reform

By Ta-Nehisi Coates
The Atlantic, April 15, 2015

There is a tendency, when examining police shootings, to focus on tactics at the expense of strategy. One interrogates the actions of the officer in the moment trying to discern their mind-state. We ask ourselves, "Were they justified in shooting?" But, in this time of heightened concern around the policing, a more essential question might be, "Were we justified in sending them?" At some point, Americans decided that the best answer to every social ill lay in the power of the criminal-justice system. Vexing social problems—homelessness, drug use, the inability to support one's children, mental illness—are presently solved by sending in men and women who specialize in inspiring fear and ensuring compliance. Fear and compliance have their place, but it can't be every place.

When Walter Scott fled from the North Charleston police, he was not merely fleeing Michael Thomas Slager, he was attempting to flee incarceration. He was doing this because we have decided that the criminal-justice system is the best tool for dealing with men who can't, or won't, support their children at a level that we deem satisfactory. Peel back the layers of most of the recent police shootings that have captured attention and you will find a broad societal problem that we have looked at, thrown our hands up, and said to the criminal-justice system, "You deal with this."

Last week I was in Madison, Wisconsin, where I was informed of the killing of Tony Robinson by a police officer. Robinson was high on mushrooms. The police were summoned after he chased a car. The police killed him. A month earlier, I'd been thinking a lot about Anthony Hill, who was mentally ill. One day last month, Hill stripped off his clothes and started jumping off of his balcony. The police were called. They killed him. I can see the image of Tamir Rice aimlessly kicking snow outside the Cleveland projects and think of how little we invest in occupying the minds of children. A bored Tamir Rice decided to occupy his time with an airsoft gun. He was killed.

There is, of course, another way. Was Walter Scott's malfunctioning third-brake light really worth a police encounter? Should the state repeatedly incarcerate him for not paying child support? Do we really want people trained to fight crime dealing with someone who's ceased taking medication? Does the presence of a gun really improve the chance of peacefully resolving a drug episode? In this sense,

© 2015 The Atlantic Media Co., as first published in The Atlantic Magazine. All rights reserved. Distributed by Tribune Content Agency, LLC

the police—and the idea of police reform—are a symptom of something larger. The idea that all social problems can, and should, be resolved by sheer power is not limited to the police. In Atlanta, a problem that began with the poor state of public

> **Police officers fight crime. Police officers are neither case-workers, nor teachers, nor mental-health professionals, nor drug counselors. One of the great hallmarks of the past forty years of American domestic policy is a broad disinterest in that difference.**

schools has now ended by feeding more people into the maw of the carceral state.

There are many problems with expecting people trained in crime-fighting to be social workers. In the black community, there is a problem of legitimacy. In his 1953 book *The Quest for Community,* conservative Robert Nisbet distinguishes between "power" and "authority." Authority, claims Nisbet, is a matter of relationships, allegiances, and association and is "based ultimately upon the consent of those under it." Power, on the other hand, is "external" and "based upon force." Power exists where allegiances have decayed or never existed at all. "Power arises," writes Nesbit, "only when authority breaks down."

African Americans, for most of our history, have lived under the power of the criminal-justice system, not its authority. The dominant feature in the relationship between African Americans and their country is plunder, and plunder has made police authority an impossibility, and police power a necessity. The skepticism of Officer Darren Wilson's account in the shooting of Michael Brown, for instance, emerges out of lack of police authority—which is to say it comes from a belief that the police are as likely to lie as any other citizen. When African American parents give their children "The Talk," they do not urge them to make no sudden movements in the presence of police out of a profound respect for the democratic ideal, but out of the knowledge that police can, and will, kill them.

But for most Americans, the police—and the criminal-justice system—are figures of authority. The badge does not merely represent rule via lethal force, but rule through consent and legitimacy rooted in nobility. This is why whenever a liberal politician offers even the mildest criticism of the police, they must add that "the majority of officers are good, noble people." Taken at face value this is not much of a defense—like a restaurant claiming that on most nights, there really are no rats in the dining room. But interpreted less literally the line is not meant to defend police officers, but to communicate the message that the speaker is not questioning police authority, which is to say the authority of our justice system, which is to say—in a democracy—the authority of the people themselves.

Thus it was not surprising, last week, to see that the mayor of North Charleston ordered the use of body cameras for all officers. Body cameras are the least divisive and least invasive step toward reforming the practices of the men and women we permit to kill in our names. Body cameras are helpful in police work, but they are also helpful in avoiding a deeper conversation over what it means to keep whole swaths of America under the power of the justice system, as opposed to the authority of other branches of civil society.

Police officers fight crime. Police officers are neither case-workers, nor teachers, nor mental-health professionals, nor drug counselors. One of the great hallmarks of the past forty years of American domestic policy is a broad disinterest in that difference. The problem of restoring police authority is not really a problem of police authority, but a problem of democratic authority. It is what happens when you decide to solve all your problems with a hammer. To ask, at this late date, why the police seem to have lost their minds is to ask why our hammers are so bad at installing air-conditioners. More it is to ignore the state of the house all around us. A reform that begins with the officer on the beat is not reform at all. It's avoidance. It's a continuance of the American preference for considering the actions of bad individuals, as opposed to the function and intention of systems.

Is a New Crime Wave on the Horizon?

By Mariano Castillo
CNN.com, June 4, 2015

After decades of a downward trend in crime, residents in some large U.S. cities wonder if a reversal is coming.

If you live in Baltimore, you know that May [2015], with 43 homicides, was the deadliest month since 1972. Or if you are a Houstonian, you've probably heard that murders were up 45% through April compared to the same period in 2014.

The latest statistics in Milwaukee show a 103% spike in murders year-to-date compared with a year ago. In Atlanta, 41 people were killed in the first five months of this year compared with 27 in the same period last year, an increase of 52%.

The spike in killings in these major cities would be troubling in itself at any time, but it is especially troubling now, when policing practices, race and social policies are regularly in the news.

The video of a gunman brazenly opening fire on another man in the Bronx in May, or another gunman caught on camera firing across the street at someone in Harlem in April, spread so swiftly online that it is fair to ask if a crime wave is on the horizon.

A review of murder statistics in major U.S. cities so far this year shows an unclear picture.

While Baltimore and Houston appear to be experiencing a crime wave, comparable cities like Dallas and Los Angeles are trending in the opposite direction.

In short, it is too early to draw conclusions of a shift in the trend for violent crime.

Anecdotal Evidence

How telling is Baltimore's deadly month of May?

Of the 119 homicides recorded in Baltimore this year, more than one-third happened in May.

As the *Baltimore Sun* put it in an editorial, "We don't think it is at all unreasonable to start asking questions about leadership in a city that, over the last month, was less safe by some measures than it has been at any point in recorded history."

On Wednesday, Baltimore Police Commissioner Anthony Batts said his office is asking for more federal resources—prosecutors and law enforcement officers—to boost the city's response to the recent uptick in crime.

From CNN.com, June 4 © 2015 Turner Broadcast Systems, Inc.. All rights reserved. Used by permission and protected by the Copyright Laws of the United States. The printing, copying, redistribution, or retransmission of this Content without express written permission is prohibited.

Speaking at an event remembering a toddler who was killed by a stray bullet last year, Baltimore Mayor Stephanie Rawlings-Blake said last month

> **"Why should the black community have to choose between police abuse and police neglect? That's a false choice."**

that it is a "very, very painful time in our city."

On the other extreme is Los Angeles. Because of its large population, the city notches one of the nation's highest numbers of murders, but the trend has been shrinking violent crime.

CNN requested murder statistics for 2015 from a number of large U.S. cities. Some departments cooperated right away, while others asked for more time or formal open records requests. Among the departments that released statistics, the numbers reflected different periods. Some cities had murder statistics through May, others just through April.

For the cities where crime does appear to be trending upward, how can one know if it is a blip or a historic reversal?

"It's a little bit like the stock market. These statistics go up and down," said Harold Pollack, co-director of the University of Chicago Crime Lab. "It's like asking why did the stock market go up 75 points today."

But numbers have the power to sway, and many of these figures are being used already to bolster arguments for stronger police enforcement or a reformed police presence.

Explaining the Downward Trend

As policing has changed over the years, the question of what the nationwide decreases in violent crime means has been debated.

There is general agreement that larger police departments—and more officers in the streets—has had a positive effect on lowering crime, Pollack said.

The quality of policing has also improved over the past 20 years and the departments are better managed, he said.

Other factors are harder to quantify.

The end of the crack epidemic is believed to have contributed to the decrease in violent crime, as have other reasons ranging from the legalization of abortion to changes in the illegal drug market.

This year "may not be shaping up to be a terrific year in many cities, and it may be part of a larger pattern, but we really don't know that," Pollack said.

So What's the Debate Right Now?

One obvious difference between last year and this year is the tensions between police officers and certain communities.

The high-profile instances of police officers killing unarmed black men stirred outrage and protests.

There is an understanding that somehow things have changed—or must change—in a post–Michael Brown, post–Freddie Gray, post–Eric Garner America.

The debate on whether police reform is needed or whether more aggressive policing is necessary is often political. The early 2015 murder statistics are providing evidence for both sides.

"If there's a national mood that starts to see police as the bad guys, the police as the enemy responsible for these problems, it makes it a hell of a lot harder to police," said Peter Moskos, a former Baltimore police officer and professor of policing. "One way that cops deal with that is that they just stop policing those people."

A former New York Police Department officer, Bill Stanton, agreed that an uptick in crime can be linked to police being less assertive.

"When you take away police pride and you take away giving them the benefit of the doubt. . . and you're going to call them racist and you're going to prosecute them for doing nothing wrong," Stanton said, "then what happens is they're going to roll back. They're not going to go that extra mile."

CNN Political Analyst Van Jones said tying the protests over the deaths of unarmed black men to increases in crime is disingenuous.

"Police unions are trying to link any crime to First Amendment protests and cherry-picking data," he told CNN's Erin Burnett.

"This is all part of an attempt to tell black people that if we exercise our First Amendment rights, we are somehow now responsible for people who engage in crime," he said. "Why should the black community have to choose between police abuse and police neglect? That's a false choice."

The Fundamentals

The bottom line, statisticians say, is that there is not enough data to conclude if a new crime wave is upon us, or if there is, what factors are behind it.

Pollack suggested that looking at the available data through a political lens can distract from a focus on the fundamentals.

Nearly without exception, the protests over the killings of unarmed black men have been examples of police misconduct or mistakes, Pollack said.

All communities need and want good policing, and the focus should be on factors that are known to have lowered crime, he said.

Things like community policing and addressing other social issues in the communities have worked, he said.

"Public safety is a joint product of the police and the community, and each side has to trust each other, and when that trust breaks down, it's very hard for police to do its job and for the community to do its part as well," he said.

But with the current political climate, don't be surprised if crime statistics become part of the discussion on race and policing.

"The premise of the Black Lives Matter movement, that the police are the biggest threat facing young black males today, is simply false, and the animosity that's directed to police on the streets today is having an effect," Heather Mac Donald of the Manhattan Institute told CNN's Chris Cuomo. "I've heard from many officers that they are reluctant to engage in actions that could be misinterpreted on cell-phone cameras."

The accusation from the other side is that there is an intentional effort to undermine the political support black protesters have garnered.

"Conflation of the protests with a rise in crime and criminality itself kind of defames what the protests are about," *New York Times* columnist Charles Blow told Cuomo.

5

Architecture and the Arts

© Colin Miller/Corbis

The exterior of New York City's new Whitney Museum of American Art, photographed from the High Line on May 13, 2015.

Urban Beauty, Functionality, and Culture

Since the pre-industrial era, cities have been hubs of artistic expression and industry. Density, tourism, and diversity help to support generations of artists and the creation of thriving commercial industries that support the culinary, visual, and performing arts industries. Though the digital age is rapidly transforming the American economy, the primacy of cities for artistic innovation and industry has remained unchanged, while cities are also embracing uniquely urban forms of art and architecture in response to the changing tastes and values of the urban population.

Cities as Monuments and Economic Centers

Archaeologists have identified the first human developments that qualify as "cities" in the ruins of ancient China, India, and Iraq, stretching back as early as 7500 BCE. One example is Uruk, sometimes called the "first city," which was an ancient settlement in what is now Iraq with hundreds of mud-brick buildings, the most prominent of which rose above the city, intricately decorated with sculptures and mosaics.[1]

The architecture of cities has always blended utilitarian and less prosaic goals. In most societies, agriculture and animal husbandry was the backbone of survival. Cities, by contrast, served as meeting places for farmers, ranchers, and consumers, and thus as economic hubs, and also served as centers for religion and administration. Urban architecture reflects economic concerns with streets and channels designed to facilitate trade and shipping. For most of history, the largest, most prominent buildings in cities were either churches/temples or "city halls," both of which tended to be extensively decorated with statues, mosaics, paintings, and other features designed to convey visually the communal importance of the structure.[2]

From the mid-1800s to the mid-1900s, the Industrial Revolution dramatically altered urban environments. Increasingly, urban design came to reflect the use of cities for industry, with simple stone structures built to house factories of various types. The Industrial Revolution also led to massive urban growth, with an increase in simple, functional housing to accommodate growing populations of working-class residents. However, even as the urban look became more prosaic, U.S. cities continued to use art and design to express cultural significance. Drawing from the traditions of ancient cities around the world, a number of American cities erected "monuments," like the Statue of Liberty, which was given to the U.S. government by the government of France in 1886. The Statue of Liberty harks back to the ancient statues of kings and queens erected in Egypt and other prominent city-states to signify wealth and societal importance. Placed on Ellis Island, the Statue of Liberty, for instance, signified the United States' commitment to becoming a home for refugees seeking opportunity in the new world.[3]

The architectural development of a city is also governed by history, as the early street grids and functional pathways used when a city is born often determine how traffic and development proceed over subsequent generations. Cities that established mass transit systems during the early industrial era, for instance, have developed around the tunnels, raised platforms and tracks, and other facilities used in the transit system. Newer cities, developed after the Industrial Revolution, tend to be far more "regular" in design, with parallel street grids and other logically planned designs made possible by the technological advancements in architecture and construction that developed in the 1900s.[4]

From the Skyline to the High Line

Population growth and density inspired cities to expand vertically, leading to the first "skyscrapers," like the 10-story Home Insurance Building in Chicago, Illinois, which was the tallest building in the world from 1884 to 1889.[5] The first skyscrapers changed the look and feel of the city, giving urban centers a characteristic that architectural critic Montgomery Schuyler dubbed, in the 1890s, the city's "skyline." Schuyler, whose writings about urban design are seminal in the field, wrote famously that the urban skyline, with its combination of shapes and colors, which didn't represent a single, unified design, but were a combination of individual pieces coming together in unexpected ways, was a unique feature of the urban aesthetic, and one that Schuyler said, "looked like business."[6]

From the birth of city skylines, urban architecture progressed through numerous trends, often developing in widely divergent directions inspired by utilitarian criteria on one hand, and aesthetic and artistic criteria on the other. Beginning in the 1980s and 1990s, increasing population density and a sea change in American environmental consciousness inspired a new era in urban design. Increasingly, city planners and architects focused on "sustainability" and new ways to maximize urban space. For instance, in Milan, Italy, architect Stefano Boeri created an innovative plan for two new residential skyscrapers that have extended "shelves" at each level planted with trees. Each of the towers holds as many trees as would be found in a hectare of Italian woodland, creating what the designers called a "vertical forest." Similar designs have been planned in China, Germany, and the Middle East, creating buildings that help sustain wildlife, reduce pollution, and create innovative opportunities to increase green space within crowded urban areas.[7]

In the United States, an example of sustainable architecture can be found in New York City's High Line, a combination museum and urban park constructed along the architecture of an unused elevated rail line running through Manhattan's West Side.[8] Planted with thousands of trees, bushes, and flowering plants, the High Line is an example of a trend that will likely increase in coming years: repurposing space in urban environments for sustainable development and urban recreation. On a far simpler level, urban planners in the twenty-first century have been increasingly focused on maximizing and developing green spaces within cities. This includes simple measures and efforts from tree plantings on residential and commercial streets, to attempts to protect, expand, and redevelop municipal parks.

With space and real estate becoming increasingly expensive, increasing green space in cities requires innovative design.

Art and Industry

While the economic importance of U.S. cities has waxed and waned over the past 200 years, cities have remained unchallenged as hubs for visual and performing arts. The density of residents, and the fact that cities are the primary entrance point for tourists, makes cities the only viable place to establish thriving commercial arts scenes. From galleries and public installations to museums and educational institutions, cities are the nerve center of a nation's artistic industry.

Art museums in cities across the United States rely on tourism for revenue, and the art collections housed in these institutions constitutes a tremendous source of value for the city. Visitors from around the world visit New York's Metropolitan Museum of Art or the Philadelphia Museum of Art to see works from historically important artists from around the world. Though the collections contained in art museums were once symbolic of imperialism and elite oligarchic societies, through the twentieth century, art collections have increasingly been seen as part of a public trust: a cultural resource stored and displayed for the benefit of the city and the global population.[9]

Especially in the larger cities, art galleries provide another level of urban support for the art industry. Galleries range from prestigious and internationally famous locales open only to prominent artists, to independent alternative galleries often located in urban "art districts" where emerging and outsider artists can begin attempting to transform their creative output into income. Added to this are the numerous galleries owned or supported by colleges and universities, through which students can also display their art. Suburban and rural areas, with more spread out populations and fewer walkable avenues, simply cannot provide the same or similar level of exposure for artists. Though suburban art venues exist, there has been no substitute for the urban arts scene.[10]

Cities also provide an unparalleled level of exposure and support for the performing arts. For musicians, cities provide a wealth of venues for performance and a convenient place for established artists to attract larger audiences. Large urban concerns have become increasingly important as the digital distribution of recorded music has increased the importance of concert revenues.[11] While music doesn't necessarily need to be "seen" to be enjoyed, performing theater, including musicals, plays, orchestra performances, and opera require physical audiences, and it is only in cities that these venerable, ancient institutions of creative performance can find sufficient audiences to sustain their endeavors. Like art museums, the products of these cultural institutions, like the world famous Broadway theater district in New York or the live music venues of downtown Austin, New Orleans, Memphis or Nashville, provide a commodity for the city, encouraging tourism and enriching the artistic environment for residents alike.

Tourism, population density, and the aesthetic/cultural realities of urban life inspire art as well, not just among "professional artists," but also within the public.

For instance, the performance art seen on commercial streets in cities around the world (when not prohibited by local laws) provides one example of a unique form of artistry inspired by the particularities of urban living. The "subway" musicians and performers who perform for gratuities inside New York's subway system are probably the most famous example in the United States, but also well known are the many street musicians who perform in the entertainment districts of New Orleans and in the streets of downtown Chicago. Though street performing, or "busking," has often been seen by metropolitan authorities as a nuisance, attitudes are changing as urban residents increasingly view busking and street performance as a unique and potentially valuable draw for tourism and source of income for artists.[12]

Another example of art that came out of cities is graffiti, writing or drawings displayed illicitly in public spaces and often associated with criticism of society or the state. Graffiti is an ancient practice, with examples found by archaeologists in ancient Rome and other early cities. In the United States, urban graffiti became popular in the 1970s, and in the 1980s was heavily associated with youth gang activities. Though seen as a form of vandalism and property destruction, American graffiti evolved into a complex, unique art form, and many cities have begun to embrace the process, encouraging planned "street art" programs to encourage the responsible use of the art form.[13]

Cities are also essential for the culinary industry, and have long been hubs for the nation's most innovative and experimental cuisine. While an increasing number of restaurants now appear in suburban locations, the concentration of urban environments cultivates an unparalleled level of culinary diversity. From fine dining and emerging trends like "molecular gastronomy" to the prevalence of small, ethnic dining establishments, urban commercial avenues are the cornerstone of a huge industry that provides essential income for thousands of workers. In the 2000s, many cities have seen an expansion of the "food truck" business, a uniquely urban trend that involves restaurants and independent purveyors using mobile kitchen vehicles to sell food on busy city streets and near tourist/students/commercial venues. The food truck trend, which spread from larger cities in the West to many of the smaller cities across the nation in the 2000s and 2010s, is just the latest dimension to the richness and diversity of urban dining, which for many residents and promoters of urban living ranks highly among the list of advantages to urban life.

The Digital Era and Beyond

While cities have remained unchallenged as hubs of artistic expression since ancient times, the digital era has changed the medium of delivery for visual art, literature, and music and thus poses a new challenge to the primacy of cities in arts culture. Increasingly, it is possible for an emerging artist to gain success through the Internet, without utilizing the urban art districts and venues that have been centrally important to previous generations.

However, cities remain centrally important for art forms that require physical experience and direct interaction. A recording of a popular opera or play can be shared, for instance, but is not a true substitute for the experience of a live performance, whether in one of the nation's famous concert halls or in small venues or clubs. Likewise, images of visual arts can be reproduced and shared but do not diminish the appeal of viewing art in person, on display, and through the institutions that have long made this process possible. So even with trends of digitization, cities likely will continue to capitalize on their direct experience of art and may increasingly concentrate on supporting and encouraging art forms that are enhanced by involvement. Like the repurposing of industrial spaces to create parks and public recreation, urban artistic spaces are flexible and can be repurposed to serve a new generation.

Micah L. Issitt

Notes

1. "Uruk: The First City," Metropolitan Museum of Art.
2. Hollingsworth, *Art in World History.*
3. "Statue of Liberty," UNESCO.
4. Levy, *Contemporary Urban Planning.*
5. Douglas, *Skyscrapers*, 24–25.
6. Boyer, *Meditations on a Wounded Skyline and Its Stratigraphies of Pain*, 111–112.
7. Woodward, "The Age of Flower Towers."
8. "NYC Parks: The High Line," *Museum of the City.*
9. Straughn and Gardener, "Goodwork in Museums Today. . . And Tomorrow."
10. Currid-Halkid, "Evolving Perspectives on the Arts, Place, and Development," 373–392.
11. Hogan, "How Much Is Music Really Worth?"
12. "Busking It," *The Economist.*
13. De Melker, "'The History of American Graffiti: From Subway Car to Gallery."

Why Public Art Is Important

By Jared Green
The Dirt, October 15, 2012

Susan Weiler, FASLA [Fellow of the American Society of Landscape Architects], OLIN [an international landscape architecture, comprehensive planning and urban design firm], successfully made the case that "public art is important," at a session on art and landscape architecture at the 2012 ASLA [American Society of Landscape Architects] Annual Meeting. In a review that ran from the early history of American public art, which began in Philadelphia, to evocative examples across the country, and then back to an exciting contemporary project in Philadelphia, Penny Balkin Bach, Fairmount Park Art Association; Marc Pally, a public arts consultant; Janet Echelman, one of the more exciting public artists working today; and Weiler walked the audience through where public art has been, where it may be headed, and why it will always be important.

For Bach, public art occupies a unique position within the art world. In comparison with big-name gallery shows, public art is often "under appreciated" much like landscape architecture is. But there's lots to applaud: "It's free. There are no tickets. People don't have to dress up. You can view it alone or in groups. It's open to everyone."

Community art can also create attachment to one's community. According to Bach, studies have looked at the economic development benefits of art, but only just recently have there been wider examinations of the effect of art on a community's sense of place. The Knight Foundation's Soul of the Community initiative surveyed some 43,000 people in 43 cities and found that "social offerings, openness and welcome-ness," and, importantly, the "aesthetics of a place—its art, parks, and green spaces," ranked higher than education, safety, and the local economy as a "driver of attachment." Indeed, the same story may be playing out locally in Philly: a survey of local residents found that viewing public art was the second most popular activity in the city, ranking above hiking and biking.

The Fairmount Parks Art Assocation—which has been renamed the Association for Public Art given its new broader, national purview—was formed in 1872. Back then, along the Benjamin Franklin Parkway, sculptor William Rush, perhaps the original American public artist, was the first to be commissioned to do art in public spaces in the U.S. Then, as now, "public art was viewed as the nexus for gathering," while people promenaded. In this instance, that nexus was a decorative fountain

Reprinted with permission.

designed for the public. And then, as now, Bach said, public art was controversial. The clinging clothes of the marble nymphs in the sculpture caused a bit of a "scandal."

Bach had lots of kind words for Rush, who is now known as the "father of public art, the first artist as planner, and the negotiator of public spaces." He understood that public spaces are the result of "collaborative effort between many design and artistic disciplines, anticipating the future direction of public art."

The Art Association was formed prior to the big Philadelphia Centennial and undertook many artistic initiatives to make the event a hit. Bartholdi's arm for the Statue of Liberty was featured, serving as one of the main draws. The group has always worked with some of the best artists of the era, making sure it's contemporary in its commissions. Bach said, "We take a leap of faith with artists and commission the art of our time." In 1908, the group commissioned Remington's largest bronze sculpture. Today, that site has a site-specific poem written for the Schuykill River. Another project called *Pennypack* by artist Ed Levine along the Pennsylvania Park Trail helps bring that trail to life.

Bach also made a point of discussing the "afterlife of public art," what happens once it's out there. As an example, she pointed to a work by Pepon Osorio, a pavilion at a Latino community center that features historical photos of people from the community. Today, kids from the neighborhood take photos of themselves with photos of their ancestors. Another project called *Common Ground* in a footprint of a church that burned down was hosting weddings just a week after it opened. While these works became part of their communities, Bach said the group still has to work hard to ensure that all works remain relevant to their communities and aren't "orphaned." "We have to keep the stories about these art works alive." That involves conservation—making sure the work stays in good

The Knight Foundation's *Soul of the Community* initiative surveyed some 43,000 people in 43 cities and found that "social offerings, openness and welcome-ness," and, importantly, the "aesthetics of a place— its art, parks, and green spaces," ranked higher than education, safety, and the local economy as a "driver of attachment."

shape—and interpreting the art for a contemporary audience through signage, lighting, and public education programs, with volunteer public art ambassadors providing interpretive programs on the street. Works now have telephone numbers next to them people can call to hear "first person narratives" from people with some connection to the work. "We have both high tech and low tech ways to make connections."

A new piece that just launched promises to upend what cities can do with art at night. Mexican artist Rafael Lozano-Hemmer's *Open Air* just had its world premier. Believing—like Marcel Duchamp—that art requires an audience to make it complete, Lozano-Hemmer has a set of 24 high-powered search lights coursing through the night. The lights are activated by the voice and GPS location of the crowd, who leave messages via a Web site. Messages are converted into light arrays every night from 8–11.

Groups in cities beyond Philadelphia are also commissioning fascinating works. For Marc Pally, a public arts consultant, these new public art works can have "unanticipated" impacts on viewers. Public art can be "provocative, joyous, or annoying." The art can be a "rupture in pedestrian life." In fact, it's designed to do this: as you view the art, "your progress through the space is slowed down."

In Sony Studios in Culver City, a new four-year project on the 40-acre campus has transformed the day-to-day experience. A 94-foot rainbow by artist Tony Tasset now welcomes visitors. Where the art hits the ground plane, there's an interesting "conversation between art and landscape." Meanwhile, the actual rainbow is viewable from miles around. Pally said people were actually "giddy" during the rainbow's opening ceremony, believing it "can't be real," which actually fits right in with how people experience real rainbows.

Another project Pally highlighted, a work in a small pocket park in Pittsburgh, offers a new bronze tree, with thousands of hand-painted flowers and leaves. For a short window of time, the piece actually synchs up with the natural trees in bloom. The rest of the year it's a "layer of disruption, intellectually dissonant." Pally said for those working with public artists, the "sheer terror of not knowing how these pieces will work out" actually makes the works exciting.

In Santa Monica, a major arts festival called *Glow*, an all-night event on the beach, is a prime example of terror-inducing art. That's because the organizers were expecting a few thousand people and 250,000 showed up. The Santa Monica event, which was modeled after the global version, aimed to "remake the coordinates of time and space." The beach was "invaded with art." In contrast to gallery works, much of the work took advantage of the open space, "creating interactions the exact opposite of individual experiences in museums."

So what role do landscape architects play in helping public art work its wonders? According to Weiler, landscape architects help frame these creative experiences or even implement them. In the case of Sol LeWitt's *Lines in Four Directions on Flowers*, a landscape work the artist created many years ago for the space in Fairmount Park in front of Philadelphia Museum of Art, it was OLIN who made the work actually happen. OLIN translated the conceptual work into plants, creating "an appropriate palette" for the site-specific work. For OLIN, Weiler said, the job is to "honor gems of another nature, not distract or add to the experience." In fact, for their recent work updating the gorgeous Rodin museum in Philadelphia, they undertook a "subtraction of the landscape."

For a new project with Janet Echelman, whose giant jellyfish-like sculptures woven of high-performance fishing wire dot many cities, landscape architects can play a leadership role in creating space for art. She said Phillips Farevaag Smallenberg (PFS), who was in charge of the landscape architecture for the Vancouver convention center that is capped with a 6-acre green roof, was central to creating the space for her work, and even integrated her ideas and concepts into the landscape. With

PFS, Echelman redrew the plan for the water garden so that her art forms became "aerating, remediating."

Working with EDAW (now AECOM) [a landscape architecture firm] and Christine Ten Eyck, FASLA, in Phoenix, she found the landscape architects were once again in her court. *Her Name Is Patience*, which is set in a plaza next to the main light-rail transit center and the downtown Arizona State University campus, was initially cancelled due to the economy. The public "protested in favor of this art" to such an extent that it ended up being financed. It's now the highlight in the downtown walking experience, a destination in a downtown that doesn't have many. At night, the work really seems to come alive.

And now, returning to Philadelphia, Echelman has begun work with Weiler at OLIN on *Pulse*, a new $50 million project that will add a welcome contemporary element to Dilworth Plaza, at Philadelphia's historic City Hall, with its glowing yellow clock. Echelman and OLIN are adding to the "beloved work of historic architecture" by creating a "physical Rothko painting in the landscape." Layers of colored lighting, glowing in water mist that will amazingly leave no water trace on people who walk through it, will illuminate the path of the green, orange, and blue subway lines running under the city, tracing the path of the trains in real time. An exciting hybrid space will appear, with public art, transportation, and landscape combined.

Local Urban Culture Goes Global

By Jeroen Beekmans
Pop-Up City, January 15, 2013

We all know what the process of globalization stands for. Capital flows around the world as if there are no borders, individuals become cosmopolites, and my banana was grown 12,000 kilometers away from my salad bowl. In recent years we've seen a trend of globalization that's relatively new: local bottom-up culture, events and ideas spread virally around the world and become branded products.

The globalization of creativity is becoming increasingly visible on the streets of the 21st century city. All hipsters look the same, no matter if you're in East London, Stockholm, Brooklyn or Amsterdam. The same goes for ideas to improve the city and alternative ways of urban planning. A great example in this regard is Candy Chang's "Before I Die" initiative that enables citizens to write their dreams on a neighborhood chalkboard. The project started in New Orleans, but over last years we've seen exactly the same chalkboard design popping up in cities like Berlin, Melbourne, Budapest, Johannesburg, Amsterdam, Buenos Aires and Beirut. Due to the Web, urban culture, events and ideas are slowly turning into branded products that flow around the globe. Local becomes global.

Especially urban events are things that have proven to go viral easily. We all know Park(ing) Day, the annual worldwide event where artists, designers and citizens transform metered parking spots into temporary public parks. The project began in 2005 when Rebar, a San Francisco art and design studio, converted a single metered parking space into a temporary piece of public space in downtown San Francisco. The project inspired such a large group of people around the world that we can speak of a global movement today.

Also Jane's Walk is an initiative that goes hand-in-hand with the trend. Jane's Walk is a series of free neighborhood walking tours that helps put people in touch with their environment and with each other, by bridging social and geographic gaps and creating a space for cities to discover themselves. Since its inception in 2007, Jane's Walk has happened in cities across North America and is growing internationally. Another interesting project is the famous street piano project "Play Me, I'm Yours." In 2008, British artist Luke Jerram decided to install pianos in parks, train stations, markets and other urban public spaces, and invite passers-by to play and enjoy. Over the last years, Jerram installed some 700 pianos in 34 cities around the globe, from New York City to São Paulo.

Reprinted with permission.

Does your city already have its annual Nuit Blanche festival? No? Be patient, because there's a big chance it will come to your city. Nuit Blanche is an annual night-time arts festival that will typically have museums, art galleries and other cultural institutions open, with the city center itself being turned into one big art space with installations, performances, social gatherings, and other activities. Over the last years the festival has spread its wings from cities in France to cities in all corners of the world. PechaKucha is another great example of an initiative that started in Tokyo in 2003 as a presentation night for young talented people. The 20 slides × 20 seconds format has gained international fame inside and outside the creative world. As of today, more than 600 (!) cities worldwide have their own PechaKucha Night.

> **The big challenge for cities is to stay creative and maintain a unique identity in a world in which even local urban culture is globalized.**

What characterizes this major trend is that we can speak of a form of globalization that's not driven by governments or international companies, but by the local community itself. The majority of these characteristic bottom-up projects has only spread over the last years—something that may be due to the rise of social media. If you look at this global development from a marketing perspective, you could say that urban culture is slowly turning into a "me-too" product that's a result of today's online copy culture. As soon as a good idea pops up in one city, it almost automatically gets picked up by hungry communities in other cities.

The big challenge for cities is to stay creative and maintain a unique identity in a world in which even local urban culture is globalized. Helsinki is a city that has tried to come up with its own ideas—21st century traditions as we call them. Restaurant Day is such an initiative that has put the city's innovative, idea-driven environment on the map. This food festival invites everyone to a restauranteur for a day. You can set up a pop-up restaurant, café or a bar in your home, office, the park, or even the beach. This food-focused initiative, initially meant to revitalize Helsinki's urban community, has spread over the world since 2011. Still, everyone knows it was a Finnish idea. The same thing is likely going to happen with Cleaning Day, a Helsinki bottom-up initiative that turns the city into one big second-hand market.

Pop-Up Salvation

By renée e. hoogland
Art in America, December 1, 2013

News stories about art in Detroit these days tend to focus on the city's possible sell-out to a ruthless market economy. To help pay off municipal debts, the impressive collection of the Detroit Institute of Arts (DIA) is threatened with the auction block. Diego Rivera's revolutionary Detroit Industry murals have become little more than a liquid asset, potential appeasement for creditors who forced the city of Detroit to file for bankruptcy this summer. Perversely, to some this represents a welcome change, shifting the attention away from Detroit as a Mecca for "ruin porn," a relatively new genre of photography that aestheticizes urban decay. Instead, most people are preoccupied with the potential privatization of the DIA's Rembrandts, Breughels, van Goghs, van Eycks and Caravaggios, an issue that has newly stirred up discussions on the function of art in our society. As Roberta Smith put it in the *New York Times* on Sept. 10: "The Detroit Institute will be the most prominent victim of the separation of daily existence and culture that so darkens American life."

In Detroit, however, word on the ground is not so much buzzing around the lofty ideals underlying the traditional fine-arts museum, or the DIA's collection as a political bargaining chip, but the city's flourishing pop-up movement. In the D, "pop-up" is the new "ruin porn."

Pop-ups are hardly new, their forebears the annual Christmas tree, pumpkin or fireworks bazaars that have for so long conveniently appeared and disappeared in lots or tents during holiday seasons. In the current urban trend, temporary businesses occupy the many storefront spaces left empty by the recession and overall postindustrial decline. Pop-ups bypass the complex rules and regulations that govern fixed locations. With Detroit's surplus of underused or abandoned buildings, its low-cost real estate, its dense neighborhoods lacking small retailers and its recent influx of young professionals (in the last 10 years, the downtown area saw a 59 percent increase in the number of college-educated residents under the age of 35), the city would appear to be the perfect testing ground for the entrepreneurial talents, artists and hipsters who are rediscovering unique urban business opportunities. And most of the pop-ups are, indeed, businesses. Despite the breathless reports in local media on the "pioneering," "anarchic" and "creative" aspects of the pop-up model, proprietors seek to evaluate local markets for consumer interest and long-term viability, just as they do in any other form of free-market activity.

Originally published by Art in America, December 2013. Courtesy BMP Media Holdings, LLC.

Yes, the pop-up movement is "hip," yes, it is "creative," and, yes, it might help revitalize destitute urban centers. Alongside trendy brick-and-mortar restaurants, coffee shops, clothing boutiques, yoga studios, bike stores and mercantile retailers, pop-ups increasingly incorporate artistic and/or creative ventures. Pop Up Detroit, for instance, is a roving art gallery that places projects in vacant buildings: it has popped up in various downtown and midtown locations, most recently as a green live-work space for artists in the Sugar Hill Arts District. But do pop-ups truly offer opportunities to connect "Detroit's creative talent to global markets"? That's the scenario suggested by DC3 (the Detroit Creative Corridor Center), an "economic development center," which houses, among its other components, DC3 Gallery, described on the organization's website as "a forward thinking gallery space showcasing the visual work of a variety of local Detroit creative practitioners." Will pop-ups ever lead to a general shift in attitude, one that might nourish and protect the kind of artworks—the "jewels" of the DIA— that are so passionately defended in (inter)national news coverage? The ties between entrepreneurship and creative production are both indissoluble and vexed.

Champions of art as a resistant or radical practice have always struggled with art's dependency on money. The connection shapes a paradox inherent in Detroit's surge in "creative industries." It is not too much of a stretch to say that cities like Detroit, plagued by urban blight, white flight and collapsing mono-industries, have generated the quintessential pop-up culture in its most resistant forms: street art, graffiti and grassroots visual creativity in the public domain. Yet even in an increasingly hybrid urban environment, where heterogeneous flows and processes of economic, political and creative energies prevail over structured business and market strategies, the fate of such artistic practices is never predictable.

Take, for instance, the once controversial but nowadays renowned open-air Heidelberg Project, a colorful "art environment" made up of painted houses and sculptures constructed from salvaged everyday objects, spanning about a block amid abandoned houses and weed-covered lots on Detroit's depressed East Side. Its founder and artistic director, Tyree Guyton, has seen his work collected by the DIA and other prestigious art museums. Does the Heidelberg Project constitute capitalist co-optation—(sub)cultural mainstreaming—or, as its website has it, a "demonstration of the power of creativity to transform lives"? In contrast, while GRCC Detroit, a neighborhood revitalization project consisting of over 100 murals on 15 buildings on Grand River Avenue between Rosa Parks Boulevard and Warren Avenue, may offer the occasional background for bride-and-groom pics, it is situated in a neighborhood where lots of (white) people and hipsters are still afraid to get out of their cars. I am not sure which of these two projects better represents a resistant art practice in the 21st century.

I recently attended the opening of Light Up Livernois, a pop-up storefront on Livernois Avenue, which marks the abrupt breaking point between (Eminem's) 8 Mile and the beautiful neighborhood of Sherwood Forest, known for its striking domestic architecture and quiet, winding streets. The opening was promoted as "celebrating the next chapter on Detroit's historic 'Avenue of Fashion' with an evening

> **Cities like Detroit, plagued by urban blight, white flight and collapsing mono-industries, have generated the quintessential pop-up culture in most resistant forms: street art, graffiti and grass-roots visual creativity.**

of design, art, shopping and entertainment." The organization behind the project, REVOLVE, "partnered with local leaders and property owners to bring new businesses and artists" to Livernois, and was awarded a $200,000 grant from Artplace America and $50,000 from the Michigan Economic Development Corporation to support the Livernois Community Storefront project. Part block party, part art fair, part shopping adventure, the Livernois project currently showcases several large-scale murals and outdoor sculpture installations. The spaces designated as galleries appear to be focused on community building and retail: you can learn to make pottery at a ceramics studio, Art in Motion, or buy costume jewelry at the Glam Shoppe and hand-hooked bags at Love. The Sherwood Forest Art Gallery presents a mixed bag of Hallmark-gift-shop-style paintings, prints, figurines and collectibles. Detroit Fiber Works offers fiber and felting workshops. Jeweler on Deck, an initiative of the Detroit-based artist Tiff Massey, was the only true gallery in Light Up Livernois, but it popped up on the opening night and out again after just three days. Most of the other storefront spaces will remain open for business for at least three months.

Perhaps this kind of community-oriented, hands-on, art-as-festival event will begin to bridge the gap that Roberta Smith so deplores between daily existence and culture in American life. And maybe the hybrid, ephemeral, processual model of the pop-up is setting the stage for changing art practices in the 21st century. But whether any pop-up in Detroit will generate the "real" or, if you will, "elitist" art that is stored and preserved for posterity in 19th-century fine-arts museums like the DIA remains to be seen. The jury is out.

Can Chicago Become America's Next Great City for Artists?

By B. David Zarley
Citylab, February 15, 2013

Chicago is losing its artists, to New York City and Los Angeles and San Francisco. This is admitted, from various members—with varying statures—of the art community, either begrudgingly or with ease, but in the end, is always admitted.

"It's difficult for me to generalize this, because people move for different reasons," explains Jason Foumberg, contributing art editor at *Newcity* (where I've freelanced in the past) and *Chicago* magazine's art critic. "The art market here is smaller, so people tend to follow the money if they want to have an art career."

Many art collectors who live in Chicago do the bulk of their buying from New York galleries and from art fairs in Miami. New York's better established peripheral infrastructure attracts artists too. "Take a look at the various types of jobs that artists tend to take: adjunct lecturer at an art school, preparator at a gallery. We have plenty of art schools in Chicago, but the politics and unions tend to make the hiring process very difficult. Preparator jobs, not enough galleries to sustain full-time employment."

Recent BFA and MFA grads also seek work as studio assistants, something else which New York City can provide in greater abundance.

But though the weaknesses of Chicago's art scene are obvious, there are strengths too. Its comparatively cheap rents and abundant factory and warehouse spaces make it an ideal place for a studio, while the lower cost of living frees up money for artistic pursuits. And Chicago's art community is particularly accommodating to experimentation.

"The scene is very collaborative," says Chuck Thurrow, former chairman of the board of the Hyde Park Art Center, one of the city's most public proponents of the visual arts. "You can be experimental. No one is looking over everyone's shoulders."

Meg Duguid agrees. Broadly categorized as a performance artist, Duguid obtained her BFA from the School of the Art Institute of Chicago, and has lived and worked in various locations across the U.S., including New York City. Duguid is a firm believer in Chicago as a place for an artist to flesh out his or her work. "You have a better opportunity of building a richer portfolio," Duguid explains. And there [is] an abundance of small scale, DIY apartment galleries which allow artists a freedom that may be hard to come by in Gotham.

Reprinted with permission.

The trick, she and others say, is creating a unique set of patrons and collectors interested in the bold ideas Chicago artists have to offer. The Hyde Park Art Center is trying to do just that with a program called Not Just Another Pretty Face.

"[Mihaly] Csikszentmihalyi, the great expert on creativity, was living two doors away from the Hyde Park Art Center," Thurrow says. "We'd have lunch regularly, and talk about what I should be doing to foster creativity in Chicago. He very much believed that. . . the community supporting visual arts had to be a broader, middle class community. It couldn't be just a bunch of super rich guys. So Not Just Another Pretty Face came out of a combination of artists saying 'You need collectors' and this guy saying that unless the arts reach the middle class, they are a failure."

> As the internet allows artists from anywhere to show their works to massive audiences, Duguid believes that the "geopolitical inclusion" that is occurring in the art world will only allow Chicago to become that much more of an attractive destination, as well as defuse the geographic biases that serve to divide.

By acting as go-betweens for artists and potential patrons, Not Just Another Pretty Face can streamline and demystify the world of art collection, offering a perfect jumping in point for those who want to live with art. With a sliding payment scale, the idea of commissioning a piece from an artist was made accessible to those who had only thought the art world to be the playground of plutocrats and business czars. Furthermore, artists are paid for their efforts, something which would seem a given in anything but the creative career fields.

"Our mission, as stated, is to stimulate and sustain the visual arts in Chicago," HPAC executive director Kate Lorenz said. "Our goal is to make this a very artist friendly place."

Another way to achieve that is to provide assistance to artists on the verge of becoming established. To this end, the Center and the University of Chicago's Graham School of Continuing Education put together a visual arts certificate program, a 12-month course that provides business acumen and practical, art-related knowledge that may have been found wanting in the artist's BFA and MFA programs.

Mike Nourse, HPAC's director of education, believes that Chicago is already turning the tide. Local artists like Theaster Gates and Tony Fitzpatrick have the clout to draw others to the city, he says.

To Nourse, Chicago only must realize its already abundant potential to become a locus point for visual arts. "All the parts are right here," he said. "It's not far away. It is just a matter of some of these dots being connected."

As the internet allows artists from anywhere to show their works to massive audiences, Duguid believes that the "geopolitical inclusion" that is occurring in the art world will only allow Chicago to become that much more of an attractive destination, as well as defuse the geographic biases that serve to divide. "We're just all artists who happen to live in different cities," she said.

Duguid's advice for those wishing to see Chicago hold on to its aesthetic life-blood is simple and firm: "Stop asking yourself why you're not New York City, and focus on being Chicago."

Why Cities Can't Afford to Lose Their Artists

By Richard Florida
Citylab, December 4, 2014

The Art Basel Miami Beach art fair kicks off this week [in December 2013], an event that drew 75,000 people and 140 international museum and international groups in 2013. The art fair is widely credited with kick-starting the economic resurgence of the Miami area, so it seems like a good time to ask: What do we really know about the role of art in the city? Does it help to drive economic growth and development or does it contribute to gentrification? Are leading edge arts clusters found just in big cities, like New York and Los Angeles, or can they spread to smaller and medium sized ones as well?

A recent study published in the journal *Urban Studies* takes a close look at the connection between the arts and city building. The study, by Carl Grodach of the Queensland University of Technology, Elizabeth Currid-Halkett of the University of Southern California, and Nicole Foster and James Murdoch III of the University Texas at Arlington, examines the economic and demographic factors most closely associated with arts clusters and the kinds of metros where arts hubs are found. The researchers scrutinize the concentration of arts clusters (using the standard location quotient measure) across all 366 U.S. metros areas and nearly 14,000 ZIP codes, which account for nearly 90 percent of all arts employment. Grodach et al. also look at the relationships between the arts clusters and a series of 33 social, economic and demographic factors across four types of metro areas: large metros with over 1,000,000 people, mid-sized ones with 500,000 to 1,000,000 people, small metros home to 250,000 to 500,000 people, and the smallest ones with less than 250,000 people. The researchers define arts clusters as comprised of 22 key industries that produce artistic content, spanning arts, music, theater and design, but excluding industries like radio or TV broadcasting.

The researchers use a series of statistical techniques, including correlations and regression models, to identify the types of places that are home to arts clusters and the key locational factors that are associated with them.

They find that arts hubs are considerably concentrated, taking the form of a "winner-take-all geography." Just 28 out of 366 U.S. metros, less than one in ten, have substantial arts hubs with LQ's of 1.2 or higher. The chart below shows how

© 2014 The Atlantic Media Co., as first published in Citylab. All rights reserved. Distributed by Tribune Content Agency, LLC

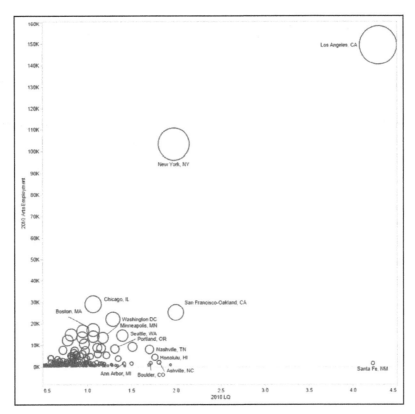

Figure I. 2010 metro arts cluster employment size and concentration.

(Grodach et al.)

metros stack up in terms of the total arts employment (along the Y axis) versus their relative concentration of arts industries based on their LQ (across the X-axis).

Metros to the upper right, like L.A., have high levels of highly concentrated arts employment. Metros to the lower right have high concentration but less arts employment overall (notice smaller Santa Fe way out on the lower [right]). New York City and San Francisco have high arts employment that is relatively concentrated. Smaller metros like Asheville, Boulder and Ann Arbor register as significant arts hubs for their size, while Nashville, Honolulu, and Seattle also punch above their weight. But many metros, including large metros like Chicago and Boston, have smaller arts clusters (based on their LQs) than their levels of arts employment suggest.

Overall, the study finds that arts clusters occur in "urbanized, relatively diverse regions," and that arts hubs are indeed associated with strong economies.

But the factors that are associated with arts hubs vary considerably between large, medium-size and smaller metros. And things get even more complex when the researchers take the analysis down to the neighborhood, rather than metro, level. First off, the results of their statistical analysis get considerably weaker: Their neighborhood level analysis explains just 14 percent of the variance in where arts hubs are located, compared to 59 percent for the metro models. In particular, the associations between arts clusters and urbanization, density, highly educated populations and diversity are much weaker or disappear entirely at the neighborhood level.

While much has been made of the connection between arts and gentrification, the researchers find little evidence of it, noting that "art clusters are tied less to conventional signs of gentrification and 'urban' characteristics but rather they may be found where other related industries that rely on specialized expertise and knowledge abound." They find a negative correlation between arts clusters and poverty.

> **Mayors, arts and cultural policy-makers and economic developers would be better served by taking a more localized, place-specific approach to arts initiatives.**

Two important implications flow from the study's key findings. For one, mayors, arts and cultural policy-makers and economic developers would be better served by taking a more localized, place-specific approach to arts initiatives and creative placemaking. As they put it:

> [A] comprehension of arts clusters requires specificity and particular attention to the uniqueness of the type of art and place itself. Targeted local development may be the most important means by which to support the arts, rather than broader federal, state or regional efforts. Distinctions between arts clusters occur at [the] localized level and thus ought to be supported as such.

Second, the study notes the benefits that flow from better connected arts and innovation clusters. "While many of the variables linked to arts clusters are incredibly place specific," they write, "the arts are linked to broad measures of innovation and development. . . suggesting the arts can play a larger role in economic development irrespective of metro size or geographic boundaries of city and neighborhood."

Ultimately, the study notes that while arts are not a silver bullet for cities, their role in urban economic development is, in the authors' words, "highly underestimated."

Cities Create Music, Cultural Festivals to Make Money

By Chad Kaydo
Governing, January 2014

In 1871 the Great Chicago Fire killed more than 300 people, leveled the city's central business district and left more than 100,000 people—a third of its population—homeless. A massive rebuilding effort followed, re-establishing the city's status as a center of transportation and trade. By 1893, the Chicago World's Fair drew 27 million visitors and profoundly influenced art, architecture and design.

Tapping into that history, Chicago will introduce the Great Chicago Fire Festival this fall, with a parade, live music and a symbol-laden centerpiece: Fifteen floats representing local neighborhoods will bob in the Chicago River and be burned in effigy. As the 19th-century fire led to Chicago's rebirth, the burning floats will reveal interior designs to showcase hope for the future. Michelle Boone, the commissioner of Chicago's Department of Cultural Affairs and Special Events, says the festival could become "Chicago's Mardi Gras."

The celebration is part of a movement to use events as economic drivers and urban brand builders. Municipal officials and entrepreneurs see the power of cultural festivals, innovation-focused business conferences and the like as a way to spur short-term tourism while shaping an image of the host city as a cool, dynamic location where companies and citizens in modern, creative industries can thrive.

The leading example is South by Southwest (SXSW), the annual music, film, and digital conference and festival in Austin, Texas. Launched in 1987, the juggernaut not only draws visitors who spend money in hotels and restaurants, but now has become an entire microeconomy. As music executives, film producers and tech startup founders come to town—along with fans looking for the next big thing—those attendees lure marketers seeking to reach influencers. Companies host lavish parties, pop-up stores and guerrilla marketing stunts, all of which requires the services of florists, caterers, carpenters and real estate owners. The festival's economic impact has grown steadily over the past few years. In 2007, it poured about $95 million into the Austin economy. Last year's event [in 2013] topped $218 million.

The Coachella Valley Music and Arts Festival in California's Inland Empire is another influential cultural event, drawing big-name bands, thousands of music fans and marketers who want to reach festivalgoers. Since 1999, the concert

Copyrighted 2015. e.Republic, Inc. 119104:0815RR

promotion and festival production company Goldenvoice has expanded Coachella into a two-weekend giant, drawing 80,000 people per day.

In August Goldenvoice launched the First City Festival in Monterey, a smaller music event meant to draw on the city's history as host of the long-running Monterey Jazz Festival. "We were designing this to be a laidback festival that fits in the city of Monterey," says co-producer Paul Billings. In addition to live musical performances, Goldenvoice staged a carnival with games and rides and invited 20 local vendors to show art, furniture and clothing. The event drew 11,000 people each of its two days, about half of them from Monterey County and surrounding areas. According to surveys, most non-locals stayed in a hotel or a rented house and visited local restaurants and attractions.

While the event had no formal relationship with the city, Goldenvoice got marketing support from the Monterey County Convention and Visitors Bureau. When considering locations for its festivals, Goldenvoice looks at a city's willingness to help with festival logistics and to reassure citizens more worried about traffic jams and concert noise than cool bands or hotel sales. "It ends up being a huge factor," Billings says.

In Las Vegas, events are part of a new effort to revitalize the city's downtown. Tony Hsieh, the CEO of online retailer Zappos—the company's headquarters are located in the old center of town—wants the place to feel more like a creative community in the vein of Austin or Brooklyn, N.Y., than the more-traveled Strip. Hsieh has put $350 million into the so-called "Downtown Project," which is funding start-ups, local businesses and community-building endeavors. It also has developed monthly First Friday festivals that feature food trucks, music, dance performances and art installations. The festivals lure some 20,000 people downtown.

The area's biggest event is Life is Beautiful. It drew 60,000 attendees in October to venues spread across a 15-block footprint within the historic city core. There was a music festival with big-name bands, a food fair with high-profile chefs, an art program and a speaker series.

Festival founder Rehan Choudhry says Las Vegas Mayor Carolyn Goodman saw the event's potential and consistently worked to ease the planning process. "Her entire organization had a very 'We're going to make this happen' attitude," Choudhry says. A year before the festival, Goodman met with the city's police, fire and traffic officials to encourage them to help festival organizers. A task force met every three weeks to keep everyone informed of festival plans. "We didn't have to do a lot of research for permits," Choudhry says.

He sees that kind of public-private partnership as the best way to facilitate ambitious events. Launching a large festival requires a focus on the long-term financial rewards and an acceptance of a high failure rate that municipal governments aren't likely to tolerate. "The biggest piece of advice to any city trying to do this is, 'Don't think year one, think year five.' If it's not long-term, it's not worth the resources."

In Chicago, the Fire Festival is being developed as part of Mayor Rahm Emanuel's Chicago Cultural Plan, an initiative launched in 2012 to drive the city's cultural and economic growth. While the area already hosts independently run music events such as Lollapalooza and the Pitchfork Festival, the planners suggested the city develop its own large, city-specific cultural festival with global impact.

Combining references to the historic fire with contemporary neighborhood issues was the idea of Jim Lasko, the executive artistic director of the local theater company Redmoon. He says events can have more immediate and lasting effects than typical economic drivers, like, say, a building, landmark or park. "They are also much less expensive, and they never disappear," he says. Even after the streets are cleaned, festivals live on in the memory of participants.

In assessing the success of the new festival, the city will take into account such financial measures as attendance numbers and hotel room sales. But it is also keeping an eye on what Commissioner of Cultural Affairs Boone calls "artistic assessments." Measures on her list: How does this stimulate the imagination of young people? How has it ignited new interest in Chicago history? How does it stimulate other artists to think about how they can program or activate the river in their own unique ways?

Those evaluations are less tangible, but can ultimately lead to measurable results. "When they're well executed and they capture the city's imagina-

> **Municipal officials and entrepreneurs see the power of cultural events. . . as a way to spur short-term tourism while shaping an image of the host city as a cool, dynamic location where companies and citizens in modern, creative industries can thrive.**

tion and the nation's imagination, events generate an enormous amount of revenue for the city," Lasko says, partially by making the city "look like a place where people want to live and bring their creative enterprise."

Boone doesn't see the city owning the new event forever. The city's role, she says, is to be an incubator. It can't "maintain a competitive edge against for-profit companies that are able to run these as part of their business. It makes more sense for us to be more of a partner."

The same goes for other events. Chicago has partnered with Lollapalooza on a program that gives college students from across the country concert tickets and exposure to local tech companies, including a business plan competition judged by Emanuel. In September the city hosted the first Chicago Music Summit, a day of panels, discussions and performances meant to showcase the city's diverse talent pool and help music professionals—performers, producers, club owners—discuss ways to work together better.

Boone says she works with officials across other city departments to consolidate licensing applications, advocate for events and act as a liaison for event hosts navigating city bureaucracy. "I don't turn down a meeting with anybody."

High Line Your Museum

By Jonathan Massey
Art in America, May 1, 2015

Walk the High Line, the elevated park that snakes through the West Side of Manhattan, and you'll find much to reward the eye. Lofted a story or three above the pavement, the mile-and-a-half-long promenade cuts through the city's grid as it runs above, beside and through buildings. When it crosses a street, makes a turn or punctures a warehouse, the High Line offers views through the middle of city blocks, into upper-floor offices and apartments, and down into construction pits. At intervals along the walkway are overlooks framing vistas, and stepped seating is positioned to allow visitors to watch the flow of traffic along Tenth Avenue.

This urban panorama reflects the shipping requirements of meatpackers, produce distributors and other industrial businesses that dominated the area 80 years ago, when the viaduct was built to lift trains above streets filled with automotive, truck and foot traffic. After its completion, in 1934, the West Side elevated railway spurred construction o f modern factories, packing facilities and warehouses along the rail line and in surrounding blocks.

The neighborhood was remade in the past decade by a flood of new construction as developers transformed the area into a mecca for shopping, entertainment, business and upscale living. A rezoning in 2005 allowed property owners along much of the High Line's route to transfer development rights among parcels, spurring a rush to build luxury residential units throughout the district. As a result, the promenade takes you past buildings by some of the world's most famous architects, including Frank Gehry, Shigeru Ban and Annabelle Selldorf, soon to be joined by Zaha Hadid, Rick Cook and Rem Koolhaas. Owners have renovated older buildings to serve new uses, and the northern section of the park runs through the Hudson Yards Redevelopment Project, a massive undertaking on nearly 28 acres that will yield towers containing some 13 million square feet of offices, condominiums and retail space.

The new buildings in West Chelsea have an exhibitionist character as they address the High Line and the pedestrians who stroll along it. A metal-clad residential tower by Neil Denari appears to shrink from the High Line at its base but angles distinctively outward as it rises, hugging the park. Twin condo buildings flanking the viaduct at 19th Street, by Thomas Juul-Hansen, invite visitors on the promenade to exchange glances with residents through faceted full-length windows. A half-block away at 11th Avenue, Jean Nouvel has multiplied mullions to create a deliriously

Originally published by Art in America, May 2015. Courtesy BMP Media Holdings, LLC.

jumbled facade of window frames. Though offering a vision of spare luxury, these iconic buildings compete for attention, constitute memorable figures and produce visual relationships.

The viaduct-turned-promenade is one of New York's most popular tourist destinations, drawing an estimated 5 million visitors last year [2014]. On a fine day its walkway, benches and lawns are packed with people looking around and at one another. The High Line primes these visitors for viewing exhibitions, too. When the first section of the park opened in 2009, a neighbor turned her adjacent fire escape into the stage for Renegade Cabaret, partly to protest her loss of privacy. Soon the High Line became known as a good place for other kinds o f watching. The Standard Hotel, with its giant wall of floor-to-ceiling windows that straddles the park, became famous for the naked guests who put on shows for viewers below. "Take a photo of yourself from here," invites the sign on a nearby fire escape outfitted with a webcam. But who needs a webcam? The new park has made the neighborhood an archipelago of hotspots on Instagram, Facebook and Flickr.

Interspersed among the park's gardens and throngs of pedestrians are works of art. West Chelsea hosts the world's largest contemporary art market, with more than 300 galleries that occupy buildings beneath and beside the High Line, and the rezoning was designed to protect them from being priced out even as it allowed other property owners to realize the increased value of their parcels. Some have installed sculptures and murals along the promenade. High Line Art, an offshoot of Friends of the High Line, the nonprofit group that imagined and planned the park, runs a substantial program of site-specific installations, exhibitions and performances. Joel Sternfeld's commissioned photographs were instrumental to fundraising for the railbed conversion, and the park opened with a stained glass piece by Spencer Finch in the passage that runs through the Chelsea Market. It has since hosted work by John Baldessari, Thomas Dem and Faith Ringgold, Ed Ruscha and Sarah Sze, among many others.

The art along the High Line can sometimes seem like no more than changing decor for the tourist crowd. At its best, though, this program spurs us to reflect on Chelsea's distinctive confluence of art, architecture and capital investment, as it did four years ago when High Line Art restaged Trisha Brown Dance Company's 1971 Roof Piece. In the original performance, dancers on various SoHo rooftops improvised responses to each other's movements. Repeated on rooftops adjacent to the High Line by dancers in bright red costumes, the piece evoked the displacement of the city's contemporary art market from SoHo to Chelsea as boutiques priced out artists and galleries. Beckoning to each other among chimneys and water tanks, the dancers prompted viewers to consider the economies of experience and attention created by commercial gentrification, urban spectacle and art-centric redevelopment.

This complex neighborhood is now the home of the Whitney Museum of American Art. The museum's new building, designed by Renzo Piano Building Workshop, sits alongside the elevated park on the north side of Gansevoort Street between Washington and West streets in the Meatpacking District. As it steps down toward the High Line, the eight-story structure includes a series of roof terraces, walkways and stairs designed for outdoor exhibitions, installations and performances—as well as for the reciprocal views they afford to the surrounding buildings. The new Whitney intertwines visually with the promenade and adopts attributes of the architecture characteristic of its neighborhood. "High Line Your Business," exhorts a banner at West 22nd Street, recruiting prospective office tenants with the added value of being at the center of a cultural and commercial hub. In moving here, the Whitney, I believe, aims to High Line itself: to gain attention, audiences and fundraising clout by leveraging a site along one o f the city's leading attractions, an urban space in which art sits at the nexus of public and private interests.

A new building affords an institution the opportunity to reshape its identity, as the building by Marcel Breuer did when the Whitney moved to Madison Avenue in 1966. Even if it nodded to precursors in Greenwich Village and Midtown with the domestic scale of its smaller galleries and its scarcity of windows, the Breuer building transformed the museum's profile by heralding the Whitney's ambition to stand out among New York museums.

Received by critics as a "harsh and handsome" assertion of contemporary art against Upper East Side "tearooms" and International Style office towers, the building was assertive, monumental and memorable.[1] It pulled the Whitney out of the Museum of Modern Art's shadow and gave the institution prominence among the other museums and galleries in

> **Whereas Breuer's Whitney emphatically separated its... galleries from the city beyond, Piano's design programmatically interweaves the museum's art with the outside world.**

its art-filled neighborhood. By reimagining traditional forms such as the ziggurat, the canopy and even the moat, the building imbued the Whitney with an image of boldness that reputedly inspired curators to follow its tone. By raising the institution's profile and demonstrating its capability, the move initiated growth in collections and endowment that soon outpaced the building's capacity.

These successes brought a new challenge: to allow for growth in a tightly regulated historic district. Over the years, the museum expanded into adjacent brownstones, a building around the corner and an addition hidden within the block. It also established satellites around town, including in the lobbies of corporate offices, notably in Philip Morris's (later Altria's) Park Avenue headquarters. But the antagonistic relationship to its primary neighborhood remained constant for nearly 50 years. Neighborhood groups and preservation coalitions blocked attempts to build a large expansion on Madison between 74th and 75th, rejecting successive designs by Norman Foster, Michael Graves and Rem Koolhaas. Just as it seemed finally to prevail, in 2006, when it received planning authorization and zoning variances for a tower by Piano, the museum chose another course. After negotiations by the Dia Art Foundation to take over a city-owned meatpacking property stalled, Whitney director Adam Weinberg convinced the museum's board to step in. Nine years later, the museum moves into a new flagship as the Metropolitan Museum occupies the Breuer building on a multiyear lease.

The Whitney's new building contains more space for galleries, conservation labs, offices and other facilities the museum could not accommodate on Madison Avenue, and the Whitney has provided for potential expansion onto adjacent property to the north. With prominent exposures onto the High Line and West Street—along with the river and New Jersey beyond—the new Whitney is a far more visible presence in the city than the Breuer structure tucked away on Madison Avenue. The Gansevoort site is near the biggest and most important cluster of contemporary art galleries in the world, including Gagosian, David Zwirner and Hauser & Wirth, which mount historical shows that can resemble those offered at the city's art museums. If it can distinguish itself from these potential rivals, the Whitney will take over from the Dia Art Foundation the mantle of being the biggest institutional presence in the West Side art world. Much as the New Museum—the Whitney's secessionist offspring—presides over the growing Lower East Side gallery scene from its site on the Bowery, the Whitney has the potential to anchor the much larger Chelsea gallery constellation.

Its new site also puts the museum in the midst of Meatpacking District luxe, amid the upscale hotels, restaurants, nightclubs, boutiques, design showrooms, fashion enterprises and private clubs that have displaced meatpackers. The Piano building draws this milieu in with an eatery owned by famed restaurateur Danny Meyer that offers seating on the sidewalk and in the lobby. As the museum's lofted mass angles inward and down to open the lobby for views to and from the High Line, pavement and plantings reinforce continuity between the art displayed in the lobby and the commercialized leisure zone on the other side of an unobtrusive glass wall.

This interpenetration of inside and out beneath angular forms recalls the work of Diller Scofidio + Renfro, the architects on the High Line team who also completed a recent renovation of Lincoln Center. Other aspects of the Whitney evoke the firm's design for the Institute of Contemporary Art in Boston, where galleries offer spectacular views as they cantilever above a public promenade in a redevelopment zone. From west and south, by contrast, the building evokes Breuer in its massing. But whereas Breuer's Whitney emphatically separated its nearly hermetic galleries from the city beyond, Piano's design programmatically interweaves the museum's art with the outside world. The spacious galleries on the fifth through eighth floors offer expansive views that stretch to New Jersey and the Statue of Liberty on the west, upriver to the north, and into the city to the east, where intersecting streets and the low profile of the Gansevoort Market Historic District afford a deep and varied vista toward the Empire State Building.

On each of the top three floors, the east-facing wall of windows opens onto the cascading terraces. As these are linked by generous outdoor catwalks and stairs, it seems likely that many visitors will take one of the elevators to the top and then work their way down in a circuit that spirals from river view through gallery to city view and back again a few times over. City sights, sounds and smells will punctuate engagement with the art inside, amid changing rooftop exhibits, installations, fund-raising parties and performances.

What implication does this intertwining of gallery with shopping district have for the Whitney's art program? The Piano building does not seem conducive to the focused looking that. . . Timothy M. Rohan finds in Breuer's inward-looking precursor. The new Whitney's imbrication of art exhibition with urban spectacle points instead toward a curatorial vision that aims for visual and experiential impact. (The opening a few years hence of the Culture Shed, a vast art-and-culture emporium planned by the Related Companies for a site at the northern end of the High Line, with a design by Diller Scofidio + Renfro, will likely challenge the Whitney to either compete on experiential intensity or present art on more autonomous terms.)

Notwithstanding this propensity, the Piano building is anything but iconic. The museum will reopen with a show titled "America Is Hard to See." In some ways, both literal and not, the new Whitney can be comparably elusive. The building is clearly organized, with galleries and other public areas along the south of the L-shaped site separated from offices and other back-of-house facilities by a services-and-circulation spine. But as the architects addressed site constraints and visual connections, they complicated and unsettled the museum's blocky mass, further disjoining it into disparate parts and materials.

The form is chunky and clunky, but also dynamic in its splay—particularly from the east along Gansevoort, where the end of the main gallery projects forward from stepped and angled facets that rhyme with the sawtooth roof and steel balconies in buzzing angularity. Bluegreen-gray metal panels perforated by slightly rounded windows clad the building's angular form, evoking the work of Piano's mentor Jean Prouve and associating the building with the historical shipping industry.

Overlaid onto this nautical imagery are distorted and rescaled references to other forms of industry: smokestacks, metal grates and fire escapes, along with the exposed chillers. The intent may be to affiliate the building with its context, but these elements have the opposite effect because they reference a general corpus of industrial architecture more than they engage the specificity of the facilities along the High Line and in the Meatpacking District.

The Cudahy Packing Company branch plant, which previously occupied one part of the museum property, was typical in its horizontal massing, rectangular structural bay, reinforced-concrete construction, flat roof, pressed brick walls and steel sash windows. (The Cudahy structure is recalled in the Diller–von Furstenburg Building, the unobtrusive maintenance facility and Friends of the High Line headquarters adjacent to the museum, also designed by the Renzo Piano Building Workshop.) Sawtooth roofs are a hallmark of factory architecture, but you won't find them in this neighborhood, and you'll see fire escapes mostly on tenements, as the area's industrial facilities were built to modern fire codes. These elements gesture less toward the neighborhood and its history than toward the generalized appropriation of formerly industrial infrastructure for "creative economy" activities, as can also be seen in the Googleplex around the corner in the former Port Authority Building. In this respect, the new Whitney seems to confirm Hal Foster's diagnosis of Piano as an architect of "banal cosmopolitanism" producing superficial tokens of local culture for global circulation.[2]

Even as Piano's multifaceted Whitney refuses to settle into an iconic brand-image, it is optimized for our viewing in another sense. Some of its most pronounced forms, such as the projecting ends of the grandest gallery, on the fifth floor, serve as frames for looking that resemble similar viewfinders along the High Line. The exterior metal decks echo the park's vista-oriented catwalks. Narrow balconies that project from the terraces on the seventh and eighth floors bring the museum's scopic invitation to a point as they suspend you above the neighborhood's carnival of consumption.

Visitors may have difficulty under these circumstances giving art the sustained attention it sometimes demands. For many, taking in the collections will merge into an afternoon of shopping, eating and strolling. Not all art relies on detachment and focus, though. As he toured me through the fifth-floor gallery, the giant rectangular hall that frames superb views to east and west, Weinberg described the space as a transit between Charles Sheeler and Jackson Pollock—between the jumbled cityscape of industrial Manhattan and the notional American expanse beyond the Hudson. Such a reading suggests that the museum's architecture can show us the world anew by allowing art to reframe perception of our surroundings. This capacity is strongest where the building's integration into its saturated context sets up the potential for sculptures, installations, performances and happenings to infiltrate the area's densely animated commercial sociability, as Brown's Roof Piece did. The museum heralded its move by partnering with High Line Art and building owners to program works by Alex Katz, Yayoi Kusama, Richard Artschwager and others. The groundbreaking ceremony in 2011 featured a performance by the STREB Extreme Action Company, whose founder, Elizabeth Streb, the previous year had reenacted Brown's Man Walking Down the Side of a Building (1970) on the north face of the Breuer building. The downtown Whitney may be strongest as a platform for wall and roof pieces, artworks that animate the facade for onlookers in the neighborhood and beyond.

Notes

1. Ada Louise Huxtable, "Harsh and Handsome," *New York Times*, Sept. 8,1966.
2. See Foster's *The Art-Architecture Complex*, New York, Verso, 2013.

New York City Rethinks Art for the Masses

By Jennifer Smith
The Wall Street Journal, May 18, 2015

New York City's cultural-affairs budget is bigger than that of the National Endowment for the Arts.

Yet for many artists, the city has never been a harder place to make ends meet. Some complain that the city's cultural largess doesn't extend to all of its residents.

Now the city is attempting to address some of these problems, by drawing up a plan that outlines its cultural priorities and ensures they align with the needs of artists, residents and local organizations.

"Are we reaching every community? Are we providing access to culture and the arts to every child in every neighborhood?" said New York City Councilman Jimmy Van Bramer of Queens, the chairman of the cultural-affairs committee. "It just seems to me that as the largest city in the nation, with the biggest, most robust funding for the arts, we should have a plan for what we are doing."

On Monday, Mayor Bill de Blasio signed a bill requiring the Department of Cultural Affairs to come up with a plan that analyzes where arts activities occur, how they affect community welfare and how they can be incorporated into city planning and economic development.

Chicago, Houston and Denver have already adopted similar cultural plans, pitched at making cities more artist-friendly and cultural activities more accessible.

But in New York City, the initiative comes as soaring rents and other economic pressures have made it harder for many artists to live and work here.

Some activists have criticized the city and its previous mayor, Michael Bloomberg, for funneling money to major institutions and public-art projects while cutting back spending for less-glamorous measures such as arts education.

"I think it's very important for the city of New York to have a cultural plan that addresses equity across the city," said Amy Sananman, executive director of Groundswell, a nonprofit that works with at-risk youth to create murals and public art to promote social justice.

Caron Atlas, co-director of Naturally Occurring Cultural Districts New York, a group of community-based cultural organizations, including Groundswell, said it was important for the city to map out a cultural policy, and for the Department of Cultural Affairs to coordinate with other city agencies and smaller community groups.

Reprinted with permission of The Wall Street Journal, Copyright © (2015) Dow Jones & Company, Inc. All Rights Reserved Worldwide. License number 3692660615088.

The effort would also bring a welcome spotlight to smaller cultural groups, she said.

"It becomes an opportunity to really lift up the work that is being done

Chicago, Houston and Denver have already adopted similar cultural plans, pitched at making cities more artist-friendly and cultural activities more accessible.

in a whole lot of ways across the city," said Kemi Ilesanmi, executive director of the Laundromat Project, which works with artists to create interactive projects in laundromats, parks and beauty salons in neighborhoods such as Harlem, Bedford-Stuyvesant in Brooklyn, and the Hunts Point-Longwood section in the Bronx.

Councilman Stephen Levin of Brooklyn, who co-sponsored the bill with Mr. Van Bramer, said one aim is to support neighborhood groups located in gentrifying areas.

"The community culture of the Lower East Side, or the south side of Williamsburg—it's so inherent to the identity of those neighborhoods," Mr. Levin said. "We want to strengthen them and keep that intact."

The bill suggests increasing arts education and cultural activities in New York City public schools, as well as looking at artists' needs for affordable housing and studio and rehearsal space.

In the coming months, the Department of Cultural Affairs will set up a citizens' advisory committee to advise on the plan. Members will include representatives of community-based cultural groups as well as people with experience in areas ranging from business and real estate to public housing or nonprofit groups.

A final plan is expected to go before the mayor on or before July 1, 2017. The plan would be reviewed every 10 years.

"It's a two-way street," said Cultural Affairs Commissioner Tom Finkelpearl. "We have to get it out there, in the public eye, and get back the input from the public."

Embracing Graffiti Could Help Contain It, Save Tucson Money

By David J. Del Grande
Arizona Daily Star, August 1, 2015

Each year Tucsonans spend more than $1 million removing graffiti like the spray-painted scrawls that recently defaced the Fox Theatre downtown.

But other communities have found success with programs that prevent graffiti rather than paint over it—and local supporters say Tucson could do the same.

Options like graffiti walls or mural projects could provide a productive outlet for taggers, said Michael B. Schwartz, director of the Tucson Arts Brigade, an after-school program that organizes mural projects around town. Schwartz said the feedback he gets from communities that participate in mural programs is always the same.

"It was inspiring people and had kind of a ripple effect," he said. "People love the arts and love anything that brings the community together."

Supporters say public support of such efforts could cut or eliminate the amount spent on graffiti abatement: The city's Transportation Department alone issued more than 62,000 work orders last fiscal year and paid a contractor $720,000 to paint over all the tags. And that's in addition to abatement by power and phone companies, which are responsible for graffiti on their utility boxes.

Spending money on mural projects, which have proven to reduce tagging, is a better investment than increasing enforcement, Tucson City Councilman Steve Kozachik said.

"Everyone's paying for it, over and over," Kozachik said. "If we can reduce the area that's being tagged right now, and you're not going back next month and abating again, we're saving money in the long run," he said. "Plus, the city will look nicer."

Here are some graffiti prevention ideas that have proven to work here and elsewhere.

Legal Graffiti Walls

The historic Venice Pavilion in Venice, California, was a magnet for taggers.

But since 1999, after the city tore down most of the pavilion, the remains have offered a legal alternative to the formerly illegal behavior. Venice Art Walls offers

Reprinted with permission.

graffiti writers a place to paint and tag, with their creations curated by local graffiti production company Setting the Pace.

The Setting the Pace foundation began managing the Venice Art Walls in 2012, and the group has since organized mural workshops for students and young artists.

Bruno Hernandez, executive director at Setting the Pace, said becoming a mentor for young people interested in graffiti art was a major motivation for spearheading the nonprofit organization.

"It really is important to have legitimate role models," Hernandez said.

Setting the Pace uses the planning of mural projects as a metaphor for achieving long-term life goals for the students and young people who participate.

When a school district is faced with a budget deficit, art classes are the first to be cut, Hernandez said. And for students who do not excel in academics, a creative outlet like art may be what's keeping them in school, he added.

> **"Cities that have embraced not just the arts, but the creative economy as a whole, tend to be doing a little bit better these days."**

Artists interested in painting at the Venice Art Walls must follow strict guidelines.

For instance, painting is allowed only on weekends, minors can paint only with brushes or paint rollers, and all artists must have a permit.

Hernandez said he doesn't want another generation risking the many setbacks of illegal graffiti writing such as gang affiliation, violence, incarceration and the overall negativity tagging creates within the community.

Also, having a safe and legal place to express themselves helps prevent run-ins if taggers drift into another crew's territory, Hernandez said.

Utility Box Murals

A mural program in San Diego turns public utility boxes into sanctioned art spaces.

Kozachik said he is working with local utility companies to launch a similar program here [in Tucson, Arizona].

Not only could it improve urban aesthetics, it could save customers money, he said.

Taggers are more likely to deface blank walls, utility boxes or traffic control hardware, the Tucson graffiti task force says. They typically avoid defacing legitimate artwork or murals.

Private energy companies have been reluctant to agree to a mural program so far, but the Tucson Transportation and Environmental Services departments are on board, Kozachik said. He said if the program is successful, he hopes the private sector will follow suit.

"Let's get the city to lead by example," Kozachik said.

Large-Scale Murals

The Tucson Arts Brigade was formed in 1995 to introduce the creative arts in Tucson's low-income schools.

At the time, the city had many more arts organizations because of regular funding, so the Brigade focused on its City Wide After School Arts & Civic Engagement Program, Schwartz said.

During the past 20 years, it has organized multiple large-scale mural art projects throughout Tucson, including the Amphi Community Action Mural Project, the 29th Street Community Mural Project and the Together We Thrive Mural at 316 N. Fourth Ave.

From 2009 to 2013, communities that participated in one of the organization's mural programs saw nearby graffiti decline at least 69 percent, Schwartz said.

This year, the organization is set to paint five trash containers at Tucson's Environmental Services Center. It is negotiating with the Washington, D.C.–based Graffiti Resource Council to match the $5,000 of local funding.

Schwartz said many smaller cities throughout the U.S. have embraced programs like the utility box mural proposal. Not only do the projects employ local artists, but their respective neighborhoods also benefit, he said.

As long as Tucson makes abatement a higher priority than prevention, groups like the Tucson Arts Brigade will falter, Schwartz said. His only project at the moment is the trash containers, and he is looking outside Tucson for matching funds. He has no employees and says staying afloat is a constant challenge.

"The traditional forms of funding that we got used to, or that kept our work going in the field, have evaporated," he said.

If projects like the utility box program take off, he said, Tucson's arts community could thrive—and so could its economy.

"Cities that have embraced not just the arts, but the creative economy as a whole, tend to be doing a little bit better these days," he said. "The idea is to support our local artists, pay them well, and keep them in Tucson."

6
Politics and Education

© Yang Lei/Xinhua Press/Corbis

The mayor of Los Angeles, Eric Garcetti, signs the city's new minimum wage ordinance at Martin Luther King Jr. Park, South Los Angeles, on June 13, 2015. Under the new ordinance, the city's minimum wage will rise to $10.50 in July 2016 and gradually increase to $15.00 an hour by 2020. The city currently follows the state-set minimum wage of $9.00.

Managing the Future

Urban environments face significant challenges in the effort to improve education. Long a bastion for public education reform and development, cities have had difficulty maintaining educational quality as declining revenues and economic growth have stalled educational goals. Education is also deeply intertwined with urban politics and the relationship between cities and the suburbs and rural communities that surround them. Urban populations tend to be more liberal than rural or suburban populations, but the politics of cities have long been affected by majorities in the state that have different social, fiscal, and political goals. In the 2010s, urban governments are encouraging increased interest in city politics, hoping to filter progressive political interest into urban renewal.

Education as a Public Trust

The first schools in the United States, established in the colonial era (1492–1763), were generally either religious or private schools. The Boston Latin School, established in 1635, was one of the first of what would today be considered "public schools," but the concept didn't become popular until the mid-1800s. Educational reformer Horace Mann, who worked on the Massachusetts Board of Education from 1835, was a pioneer in public education, and initiated innovations that included "age based" classrooms and compulsory education for elementary school students.[1]

Mann and other education reformers of the 1800s wanted American education to reflect the goal of making the United States a haven of opportunity for immigrants and natural citizens alike.[2] Specifically, reformers wanted education to be open to the largest possible body of students, regardless of race, creed, or financial status, and for the school system to reach a level of sophistication in keeping with the stalwarts of Western intellectualism in Europe. The difference between public and private education is largely a matter of funding. Public schools are funded through state and federal tax revenues, and as such, public schools must meet state standards designed to prevent discrimination and protect the rights of teachers and school administrators.

Private schools, which are funded by donation and private investment, have more flexibility in staffing and curriculum design than public schools. Because private schools are not required to serve the "general population," they may choose to offer admission only to a specific population, such as members of a certain religious or social/economic group and are otherwise able to be far more selective in admitting students. In addition, private schools are not required to meet state hiring standards, thus enabling them to hire teachers who are not state certified but may be otherwise qualified to teach a certain subject. Private school teachers are generally paid less than their public counterparts, but may enjoy more freedom in designing their curriculum because they are not required to meet standards tied to government funding.

Since the 1990s, there has been a new option in education in the form of the charter schools. Charter schools are funded largely by state and local revenues but are managed by independent corporations or organizations under a "charter contract" with the state. Because they are essentially a blend of independent and public investment, charter schools are exempt from some state regulations. For instance, like private schools, charter schools are able to limit or promote admission to members of certain groups, and many of the companies operating charter schools advertise their institutions as "specialized" learning environments for certain types of students. However, unlike private schools, charter schools receive state funding and so must meet certain requirements regarding hiring and admission, though they are exempt from others.[3] While supporters argue that charters can be more innovative and effective at serving students with specific needs, the program is controversial and critics argue that charter schools reduce funding for public education while failing to meet the same standards of inclusiveness and diversity.[4] Charter schools are mainly in cities, where the debate over their effectiveness and what the growth of these schools means for the future of urban public education rages on.

The modern education debate also focuses on "educational standards," and how best to measure achievement. The No Child Left Behind (NCLB) initiatives established under President George W. Bush tie federal school funding to student achievement on standardized tests that are supposed to be designed to measure comprehension of core subjects. Opposition to No Child Left Behind and the more recent "Core Curriculum Standards" introduced by President Barack Obama has been substantial, with many educators and parents arguing that teaching aimed at standardized testing undermines educational quality and provides a limited measure of student capability.[5] Again, this debate is largely focused around cities, where criticism of schools has been sharpest.

Urban Challenges

Urban schools have been affected by the same demographic and economic trends that have affected other aspects of urban development. The suburbanization of America, driven by an exodus of white middle-class families from the 1950s through the 2000s, reduced tax revenues for urban schools and created predominantly minority school districts with reduced access to resources. Racial and cultural prejudice was a motivating factor in the "white flight" from urban public schools, beginning in the 1950s and 1960s. Desegregation, which began after the 1954 Supreme Court case of *Brown v. Board of Education*[6] and programs aimed at racial integration in schools inspired further waves of racial exodus, with upper-class white families who remained in cities increasingly sending their children to private schools.[7]

In the urban environment, one of the most significant aspects of the modern education debate is the disparity between white students and similar age African American and Hispanic students in U.S. schools. A vast majority of Americans recognize that there is an achievement gap, and polls indicate that 89 percent of Americans believe that addressing this disparity is an important social issue.[8] Deeper studies of educational disparity indicate that class, race, and, income gaps go and hand in hand with pervasive misconceptions regarding the equity and opportunity offered to students. In a 2009 study in the *Journal of Educational Controversy* the authors argued that textbooks and other standard educational materials, media coverage, and public "mythology" about American history served to deemphasize the effect of class and income on educational success. Class materials and textbooks also routinely focus on the success of predominantly white, male "heroes" with a disproportionately low emphasis on the contributions of women and people of color, while simultaneously perpetuating a myth of equal opportunity that essentially trains students to dismiss the substantial barriers that they face in education and employment.[9] Yet studies indicate that the economic and social challenges that students face do have a significant and lasting effect on educational success.[10] With this in mind, addressing the education gap may mean embracing broader policies aimed at improving social and economic environments for students and their families.

Liberalism in Urban Environments

Urban populations tend to be more politically liberal than rural and suburban populations. Even in traditionally conservative states like Texas, cities like Austin skew to the left, especially concerning social political issues. Pew Research studies found that political liberals are nearly twice as likely as conservatives to live in urban areas, while conservatives, by contrast, are nearly twice as common in rural communities.[11] Historical analyses indicate that, just after the Civil War, political ideology was divided more by national region than by the urban/rural divide. In the twentieth century, however, the political lines increasingly occurred along urban/rural boundaries, between the low-density racially homogenous suburbs and rural towns and the comparatively high-density and culturally diverse cities.[12]

The causes of urban liberalism have been the subject of intense debate among politicians, educators, and social scientists. Some, especially conservative pundits, explain the urban-rural divide through mechanisms like the "Curley effect," which suggests that the concentration of liberal groups like labor unions, welfare recipients, and poor populations drives urban liberalism,[13] but this does not explain cities like Boston, Chicago, and San Francisco where liberalism is dominant even among the affluent, white-collar populations. Conservatives have also, for many years, claimed a "liberal bias" in higher education, with some extreme ideologues, like conservative politician Rick Santorum, claiming that colleges and universities "indoctrinate" students with liberal values. This line of thinking carries potential implications for the urban liberalism of cities where colleges and universities are located; however, studies have shown that college and university professors are split along ideological lines and that the "liberal bias" in education is at least partially the result of the fact that young college-age students tend to be liberal, across economic and racial lines, though many will become more conservative later in life.[14] Urban liberals are far more likely to describe their attitudes as the result of their experiences living within cities rather than as the result of some kind of indoctrination. Pew Research studies indicate that individuals who are consistently liberal in politics also place ethnic diversity as a major priority in their decision of where to live.[15]

Urban Liberalism and Civic Interest

While the federal and state governments shift back and forth between conservative and liberal movements, urban governments have remained predominantly liberal since the mid-twentieth century, and the trend has shown little sign of changing. Interest in local politics, including mayoral elections, dropped precipitously in most cities since the 1960s, and in many cities like New York, Boston, and Philadelphia just over 25 percent of residents vote for the city's mayor. In the 2010s, however, voter registration and turnout for local elections has grown slowly, indicating a minor increase in local political interest.[16] This upswing has been linked to broader interest in urban renewal and also to the disparity in social and political values between urban and rural populations.

Because the political goals of cities and their parent states often differ, cities have also become increasingly distinct from their parents states in the twenty-first century in terms of passing environmental and social initiatives that have not been embraced by state legislatures. For instance, since 2003 twenty cities have increased the minimum wage for workers through urban ordinances, despite opposition from state governments.[17] While minimum wage movements are not unique to cities, the relatively high cost of living in cities has inspired city councils and governments to take a proactive stance on the issue. Though minimum wage increases have received widespread popular support from urban residents, critics argue that, over the long term, cities adopting higher minimum wages may essentially drive businesses and industries out of cities, although whether this will happen remains to be seen. Another example of a distinct urban liberalism has been evident in the nationwide controversy over "fracking," an environmentally destructive method of locating and harvesting secondary petroleum deposits. While the state of Pennsylvania has largely supported fracking on state land, resistance has come from Pennsylvania cities, like Pittsburgh, where the practice has been banned.[18]

Studies indicating that the political divide between cities and states has intensified since the 1980s reflect a simultaneous growth of rural conservatism and urban liberalism. Historically cities have been in the forefront of political and cultural change, and this will most likely continue to the extent that issues of class and the environment gain prominence in national politics.

Micah L. Issitt

Notes

1. "American Public Education: An Origin Story," *Education News.*
2. Reese, *America's Public Schools*
3. "Charter Schools—Fast Facts," NCES.

4. Sanchez, "The Charter School vs. Public School Debate Continues."

5. Koebler, "On 10th Anniversary, a Look Back at 'No Child' Legacy."

6. McBride, *Brown v. Board of Education* (1954)."

7. Zhang, "School Desegreation and White Flight Revisited: A Spatial Analysis from a Metropolitan Percepctive."

8. Strauss, "Poll: What Americans Say About Public Education."

9. Kansas State University, "Poverty Is Rooted in US Education System, Research Finds."

10. Jensen, *Teaching with Poverty in Mind*, 13–18.

11. Desilver, "Chart of the Week: The Most Liberal and Conservative Big Cities."

12. Kron, "Red State, Blue City: How the Urban-Rural Divide Is Splitting America."

13. Glaeser and Shleifer, "The Curley Effect: The Economics of Shaping the Electorate."

14. Williams, "Is There a 'Liberal Bias' in Academia?"

15. Desilver, "How the Most Ideologically Polarized Americans Live Different Lives."

16. Denvir, "Votor Turnout in U.S. Mayoral Elections Is Pathetic, but It Wasn't Always This Way."

17. Quinton, "States Battle Cities over Minimum Wage."

18. Bergal, "Cities Forge Policy Apart from States."

In Major U.S. Cities Education "Reform" Opponents Take to the Streets

By Amy Dean
The Nation, August 6, 2013

"As it stands now, if nothing changes, the schools are going to have to open without any adults in the large spaces where kids gather," predicted Philadelphia public schools parent Michael Mullins in late June. Mullins has two kids in the public schools and is secretary-treasurer of the city's hotel and stadium workers union, UNITE/HERE. In late May, the Philadelphia School District approved a "dooms-day budget" cutting almost $300 million from the schools and resulting in the lay-offs of 3,783 people—19 percent of the school system's workforce. The budget also threatened to get rid of arts, music and athletic programs, as well as librarians, secretaries, counselors and playground aides, unless the state or city council could come up with emergency funding.

In response, Mullins joined a group of parents and laid-off school workers in a fast starting June 17 in front of Pennsylvania Governor Tom Corbett's Philadelphia office. "We wanted to represent the sense of crisis we feel inside and make it public," said Mullins. "I think there is a hunger for more direct action," he added, in order for "the seriousness of this as we live it to reach the decision-makers."

More people stepped forward during the fifteen-day fast to reinforce this conviction: Philly's Fast for Safe Schools featured a rotating cast of twelve parent activists and school employees who fasted from three to eight days each. The activists chose to end the fast on July 1, after securing a partial win: Corbett put forward a new funding package that added $140 million back to the school district. The package combines loans with state and city funds, which the activists say could stave off many of the layoffs for now. But Corbett's package still doesn't cover the $180 million the district had requested to keep all the needed jobs filled.

As the showdown in Philadelphia indicates, the ongoing battle over education "reform" and school funding—topics often discussed in think tanks, political campaigns or *Waiting for "Superman"*-style media productions—is moving into the streets. Chicago and Seattle, too, have seen vigorous protests against austerity, privatization, high-stakes testing and union-busting. Such demonstrations together represent a forceful challenge to the corporate-financed push for "education reform" undertaken by the likes of Michelle Rhee, the former schools chancellor of Washington, DC. But these movements are more than mere isolated acts of resistance;

From The Nation, August 6 © 2013 The Nation Company, LLC. All rights reserved. Used by permission and protected by the Copyright Laws of the United States. The printing, copying, redistribution, or retransmission of this Content without express written permission is prohibited.

in their demands, the outlines of a coherent policy agenda can be discerned—one that looks honestly at what it will take to bring quality education to America's least privileged communities.

One thing this movement has already accomplished is exposing how the education "reform" movement provides cover to Republicans and neoliberal Democrats who are starving the public school system. In championing privately run charter schools, the (self-described) reformers paint traditional schools as failures that should be defunded—even if those traditional schools outperform charters. By bashing teachers unions, figures like Rhee have helped politicians scapegoat the unions for fiscal woes, even as many of those lawmakers advocate cutting taxes. And by claiming that those who cite poverty's impact on student achievement are merely making excuses for sub-par teaching, the "reform" camp has played down the devastating effects of ruthless budget cutting.

On the same day Philly's doomsday budget was approved, Teach for America founder Wendy Kopp tweeted, "I can't get over the progress in this city's schools in the last decade!" Although she later tried to cover for the gaffe, it illustrated how out of touch "reformers" are regarding the challenges facing public schools. The incident also suggests that adequate funding should be a basic demand of the movement for quality public education.

The Chicago Teachers Union (CTU) has made this demand a central part of its platform, which emphasizes combating inequality in the public school system. In a 2012 report titled "The Schools Chicago's Students Deserve," the union proposed a statewide solution to the city schools' funding troubles, arguing that wealthier suburban tax bases across Illinois should be tapped to fund Chicago's ailing public schools: "The most disadvantaged communities in Chicago and Illinois ought to receive as much educational funding as the wealthiest; any less should be unconstitutional." This focus has allowed the union to draw a stark contrast between its policies and those of Chicago Mayor Rahm Emanuel and his schools CEO, Barbara Byrd-Bennett, who is overseeing the closing of fifty schools to help bridge a budget gap of $1 billion. Meanwhile, the CTU points out, Emanuel is paying $55 million out of city coffers to build a new basketball arena and hotel at DePaul University.

The protests against these skewed priorities went beyond the teachers union, making a viral video star of 9-year-old activist Asean Johnson, who charged, "This is racism right here." Parents of kids at schools set to close have brought a federal lawsuit against the city, claiming that the closings violate the Americans With Disabilities Act and the Illinois Civil Rights Act. They argue that displacing kids (special needs kids in particular) from their neighborhood schools will place them at even greater risk.

New organizing among students, parents and educators fed up with endless "teaching to the test" is another area of promise. In Seattle this past January, teachers at Garfield High School engaged the city school district in a fight over high-stakes standardized testing, refusing to administer the state's Measures of Academic Progress test. They charged that the test wasted class time, produced "meaningless results" and was used improperly in teacher evaluations. Many agreed. Despite threats of unpaid suspensions and other disciplinary measures, teachers at several area schools joined the boycott.

High-stakes testing is a foundation of the education "reform" movement, but cheating scandals in at least a dozen districts have put a spotlight on the corrosive effects of test mania. Parents and students now have the opportunity to demand a rich curriculum in public schools—something that the American Federation of Teachers advocated in its 2012 proposal titled "Quality Education Agenda." Moreover, teachers unions are asserting their right to establish high standards for their own profession by proposing better ways to evaluate and support teachers—including enhanced mentoring, peer review and professional development. Models for peer review have already been developed and tested by the Cincinnati Federation of Teachers and the New York State Union of Teachers, among others. Rejecting the notion that we can fire—or scapegoat—our way to good teaching, advocates for quality public schools should insist that accountability be demanded of actors throughout the educational system, including administrators and politicians.

> As the showdown in Philadelphia indicates, the ongoing battle over education "reform" and school funding—topics often discussed in think tanks, political campaigns or *Waiting for "Superman"*–style media productions—is moving into the streets. Chicago and Seattle, too, have seen vigorous protests against austerity, privatization, high-stakes testing and union-busting.

The new wave of street protests demonstrates a type of community–labor alliance that ideally would become less an emergency response than an ingrained habit. Rather than mobilizing only at flash-point moments like a school closing or a contract negotiation, everyone with a stake in public education must be ready to mobilize on an ongoing basis, to strengthen their alliances with one another and have the conversations that will create a proactive agenda for the schools. That way, when politicians and school district officials come to slash school budgets—as we can, unfortunately, expect in cities around the country—they will be met by an organized opposition ready not only to shield students from those cuts, but to present a workable plan to keep public education alive and healthy.

Charter Schools Continue Dramatic Growth Despite Controversies

By Joy Resmovits
The Huffington Post, January 25, 2014

Charter schools remain the subject of intense debate, particularly in New York City, where incoming Mayor Bill de Blasio (D) won on a platform that was explicitly less friendly toward such schools than the policies of the outgoing mayor have been. But even as the political debate rages on, charter schools continue to grow dramatically throughout the country.

Overall, 1 in 20 students—2.3 million in total—now attend charter schools, which represents an increase of 225,000 students over the 2012–2013 school year. And that growth is particularly pronounced in urban areas, according to a new report released Tuesday by the National Alliance for Public Charter Schools that looked at market share in cities with the highest number of charter schools.

According to the report, New Orleans, whose school system was rebuilt in the wake of Hurricane Katrina, has 79 percent of its students in charter schools, which are publicly funded but can be privately and independently run. For the first time, Detroit had more than half of its students in such schools, with 51 percent. Washington, D.C., is working its way there, with 43 percent of its students now in charter schools. The top six school districts with the highest rates of enrollment—which also include Flint, Mich., Kansas City, Mo., and Gary, Ind.—each have 30 percent or more of students in a charter school.

The nation's largest cities also have high numbers of charter school students, according to the report. Los Angeles has more than 120,000 students in charter schools, which the report notes is a group larger than 99.9 percent of school districts nationwide. Cities such as Philadelphia and New York have 10 percent or more of their students in charters. And New York City ranked among the top 10 cities for charter school growth for a second year in a row.

The growth is large, percentage-wise, but since some of the numbers started low, the statistics may be overstating the reality. For example, the report found that the number of districts with more than one-fifth of students in a charter school has increased by 350 percent over the last eight years—but only seven districts had that level of enrollment eight years ago.

"It is significant when you see this dramatic of a growth. It says something is going on in those districts," said Nina Rees, who heads NAPCS

From The Huffington Post, January 25 © 2014 AOL Inc.. All rights reserved. Used by permission and protected by the Copyright Laws of the United States. The printing, copying, redistribution, or retransmission of this Content without express written permission is prohibited.

[National Alliance for Public Charter Schools]. "If I were a district official, I would see how I would keep some of these students in the system . . . The two sectors need to come together to find solutions that fit the needs of the entire district."

The news excited Andy Smarick, a former Bush administration official who supports charter schools and now works at the Washington, D.C.–based consulting firm Bellwether Education Partners. But the growth hasn't happened as he expected it to.

Ten years ago, he recalls, proponents of the nascent charter school movement came to a consensus: If charter schools could reach 10 percent of market share in big cities, the movement would reach a tipping point and create enough pressure to spur public schools to improve in order to compete for students.

"That tipping-point pressure never materialized the way I expected," he said. "We have not seen districts drastically improve even when charter school market share gets to 25 percent. . . You can't look at the performance of districts like Detroit or Gary and say, 'Now that charters have a significant market share, we've had a renaissance.' It just hasn't happened. I've given up on the idea."

"We can't say the competitive pressure has fundamentally improved what the district is doing," Smarick added. "This document forces us to have that conversation" and to consider the possibility that low-performing districts could transition a majority of their students to charter schools.

Others are also skeptical as to whether charter schools are living up to their promise of offering flexibility in exchange for greater accountability for students' results. "The findings are eye-popping, in terms of family demand for charter schools in the nation's largest cities," said Bruce Fuller, a University of California, Berkeley, education professor. "Let's hope that the average effectiveness of charters improves, and government devises a better way to regulate quality. Otherwise, the movement will become yet another false promise for millions of low-income families and their kids."

Overall, the performance of charter schools is mixed, according to the most comprehensive report on charter school quality, released this summer by Stanford University's Center for Research on Education Outcomes. CREDO studied charter schools in 25 states and two cities, and found that performance among charter school students varies dramatically, but overall, students learn at roughly the same rates as their peers in public schools. According to the study, charter school students did end the school year with reading skills eight instructional days ahead of public school children, but with comparable math instruction.

According to other studies, charter schools have outperformed analogous public schools in some urban areas—where the most vitriolic battles over the schools' future are still being waged.

In New York, outgoing mayor Michael Bloomberg housed many new charter schools within the same buildings as functioning public schools, a process known as "co-location" that has spawned many dramatic public hearings. Bloomberg also did not require charter schools to pay rent for that space, a policy that de Blasio has said he would revisit.

The market share study also has tremendous implications for students with special needs in the nation's largest cities. Charter schools have been known to offer fewer services to such students, in part because economies of scale make offering those services expensive for charter schools. But as charter schools provide an increasingly greater share of urban education, the options may dwindle for students with special needs. "More families are going [to charter schools], and we have to deal with the tough questions that come along with it," Smarick said, though he added these concerns are sometimes overblown.

Gary Miron, a professor at Western Michigan University who has audited charter schools for several states, has found that more and more charter schools are privately run—not by charter school boards, but by nonprofit and for-profit management organizations. According to a recent study Miron authored, 908,000 students attended a privately managed school in the 2011–2012 school year, up from 733,000 a year earlier.

"These are supposed to be publicly operated schools. But whether [an education management company] has 91 schools or one school. . . they employ the public school employees directly," he said. "So we don't have much of a public school left."

The Rise of the Progressive City

By Michelle Goldberg
The Nation, April 2, 2014

The Bush years were grim for progressives, but they did offer one small consolation: the hope that if only a smart and decent person could ascend to the White House, our politics could be repaired. Now, after years of destructive austerity and hopeless stalemate, that faith is dead. People on the left will debate where to lay the blame, but few will disagree that our federal institutions seem utterly unequal to the challenges of a country still reeling from economic crisis.

Indeed, our national politics are so deformed that it's hard even to imagine the steps necessary to fix things. Last year, *The Boston Globe* ran an award-winning series, "Broken City," about the entropy in Washington. The final piece noted that potential remedies for the country's problems are met with "almost complete indifference in Washington, the world's capital of gridlock, even when alternative, perhaps better, ways are already at work, some in plain sight."

At the city level, though, things are very different. Among those who study urban governance and those who practice it, there's an extraordinary sense of political excitement. An outpouring of books like *If Mayors Ruled the World*, *Triumph of the City* and *The Metropolitan Revolution* hymns urban dynamism. Not all the new urban optimists are on the left, but that's where most of the energy is. With the federal government frozen, cities are seizing the initiative and becoming laboratories for progressive policy innovation. Amid widespread despair about national politics, cities have become new sources of hope.

"It's a movement that reflects the paralyzed nature of the political system in Washington right now and the polarization of the political process," says Neal Peirce, editor of *Citiscope,* an online magazine about cities that launched [early in 2014]. "On the local level, you can have these arguments without getting as much into partisan politics. At the same time, we're having much more discussion about income inequality." The result is a raft of local legislation intended to address problems that national politicians have let fester. "It's quite a shift," says Peirce. "It's grown dramatically in the last year or so."

There's little chance, for example, that Congress will give us a living-wage law anytime soon, but the city of SeaTac in Washington State just raised its minimum wage to an unprecedented $15 an hour, and Los Angeles is considering a proposal to mandate a $15.37 minimum for workers at big hotels.* San Francisco has adopted

From The Nation, April 21 © 2014 The Nation Company, LLC. All rights reserved. Used by permission and protected by the Copyright Laws of the United States. The printing, copying, redistribution, or retransmission of this Content without express written permission is prohibited.

near-universal health coverage, including a program for the uninsured that functions like the "public option" left out of President Obama's Affordable Care Act. The federal government has done disgracefully little about the collapse of the housing market, but Richmond, California, is pushing a bold, controversial plan to take over underwater mortgages through the use of eminent domain. Obama's proposal for universal pre-K, first made in last year's State of the Union address, may not go anywhere, but New York City Mayor Bill de Blasio has promised to bring it to the country's largest city, and both San Antonio and Denver have approved sales tax increases to pay for their own expanded preschool programs.

With a group of new, progressive mayors in office this year, the era of big-city liberalism has just begun. In addition to de Blasio, there's Boston's Marty Walsh, Minneapolis's Betsy Hodges and Seattle's Ed Murray, who wants to bring the $15 minimum wage to his city. Cities have the opportunity, Murray said in his State of the City address in February, to lead on "disparity in pay and in housing, in [sic] urban policing, on the environment and providing universal pre-K." Quoting Franklin Delano Roosevelt, he called for "bold, persistent experimentation. . . . It is common sense to take a method and try it. If it fails, admit it frankly and try another. But above all, try something."

The Nation has launched a new project, "Cities Rising," in order to report on these experiments. It will serve as a space to explore and share some of the most interesting ideas bubbling up around the country. Though the right controls most of the statehouses and large swaths of the federal government, the city, increasingly, belongs to progressives. [It will] write about what they're doing with it.

* * *

A few decades ago, the idea of cities as models of public-policy vitality would have seemed bizarre. In the 1960s and '70s, urban America was seen as synonymous with chaos and decay. Manufacturing jobs flowed out of the cities in the 1960s, and by the end of that decade, a combination of economic privation and police brutality had sparked devastating urban riots nationwide. Violent crime shot up—according to Harvard economist Edward Glaeser, author of *Triumph of the City*, New York's murder rate quadrupled from 1960 to 1975. Whites fled, and people of color who had the means soon followed them. A 1976 headline in *The New York Times* read: "Black Middle Class Joining the Exodus to White Suburbia."

Many cities responded disastrously to their deterioration, razing poor neighborhoods and replacing them with federally funded urban renewal projects. Glaeser writes: "Those shiny new buildings were really Potemkin villages spread throughout America, built to provide politicians with the appearance of urban success. . . . Investing in buildings instead of people in places where prices were already low may have been the biggest mistake of urban policy over the past sixty years."

Plenty of cities never came back from the dislocations of those years. A paper by Daniel Hartley, a research economist at the Federal Reserve Bank of Cleveland, points out that the Rust Belt cities of Buffalo, Detroit, Cleveland and Pittsburgh lost more than 40 percent of their population over the past four decades. Hartley describes what happened as "reverse gentrification," in which poverty encroached into formerly high-income neighborhoods. In these places, sheer economic desperation rather than inequality is the problem. And that's even harder to address, because there's little wealth there to redistribute, although there are fascinating policy experiments under way in places like Cleveland (more on that later).

In the 1980s and 1990s, though, a number of American cities started booming again, attracting the elite knowledge workers whom celebrity urban theorist Richard Florida famously dubbed the "creative class." (In Florida's formulation, that category includes people in finance, law, business and technology as well as the media, academia and the arts—basically, anyone in a high-status job that requires a lot of thinking.) There are many theories about why certain cities turned around, but Florida's notion of hipness as an economic accelerant was particularly influential. In the preface to his bestselling 2002 book *The Rise of the Creative Class: And How It's Transforming Work, Leisure, Community and Everyday Life*, he wrote that "rather than being driven exclusively by companies, economic growth was occurring in places that were tolerant, diverse, and open to creativity—because these were places where creative people of all types wanted to live."

The upshot of this theory was that cities could prosper by making themselves attractive to trendsetters and yuppies. Across the country, civic leaders took Florida's ideas to heart, striving to make their cities hipster-friendly in the hope that it would bring economic revitalization. (Many hired Florida's consulting firm to help.) Michigan Governor Jennifer Granholm, in her 2004 State of the State address, hailed it as "a bottom-up movement in which nearly eighty of our communities have local commissions on cool that are uncorking the bottle of creativity. . . planning everything from bike paths to bookstores to attract more people and new businesses." But Jamie Peck, a University of British Columbia geography professor and one of Florida's harshest critics, pointed out that Michigan found money for a "Cool Cities" program even as it enacted the largest spending cuts in its history.

Not surprisingly, the bureaucratic effort to engineer "cool" has failed to bring economic relief to hard-pressed urban areas. It soon became clear that even in thriving meccas of the creative class like New York, Austin and San Francisco, the economic gains made by the young professionals Florida celebrated weren't trickling down to others. "The benefits of highly skilled regions accrue mainly to knowledge, professional, and creative workers," Florida wrote in a 2013 *Atlantic Cities* piece, acknowledging what his left-wing critics had been saying for years. "While less-skilled blue-collar and service workers also earn more in these places, more expensive housing costs eat away those gains. There is a rising tide of sorts, but it only lifts about the most advantaged third of the workforce, leaving the other 66 percent much further behind."

This is the backdrop for the transition from Michael Bloomberg to Bill de Blasio in New York. In many ways, Bloomberg—who once called the city "a high-end product, maybe even a luxury product"— exemplified the Florida ethos, filling New York with new parks, hundreds of miles of bike lanes and loftlike condos. "[T]he truth of the matter is: being cool counts," Bloomberg wrote in a 2012 *Financial*

Times column. "When people can find inspiration in a community that also offers great parks, safe streets and extensive mass transit, they vote with their feet."

Needless to say, there's nothing wrong with bike lanes and parks. But while Bloomberg turned New York into a paradise for well-heeled young professionals, huge parts of the city were left behind. Over his three terms in office, inequality rose dramatically, the percentage of New Yorkers in poverty inched up, and homelessness reached a record high. De Blasio's rise, in many ways, is a backlash against the failures of an urban policy focused almost exclusively on the "creative class."

"We've done the parks—not all of it, but we've done enough," says Saskia Sassen, the Columbia University sociologist known for her writing about cities and globalization. At this point, she adds, money should be used "to address the question of the bottom 20 percent in this city, which is absolutely a disaster. We need to upgrade the housing in a lot of areas that are very poor and very degraded. That's jobs—that's an opportunity to train. We have a lot of skilled workers who are unemployed; we employ them and we also teach apprentices. The money is there. We stop with the beautifying of the city, and we now dedicate ourselves to the bottom 20 percent."

* * *

There are limits, of course, to what city governments can do independently. "The background issue for all mayors is that they are compelled to deal with the consequences of a system over which they have no power," says the political theorist Benjamin Barber, author of *If Mayors Ruled the World: Dysfunctional Nations, Rising Cities*. Mayors have little say in the structures of global capitalism. De Blasio is proposing a city ID that would help undocumented New Yorkers when it comes to leases, bank accounts and other services, but he can't regulate immigration or give out visas. New York City can't even raise income taxes on its own. All this means that rather than addressing root causes, cities have to focus on "amelioration, palliation," says Barber.

That said, city governments have certain advantages. For one thing, the far right has little power in cities. Texas may be the state that gave us Ted Cruz, but its biggest city,

> "On the local level, you can have these arguments without getting as much into partisan politics. At the same time, we're having much more discussion about income inequality." The result is a raft of local legislation intended to address problems that national politicians have let fester.

Houston, is run by Annise Parker, a Democrat and a lesbian who won her third term last year. Similarly, Salt Lake City, the capital of blood-red Utah, has a Democratic mayor, Ralph Becker; last year, when a judge struck down the state's gay marriage ban, Becker officiated at rushed weddings before a stay could be issued. In 2013, the radical human rights lawyer Chokwe Lumumba was elected mayor of Jackson, Mississippi, with more than 85 percent of the vote. (Tragically, he died of a heart attack after only eight months in office.) San Diego is the only one of the nation's ten biggest cities to be led by a Republican, Kevin Faulconer, who won a special election after the Democratic mayor resigned amid a torrent of sexual harassment claims.

City government is thus largely free of the sort of conservative ideological grandstanding that has left Washington deadlocked. Of course, Democratic domination doesn't necessarily mean progressivism—decades of machine politics have shown that. But it does mean that cities are liberated from culture-war skirmishing and market fundamentalism, giving them the chance to focus on what works. "Local governments tend to attract people who are solution-oriented rather than ideologues," says Dave Cieslewicz, the former mayor of Madison, Wisconsin, and the co-founder of the Mayors Innovation Project, a network of progressive city leaders. "I don't know many Tea Party mayors. As a rule, cities tend to hang together pretty well in terms of being politically homogenous and therefore governable."

This has left our cities ideally placed to experiment with policies that mitigate, if not reverse, the ravages of poverty and widespread inequality. Consider San Francisco, where two contradictory stories about inequality are playing out at once. On the one hand, San Francisco is the second-most-unequal city in the United States, according to the Brookings Institution (Atlanta ranks first). In the *London Review of Books*, Rebecca Solnit describes a crisis "precipitated by a huge influx of well-paid tech workers driving up housing costs and causing evictions, gentrification and cultural change." Google buses have become the symbol of the city's rapid transformation, and protesters have made international news blocking them as they try to ferry the company's well-paid workers from their homes in San Francisco to their jobs in Silicon Valley.

Yet even as San Francisco exemplifies the social stratification of the postindustrial economy, it is also, more quietly, pioneering a new social safety net. Since 1996, the city has enacted some of the country's most comprehensive laws on wages, benefits, paid sick leave and healthcare access. Michael Reich, the director of the Institute for Research on Labor and Employment at the University of California, Berkeley, and Ken Jacobs, chair of the UC Berkeley Labor Center, write that these measures, taken together, "represent a new social compact among businesses, workers, and government."

Along with Miranda Dietz, Reich and Jacobs are the editors of the new book *When Mandates Work: Raising Labor Standards at the Local Level*, a careful, scholarly look at San Francisco's largely unheralded policy experiment, which picked up steam a decade ago. In 2003, a ballot initiative made San Francisco the country's first major city to enact its own minimum wage law, initially set at $8.50 an hour. (Tied to the Bay Area Consumer Price Index, it climbed to $10.55 by 2013.) Two years later, San Francisco instituted a Working Families Credit to supplement the Earned Income Tax Credit. The year after that, it became the first US city to require employers to provide paid sick leave. And it passed the groundbreaking San Francisco Health Care Security Ordinance, which mandated minimum health spending requirements for businesses with twenty or more workers and created Healthy San Francisco, which provides comprehensive healthcare to uninsured city residents.

"Although this public option is not formally considered insurance," Reich and Jacobs note in their book, "it is tantamount to a generous public insurance policy, with the significant caveat that it is restricted to a network of providers located only within San Francisco."

Although such policies will not be enough to reverse the dynamics that threaten to transform San Francisco into a playground for privileged high-tech workers, they have proved amazingly successful at improving the lives of people struggling to get by in a terribly unequal environment. As Reich and Jacobs write: "Remarkably, and despite many warnings about dire negative effects, these new policies raised living standards significantly for tens of thousands of people, and without creating any negative effects on employment. While modest by most European and Canadian standards, San Francisco's policies represent a bold experiment in American labor market policies that provides important lessons for the rest of the United States."

Elements of that experiment will likely soon be replicated in other cities. The push for local minimum wage laws, says Alan Berube, deputy director of the Brookings Institution's Metropolitan Policy Program, has "serious legs" in the wake of last year's progressive mayoral victories. "You can trace it back to the Occupy movement and [Mitt Romney's] '47 percent' and what was a broader kind of national growing awareness of inequality and its effects," he says.

Berube especially credits the Service Employees International Union, which led last year's successful campaign for a $15-an-hour minimum wage in SeaTac, the city around the Seattle–Tacoma International Airport, which has grown increasingly poor as airport wages declined. "It got attention because it was audacious, and I think that that's proven helpful to the cause of folks who are looking to do this in other places," he says. In March, for example, Chicago voters overwhelmingly passed a nonbinding referendum calling for a $15 minimum wage for companies that do business in the city and gross more than $50 million a year.

* * *

Just as reactionary ideas tend to spread from one state legislature to another—witness the recent tide of state-level anti-abortion laws—good ideas spread among the cities. "Mayors are incredibly competitive and constantly bragging on their own cities," says Cieslewicz, who founded the Mayors Innovation Project (originally called the New Cities Project) in 2005 as an alternative to the more mainstream US Conference of Mayors. "One result of that is the sharing of best practices. Mayors always want to tell you what it is they accomplished—and when they get challenged and hear that someone did it better, they want to steal that idea."

One idea that Cieslewicz wants to steal comes out of Cleveland, where a group of worker-owned green cooperatives in low-income neighborhoods have been serving the city's hospitals and college campuses since 2008. "Universities and hospitals in Cleveland are literally spending billions of dollars a year on all kinds of services: food for the cafeteria, laundry—hospitals go through an incredible amount of laundry," Cieslewicz says. "What they did was set up three cooperatives, one dealing with laundry—it's the greenest laundry service in Ohio—another producing local food, and a third one dealing with solar energy. Because every dollar that's not being spent on fossil fuel—not being exported—can be kept in the community."

The cooperatives, which receive both government and foundation support and bring in about $6 million a year, hire people from the surrounding neighborhoods and give them an ownership share, which is paid for through a payroll deduction and allows the workers to build up thousands of dollars in equity. All of this creates "a symbiotic relationship between these powerful big institutions and the neighborhoods that surrounded them," Cieslewicz says. He's now promoting a similar idea through his consulting business: "Of all the ideas I've gotten from the Mayors Innovation Project, that's the one I love the most."

For now, Cieslewicz believes that local initiatives—some modest and discreet, others sweeping and ambitious—represent the only way to make progress against poverty and inequality. "I'm a liberal Democrat," he says. "I believe in the War on Poverty, and I wish the federal government would concentrate its resources on these issues. The truth is, it's just not going to happen anytime soon. But it can happen at the local level."

Editor's Note

*In June 2015, Los Angeles enacted a $15 minimum wage across the board.

The Revolt of the Cities

By Harold Meyerson
American Prospect, April 23, 2014

Pittsburgh is the perfect urban laboratory," says Bill Peduto, the city's new mayor. "We're small enough to be able to do things and large enough for people to take notice." More than its size, however, it's Pittsburgh's new government—Peduto and the five like-minded progressives who now constitute a majority on its city council—that is turning the city into a laboratory of democracy. In his first hundred days as mayor, Peduto has sought funding to establish universal pre-K education and partnered with a Swedish sustainable-technology fund to build four major developments with low carbon footprints and abundant affordable housing. Even before he became mayor, while still a council member, he steered to passage ordinances that mandated prevailing wages for employees on any project that received city funding and required local hiring for the jobs in the Pittsburgh Penguins' new arena. He authored the city's responsible-banking law, which directed government funds to those banks that lent in poor neighborhoods and away from those that didn't.

Pittsburgh is a much cleaner city today than it was when it housed some of the world's largest steel mills. But, like postindustrial America generally, it is also a much more economically divided city. When steel dominated the economy, the companies' profits and the union's contracts made Pittsburgh—like Detroit, Cleveland, and Chicago—a city with a thriving working class. Today, with the mills long gone, Pittsburgh has what Gabe Morgan, who heads the local union of janitorial and building maintenance workers, calls an "eds and meds" economy. Carnegie Mellon, the University of Pittsburgh, and its medical center are among the region's largest employers, generating thousands of well-paid professional positions and a far greater number of low-wage service-sector jobs.

Peduto, who is 49 years old, sees improving the lot of Pittsburgh's new working class as his primary charge. In his city hall office, surrounded by such artifacts as a radio cabinet from the years when the city became home to the world's first radio station, the new mayor outlined the task before him. "My grandfather, Sam Zarroli, came over in 1921 from Abruzzo," he said. "He only had a second-grade education, but he was active in the Steel Workers Organizing Committee in its early years, and he made a good life for himself and his family. My challenge in today's economy is how to get good jobs for people with no PhDs but with a good work ethic and GEDs.

"The Revolt of the Cities" by Harold Meyerson. Originally published by The American Prospect, April 23, 2014.

How do I get them the same kind of opportunities my grandfather had? All the mayors elected last year are asking this question."

They are indeed. The mayoral and council class of 2013 is one of the most progressive cohorts of elected officials in recent American history. In one major city after another, newly elected officials are planning to raise the minimum wage or enact ordinances boosting wages in developments that have received city assistance. They are drafting legislation to require inner-city hiring on major projects and foster unionization in hotels, stores, and trucking. They are seeking the funds to establish universal pre-K and other programs for infants and toddlers. They are sketching the layout of new transit lines that will bring jobs and denser development to neighborhoods both poor and middle-class and reduce traffic and pollution in the bargain. They are—if they haven't done so already—forbidding their police from cooperating with federal immigration authorities in the deportation of undocumented immigrants not convicted of felonies and requiring their police to have video or audio records of their encounters with the public. They are, in short, enacting at the municipal level many of the major policy changes that progressives have found themselves unable to enact at the federal and state levels. They also may be charting a new course for American liberalism.

New York's Mayor Bill de Blasio has dominated the national press corps' coverage of the new urban liberalism. His battles to establish citywide pre-K (successful but not funded, as he wished, by a dedicated tax on the wealthy), expand paid sick days (also successful), raise the minimum wage (blocked by the governor and legislature), and reform the police department's stop-and-frisk policy (by dropping an appeal of a court order) have been extensively chronicled. But de Blasio is just one of a host of mayors elected last year who campaigned and now govern with similar populist agendas. The list also includes Pittsburgh's Peduto, Minneapolis's Betsy Hodges, Seattle's Ed Murray, Boston's Martin Walsh, Santa Fe's Javier Gonzales, and many more.

"We all ran on similar platforms," Peduto says. "There wasn't communication among us. It just emerged organically that way. We all faced the reality of growing disparities. The population beneath the poverty line is increasing everywhere. A lot of us were underdogs, populists, reformers, and the public was ready for us."

This isn't the first time that America's cities have collectively shifted their political identities. As political journalist Samuel Lubell documented in his 1951 study *The Future of American Politics*—most particularly his chapter "Revolt of the City"—the New Deal coalition was prefigured by the change in urban voting patterns during the 1920s. Since the end of the Civil War, the cities of the industrial Midwest and the West Coast had tilted Republican. In 1920, GOP presidential nominee Warren Harding carried the nation's 12 largest cities by a margin of 1.54 million votes. In 1928, however, Democratic presidential nominee Al Smith carried the same 12 cities by a margin of 210,000 votes. Smith was a Catholic—the only Catholic presidential nominee until John Kennedy ran in 1960—whose speech and manner stamped him unmistakably as a product of New York's Lower East Side. His candidacy brought to the polls for the first time millions of Southern and Eastern

European immigrants—predominantly Catholic, Jewish, and Eastern Orthodox—who had transformed the composition of American cities during the preceding 40 years but who had never before voted in large numbers. Four years later, they voted in still greater numbers, sending Franklin Roosevelt to the White House and cementing the nation's major cities in the Democratic column for decades to come. At the municipal level, cities long controlled by Republican machines shifted either to control by Democratic machines or by progressive reformers like New York's Fiorello La Guardia.

This pattern of demographic transformation is now repeating itself. New coalitions and the presidential campaigns of Barack Obama have brought millions of Latino, Asian, and African immigrants and the millennials to the polls, remaking the politics of cities in the process.

Even as the wave of non-European immigrants since the mid-1980s has reshaped the United States—whose white share of the population was down to 63 percent in 2012—it has reshaped its cities even more. In New York, which was 53 percent white in the 1980 census, the white share of its population dropped to 37 percent in the 2010 census. During the same 30 years, Los Angeles saw the white share of its population drop from 48 percent to 29 percent, Houston from 53 percent to 26 percent, Phoenix from 78 percent to 47 percent, San Diego from 69 percent to 45 percent, Dallas from 57 percent to 29 percent, Columbus from 76 percent to 59 percent, Boston from 68 percent to 47 percent, Seattle from 79 percent to 66 percent, and Denver from 67 percent to 52 percent.

It's not just the racial makeup of cities that is changing; it's also their generational profile: Cities have seen a marked increase in their share of 20-somethings. These changes in demographics have coincided with the change in economics. With both manufacturing and unions in steep decline, major cities have come to be characterized by levels of economic inequality—reinforced by levels of racial inequality—the nation has not experienced since before the New Deal.

In America, politics follow demographics: Voters of color and millennial voters stand well to the left of their white and older counterparts in their support for government intervention to counter the market's inequities and for Democratic candidates generally. The voting habits of major cities reflect these transformations. For example, Barack Obama's share of the vote in the 2012 presidential election outpaced Walter Mondale's share of the vote in the 1984 presidential election by 10.5 percent nationally, but the difference was far greater in cities. Obama outperformed Mondale by 20 percentage points in New York City, by 26 points in Los Angeles, 20 in San Diego, 24 in Dallas, 27 in Columbus, 22 in Seattle, and 24 in Denver.

At the level of municipal politics, the change is even starker. Twenty years ago, half of America's dozen largest cities had Republican mayors. Today, only San Diego is governed by a Republican, and he was elected in a low-turnout special election held to replace disgraced Democrat Bob Filner. Indeed, of the nation's 30 largest cities, just four (San Diego, Indianapolis, Fort Worth, and Oklahoma City) have Republican mayors, and even they have to swim with the urban tides. Mayor Greg

Ballard of Indianapolis supported increased federal aid to mass transit and opposed his state's ban on same-sex marriage.

Not every Democratic mayor is progressive, as the record of Chicago's Rahm Emanuel makes clear. Demographic recomposition has proved a necessary but insufficient prerequisite for urban political change. The newcomers to America's cities also have had to come together as an effective political force. With few exceptions, the cities that have elected left-populist governments have first reconfigured their power structures by building coalitions dedicated to greater economic and racial equity. Aided in some instances by liberal foundations, these coalitions consist chiefly of unions, community-based organizations in low-income minority neighborhoods, immigrants' rights groups, affordable-housing advocates, environmental organizations, and networks of liberal churches, synagogues, and mosques.

The unions that have been key to the formation of these new coalitions—it's labor, after all, that has the capacity to provide the lion's share of funding for these ventures—generally aren't the municipal employee locals that have a bargaining relationship with elected officials that can limit their freedom of political action. They tend, rather, to be unions of private-sector workers—janitors, hotel housekeepers, hospital orderlies, supermarket clerks. Their members and potential members are often overwhelmingly minority and substantially immigrant. Indeed, the growing importance of these unions coincides with the growth of immigrants' rights groups in most major cities. Their constituencies stand to gain the most from city policies that raise wages, create affordable housing, and establish community-based policing.

The new urban coalitions develop common strategies, register voters, regularly canvass their respective communities, groom candidates, research issues, propose policies, lobby elected officials, run their candidates' campaigns, and walk precincts. New York's Working Families Party—the organization that defined the issues and mobilized the constituencies for the campaigns that elected de Blasio and a progressive near majority on the city council—has proceeded furthest down the path to becoming a permanent social democratic and green political force. But many of the cities that went left last year have coalitions that have begun their own way down this path as well.

> With few exceptions, the cities that have elected left-populist governments have first reconfigured their power structures by building coalitions dedicated to greater economic and racial equity. . . . These coalitions consist chiefly of unions, community-based organizations in low-income minority neighborhoods, immigrants' rights groups, affordable-housing advocates, environmental organizations, and networks of liberal churches, synagogues, and mosques.

Pittsburgh, Minneapolis, Phoenix, and Seattle are among the cities that have incubated new labor-community coalitions over the past decade. In Pittsburgh, the coalition—named Pittsburgh United—began to take shape during the revitalization of the city's affiliate of SEIU's Local 32BJ, the East Coast regional local of janitorial and building-service workers. Along with Pittsburgh's union of hotel workers, 32BJ supported the city's main African American community organization's campaign to make inner-city hiring a condition for the city council's approval of the new Pittsburgh Penguins sports arena. In turn, the community group backed the unions' effort to persuade the council to enact an ordinance guaranteeing the jobs of fast-food and other franchise workers in city-owned facilities even if the franchise changed hands. These campaigns divided the city's unions—the building trades wanted to construct the arena regardless of who was hired to work inside it—but united the minority communities and the service-sector unions. In time, the alliance grew to include liberal clergy and groups devoted to cleaning Pittsburgh's air and water, particularly in working-class communities.

Initially, the coalition's sole council ally was Peduto, but that was soon to change. A group of young professionals who'd come together on John Kerry's 2004 presidential campaign set out to elect other progressives to the city council. "We didn't know the old ways of campaigning," says Matthew Merriman-Preston, the political consultant who has managed Peduto's campaigns and those of every other progressive council member for the past decade, "so we made it up as we went along. We had people on the ground talking to their neighbors year after year."

In 2009, Natalia Rudiak, a Pittsburgh native who had studied at the London School of Economics and done economic-development work in Africa, decided to run for council in a district she describes as "the most socially conservative in the city." In a city whose politics long had been dominated by middle-aged and elderly men, Rudiak, then 29 years old, wasn't taken seriously by the Democratic establishment. But Rudiak came with multiple ties to union leaders (her father ran a public-employees local) and had spent time on campaigns with Merriman-Preston. Peduto's prevailing-wage bill was pending in the council during her campaign, and she stumped for it everywhere she spoke. In return, 32BJ flooded her district with precinct walkers, as did environmental and feminist groups. Shortly after her upset victory, the council passed the bill.

Rudiak's victory was just one of several that reshaped the council between 2007 and 2013. Neither Rudiak nor Peduto received endorsements from the city's Democratic Party organizations, but the machine wasn't delivering city service as it once had. "It had kept the trains running on time and the streets plowed," Rudiak says, "but with the growing financial constraints on the city, particularly after the 2008 crash, it couldn't keep doing even those things." In the city's older working-class neighborhoods, the new alliance and its candidates proved to be better ward heelers than the machine.

Minneapolis is a city with a richer history of progressive activism than Pittsburgh. In 1948, Mayor Hubert Humphrey presented that year's Democratic National Convention with its first civil-rights platform plank. For decades, Minnesota came closer to an American version of Scandinavian social democracy than any other state.

In recent decades, however, both the city's and state's demographics and economy have been transformed. The white share of the city's population declined from 86 percent in the 1980 census to 64 percent in 2010. Minneapolis is home to the largest Somali community of any city except Mogadishu and the largest Hmong community outside Laos. "We're ahead of any other state in equitable income and health—if you're white," says Dan McGrath, who heads TakeAction Minnesota, a progressive political organization of 45,000 members, which, like New York's Working Families Party, functions chiefly as an electoral organization. "Minnesota's way down the list when you include people of color. Four out of ten Minneapolis residents are people of color. We won't have an economy 30 years from now if only half our minority students graduate high school."

Nearly a decade ago, several local progressive organizations, including the one established by Paul Wellstone, decided to merge into a single group, TakeAction Minnesota. At the same time, the city's SEIU–affiliated janitorial union and its chief affordable housing organization, ISAIAH, entered a period of rapid growth. The groups, along with the city's ACORN chapter, which was the main community-based organization in the African American community (and which has since reconstituted itself as Neighborhoods Organizing for Change), and CTUL, an organization of worker centers serving the Latino immigrant community, began meeting together regularly. In 2011, when the national SEIU decided to fund local coalitions in 17 cities across the country, the one in Minneapolis was the only such alliance to prove both effective and enduring—in part because its member groups had already forged such tight bonds.

"We're grounded in a common experience and analysis," McGrath says. "Our problem is not just Republicans. Our problem is the extraordinary imbalance of wealth, unbridled corporate power, and structural racism." The commonality of perspectives was augmented by the integration of the groups' members and staffs—attending retreats together, merging their efforts on various campaigns. "The groups had to acknowledge that none of them could get anything done just by themselves," says George Goehl, the executive director of National People's Action, a network of community organizations with which TakeAction Minnesota is affiliated. "They now have so deep a collaboration that when you go to one of their meetings, you can't tell who works for whom."

With the power of their combined numbers, the groups in the alliance—named Minnesotans for a Fair Economy—have waged a joint campaign to pressure Target, the locally based retail giant, to stop asking job applicants if they've been convicted of a felony, to cease the wage and hour violations inflicted on their largely immigrant janitorial workforce, and to hire local residents for maintenance jobs at the company's new headquarters. Target agreed to drop the question about felonies and to adopt a local hiring policy; talks continue about the unionization of their janitors. The alliance waged a successful long-shot campaign against a 2012 ballot measure that would have required state voters to provide photo IDs at their polling places. And last year, the alliance provided the staff and precinct walkers to put one of their own—council member Betsy Hodges, who had been the executive director of one of the two groups that merged to form TakeAction Minnesota—into the Minneapolis mayor's office.

Hodges, who is 44 and describes herself as a "sociologist by training," was the council's acknowledged authority on budget and funding matters. She ran on the issue of reducing the city's racial disparities. "I said the same thing in every room I spoke in," she told me when we met in her office in the cavernous city hall. "I said, 'In Minneapolis, we have the biggest racial gaps of any city by any measure. It is a moral imperative that we end that, but it's also an economic imperative.'" Hodges talked explicitly about white people, people of color, and racial disparities—terms that most campaign consultants would urge their clients to shun—and defeated her opponent, the chair of the state's Democratic-Farmer-Labor Party, by an 18-point margin.

"A whole lot of white people thought the issue she was addressing was our principal challenge," McGrath says. "That's remarkable." It's a testament to Minneapolis's enduring egalitarianism, but it's also a consequence of the door-knocking and issue campaigns of the city's liberal coalition. "There's been a lot of political space created by progressive strategic organizing here in the city," Hodges says. "It was hugely helpful to me as a candidate, but it will be even more helpful to me as a mayor. We have to make sure that everyone is at the table as we work on growing the city, and having people organized really facilitates that."

The projects on which Hodges has embarked include a "cradle to kindergarten" program of infant health care and universal pre-K. As a council member, she initiated a pilot program to provide "body cams" for police officers to monitor their encounters with the public; she now wants to mandate the cameras for the entire department. She's also seeking to route proposed transit lines to better connect minority communities to neighborhoods with jobs.

No city government may be more at odds with its governor and legislature than that of Phoenix. In 2010, Arizona enacted SB 1070, which encouraged police to stop and frisk Latinos and if they lacked documentation, to hand them over to federal agents for deportation. In response, the New York–based Four Freedoms Fund financed a massive voter-registration campaign in Phoenix's Latino communities. The backlash against SB 1070 also fueled the successful efforts of an alliance of Latino and immigrant organizations and unions to elect Greg Stanton mayor in 2011. Stanton campaigned for union rights and marriage equality and against SB 1070. Five of the city council's other eight members—three of whom are now Latinos—share Stanton's politics. The council has directed Phoenix police not to hand over detainees to immigration agents for deportation and instructed the city's lobbyist in Washington to support immigration reform.

Seattle's leftward movement commenced when local unions of janitorial, health-care, supermarket, and warehouse workers formed a labor-community-environment alliance to win a living-wage ordinance. The regional tech boom has brought thousands of young professionals to the city, who have proved supportive of the coalition's campaigns. "They're open to human rights and environmental issues, of course," says David West, who heads the alliance, "but they're also not tax-averse and are strongly in favor of raising the minimum wage." Going into last year's city elections, Seattle already had a law for paid sick leave and one of the highest municipal minimum wages in the nation. A successful SEIU–led campaign to raise the hourly minimum to $15 in the small suburban community of SeaTac, adjoining Seattle's airport, made raising the city's own minimum to $15 the major issue in November's mayoral campaign. Both candidates supported the raise, and the issue also swept a Trotskyist candidate onto the city council. The city's new mayor, Ed Murray, who was chiefly known for his successful effort as a state legislator to legalize same-sex marriage, is negotiating the specifics of the raise.

Seattle's pro-labor liberalism has trumped what many might view as its infatuation with all things techie. The city council capped the number of business licenses for such car services as Uber and Lyft after a campaign that cast the issue as a contest between outside investors and local Ethiopian-immigrant cab drivers. Last year, Murray's predecessor blocked the construction of a Whole Foods market because of the chain's anti-union stance.

The city's ability to thwart the coming of a Whole Foods illustrates the often-circuitous ways in which municipalities are able to leverage their power to win the social outcomes they seek. Seattle was able to block Whole Foods by exercising its power over streets, since building the new market would have required the elimination of an existing alley.

"Even when they're fiscally constrained, cities can set their own rules," Pittsburgh's Peduto says. By leveraging their power over contractors and developers who've received city assistance—or who may merely need city approval to close off an alley—municipal progressives are following the lead of the Los Angeles Alliance for a New Economy (LAANE), the group that pioneered the practice of requiring living wages and community hiring. Such measures are intended to accomplish indirectly and, at times, ingeniously what the federal government could accomplish directly, say, by raising the minimum wage, rewriting labor law, establishing stronger environmental safeguards, or legalizing undocumented immigrants. In the absence of such national legislation, cities are doing what they can.

The fiscal constraints to which Peduto alluded, though, are real. New York's de Blasio had to secure the funding that establishes pre-K education in his city from the state—a revenue stream the city doesn't control. Governor Andrew Cuomo, a Democrat, and Republican state senators blocked de Blasio and his city council allies from setting a municipal minimum wage in New York City, though living expenses there are far greater than they are in the rest of the state. A number of states have enacted laws forbidding their cities from raising wages or passing living-wage ordinances.

Shortly after November's city elections, President Obama invited 16 of the newly elected progressive mayors to a meeting at the White House. Peduto, Hodges, Murray, and de Blasio were among those who attended. Obama talked about his proposal for universal pre-K, which was languishing in Congress. At the federal level, it would obviously take some time to get such a measure enacted, Obama continued, or he could find 20 innovative mayors and get it done tomorrow. Provided they can scrape up the dollars.

Even within those limitations, it's in blue states and cities—certainly not in Congress—that Obama's agenda is being enacted. While increasing the minimum wage remains stymied on Capitol Hill, legislatures in Democratic states are hiking it to the level that Obama proposed, while cities have either increased theirs even more (Washington, D.C., raised its minimum to $11.50) or are considering it (San Francisco, like Seattle, to $15). While congressional Republicans resist legislation to combat global warming, cities are demanding strict energy-efficiency standards in their new buildings. While Republicans oppose legalizing undocumented immigrants, cities are ordering their police departments, in effect, to minimize deportations.

What's happening in cities can be described as Obama's agenda trickling down to the jurisdictions where it has enough political support to be enacted—but it's also the incubation of policies and practices that will trickle up. With considerable creativity and limited power, the new urban regimes are seeking to diminish the inequality so apparent in cities and so pervasive nationwide. They are mapping the future of liberalism until the day when the national government can bring it to scale.

The Gentrification Effect

By Thomas B. Edsall
The New York Times, February 25, 2015

When Marion Barry first became mayor of Washington in 1979, the city was more than 70 percent black. Whites made up 26.9 percent of residents; 2.8 percent were Hispanic.

When Barry died on November 23, [2014,] Washington had lost its claim to the title Chocolate City. The black population had fallen below 50 percent, the percentage of whites had grown to 35.8 percent and the Hispanic population had reached 10.1 percent.

In Chicago, when Harold Washington was elected the first African-American mayor of that city in 1983, blacks and whites each made up roughly 40 percent of the population, with Hispanics at 14 percent. Today, as Rahm Emanuel, the current mayor, finds himself forced into a runoff with Jesus Garcia, blacks have dropped to 32.9 percent, and whites to 31.7. Hispanics are now at 28.9 percent.

The nation's urban centers are changing rapidly. Blacks are moving out, into the suburbs or to other regions of the country. Poverty is spreading from the urban core to the inner suburbs. White flight has slowed and in some cases reversed. Nationally, Hispanics have displaced blacks as the dominant urban minority.

The political impact of these changes is primarily being felt within the Democratic Party, where the balance of power is shifting.

As well-educated, younger liberal whites gain strength in some cities, their power base will be amplified—a development partly reflected in the marginalization of Marion Barry and his brand of machine politics in Washington before his death.

The relatively upscale city-dwelling wing of the national Democratic Party already wields great power, ensuring that same-sex marriage, green initiatives, gender equality and reproductive rights are stressed as much, or more, than issues like wages and jobs.

While many cities are experiencing an influx of young whites, those gains are more than offset by the continuing exodus of working- and middle-class whites. The result is a net decline nationwide of the white share of city populations.

Hispanic ascendance is apparent in both cities and suburbs, increasing the likelihood of the election of Latinos to local, state and federal office.

Over time, blacks stand to lose leverage. Cities have been a crucial base of power for African-American politicians. Insofar as the black population becomes diffuse,

From The New York Times, February 25 © 2015 The New York Times. All rights reserved. Used by permission and protected by the Copyright Laws of the United States. The printing, copying, redistribution, or retransmission of this Content without express written permission is prohibited.

black leaders will have to grapple with a decline in black-majority districts, especially city council districts, in cities with declining black populations.

William Frey, a Brookings scholar and author of *Diversity Explosion: How New Racial Demographics Are Remaking America*, responded by email to my query about the political consequences of population changes in the cities and suburbs:

> With the new black flight to the suburbs following decades of white flight, Hispanics will have an ever bigger role to play in big city politics and even in the suburbs. In Chicago for example whose politics were for decades dictated by different black and white ethnic constituencies, Hispanics are playing a much greater role.

This process will be replicated in every region of the country, Frey wrote, "as black suburbanization is fairly pervasive and the biggest source of minority gains in many cities is Hispanics."

Frey pointed toward the rapidly increasing strength of the Latino vote in the 100 largest metropolitan areas. Between 1990 and 2010, the percentage of city dwellers in such areas who are Hispanic grew to 26 percent from 17 percent; and the share of suburban residents who are Hispanic rose to 17 percent from 8 percent. . . .

One of the most striking alterations of the urban landscape is that there are now more poor people, in raw numbers, living in suburbs than in cities.

"The economically turbulent 2000s have redrawn America's geography of poverty," Elizabeth Kneebone, a Brookings Institution researcher, wrote in July [2015]. While the national poverty rate has remained stubbornly high, the poor are moving.

"More of those residents live in suburbs than in big cities or rural communities, a significant shift compared to 2000, when the urban poor still outnumbered suburban residents living in poverty," according to Kneebone.

In February, *Governing* magazine published a study of census tracts in cities across the nation. The study defined as "gentrification eligible" tracts in which median household income and the value of homes stood below the 40th percentile for the city as a whole. To become gentrified, a census tract would have to move up into the city's top third in terms of median income and housing values.

Mike Maciag, *Governing*'s data editor, found that the "gentrification rate was 20 percent for the period following the 2000 census"—more than double the 8.6 percent rate of the 1990s.

Using data from 1990, 2000 and 2010, Maciag found that in four major cities 50 percent or more of poor census tracts gentrified from 2000 to 2010: Portland, 58.1 percent; Washington, 51.9 percent; Minneapolis, 50.6 percent; and Seattle, 50 percent.

Other cities experiencing substantial gentrification were Denver, 42.1 percent; Austin, 39.7 percent; New York, 29.8 percent; Philadelphia, 28.7 percent; San Diego, 27.5 percent; Baltimore, 23.2 percent; and Boston, 21.1 percent.

The migration of professionals, often with advanced degrees, into the core of the nation's cities is graphically illustrated in a study conducted at the University of Virginia.

Luke Juday, a research and demographic policy analyst at the University of

Virginia, found striking changes between 1990 and 2010 in income and education patterns in Charlotte, N.C.

In 1990, the highest level of education was found in the suburbs, seven to eight miles distant from the heart of Charlotte. By 2012, the Charlotte city center itself had the highest percentage of residents with college degrees. In an email, Juday said the same pattern could be found in cities across the nation. He plans to publish more comprehensive data in March [2015].

Education and income move in tandem—that is, levels of per capita income follow the same pattern as levels of educational attainment.

Using a larger database, Frey notes in *Diversity Explosion* that in 13 of 20 of the cities with the largest black populations, the number of African-Americans declined from 2000 to 2010: Detroit, down 185,392; Chicago, down 181,453; New Orleans, down 118,526; New York, 100,859; and Los Angeles, 54,606.

"Clearly, the black presence, which has been the mainstay of many large city populations, is diminishing," Frey writes.

While gentrification is accelerating, it is not characteristic of all major cities. Looking at the racial makeup of the 100 largest cities, Frey found that the number with nonwhite majorities grew substantially from 2000 to 2010, from 42 to 58.

According to Frey, of the 16 cities that became majority-minority, Hispanics were responsible for the change in 14, including Phoenix, Austin and Las Vegas.

The metropolitan areas that are continuing to experience traditional white flight from the city core are heavily concentrated in the Midwest, particularly in the central time zone, according to Frey's data. Among them are St. Louis, Kansas City, Columbus, Memphis, Houston and Dallas.

The advantages for Democrats of these population transitions are notable. First, in big cities, a transformation of the white versus black struggle for power is increasingly a three-way contest: whites versus blacks versus Hispanics. Racial conflict is becoming more diluted.

Second, as the black and Hispanic populations disperse, these heavily Democratic constituencies will influence the election outcomes in an increasing number of congressional districts. This will lessen one of the Democrats' liabilities: the huge concentration of favorable voters in city districts that vote Democratic by 3 to 1 or better margins, effectively wasting voters who would be more beneficial to the party if located in competitive districts.

On the plus side for Republicans, the influx into the suburbs of minorities and the poor—which raises the possibility of attendant tax increases, property value declines, social service demands and crime—could push local whites to the right, into Republican arms.

In addition, there is the prospect that Democratic primaries pitting a Latino candidate against an African-American candidate for local or federal office will prompt Republicans to run Latino candidates in the general election, challenging black Democratic nominees.

The issues at stake transcend elective politics. The great urban historian Thomas Sugrue, a professor of history and sociology at the University of Pennsylvania, addresses the broader question, "How can the core characteristics of big cities be mobilized to make human life more just and democratic?"

In an essay titled "Diversity, Toleration, and Space in Metropolitan America" Sugrue writes:

> In metropolitan America, particularly in those conurbations that have grown increasingly diverse by race and ethnicity in the last few decades, America's past and its uncertain future collide. On one side are deep historical patterns of segregation and hypersegregation that reinforce racial inequality and hostilities, particularly between black and white; on the other, an increasingly polyglot, perhaps majority minority nation, where the old binaries of race no longer hold.

> Some futurists contend that by 2040, America will be a brown-hued nation, its once dominant European-descended population blended into a new whole. Others look toward a post-racial America where intermarriage and intermixing will destroy the "ethnoracial pentagon," which rigidly classifies all Americans as African, Asian, Latino, Native American, or white.

It's very hard to predict one way or the other. Outcomes could be either bleak or bright. "Not all are optimistic," Sugrue continues.

> The growing trends of class inequality, combined with persistent segregation, have led some to suggest that trends point toward a United States that resembles Colombia or Brazil, places of extraordinary diversity in color, where everyday interracial contact and tolerance are commonplace but where a still-deeply entrenched color hierarchy economically and socially disadvantages those of African and Amerindian descent.

Sugrue quite reasonably declines to make predictions:

> Any one of these prognostications may be correct, but history offers no guide to the future, other than the chastening lesson that the vast majority of past demographic and economic predictions, especially those made with great certainty, are frequently wrong.

These American Cities Are Fighting for Control over Electricity and the Internet

By Max Holleran
openDemocracy, April 21, 2015

As anyone who has paid a giant electric or water bill knows, utilities are big business. Today in the United States, multinational companies have bought up these formerly public institutions. In the name of efficiency and economies of scale—not to mention profit—many cities have sold their electricity generation stations, given up on public transport, and privatized their water.

Corporate management of previously public goods has led to dreadful human costs: from scores of low income residents of Detroit having their water turned off to some of the highest internet prices in the world. It has deprived citizens of the right to collectively decide how to administer urban services, or to control levels of environmental sustainability.

This disempowerment of US urbanites has been two-fold: first, by the Reaganomics doctrine of mass privatization and, second, by state governments, which are often more conservative and less inclined to embrace policy experiments.

However, things may be changing.

With frustrations growing over the cost of municipal services and their ecological sustainability, cities have started to fight back, starting a process of "municipalization." Mayors and city councils, spurred by grassroots activism, are experimenting with green public energy, improved rail service, and even reinvesting in public housing.

From the left-wing Bill de Blasio, of New York, to more-conservative midwestern mayors, municipal governments are returning services like internet, electricity, and housing to the public domain. A signature aspect of de Blasio's vision for New York is to create hundreds of thousands of units of affordable housing in order to shrink the difference between the 'Tale of Two Cities": one defined by poverty and precarity, and the other by penthouses.

Most of the projects involve some degree of public-private partnership—in the form of social impact bonds or subcontracting—but all of them restore control to cities and their citizens.

For decades, people living in American cities have felt marginalized by divestment in housing and transport: often at the behest of state politicians unfamiliar with the routines of urban life. What's more, urbanites—who are overwhelmingly in

Reprinted with permission.

favor of Keynesian economics and social programs—have felt victimized by companies that administer state-granted monopolies for services like gas, electric, water, and internet. In contrast to Europe, public investment for solar and wind energy is abysmal. The US Department of Transportation has consistently warned that if cities cannot find funds to update infrastructure there could be fatal consequences.

The cumulative effect of divestment in municipal services and infrastructure is a sense among city dwellers that they are already living in a semi-dystopia bereft of basic services. But for this same reason, many people living in cities have embraced projects that rely on collective action and community-based decision making. On the small scale, this could be an organic garden, but others wish to scale-up these actions to include, for example, fair housing provided by community land trusts, nonprofit high-speed internet, and ecologically-sustainable and publicly-administered electricity.

Today, cities are taking advantage of their policy autonomy, unlike states—which often use their federalist powers to subvert forward-thinking legislation around racial integration, environmental protection, or healthcare. They are pushing back against Congress' lack of action on corporate profiteering from the public sector and climate change denial.

What that means for average citizens is that while their confidence in Congress plummets, they have found local governments closer to home that seem to be willing to experiment and address the harder environmental and economic issues.

> **From the left-wing Bill de Blasio, of New York, to more-conservative midwestern mayors, municipal governments are returning services like internet, electricity, and housing to the public domain.**

Towns like Boulder, Colorado, are buying back their electricity grid in the name of greener energy and lower prices, while other cities in Colorado and California are investing in rail transit. Communities are embracing this movement as a way to rekindle the notion that public ownership can help to secure services—like internet access, electricity, and housing—as social rights.

In the past two years, we have seen a bounty of new policies emanating from cities that address problems long-ignored by the federal legislature. This includes: IDs for undocumented immigrants (New York City), housing for the homeless (Salt Lake City), and a liveable minimum wage (Seattle). With gridlock as the prevailing creed of national legislatures and laissez-faire economics as the chant coming from most statehouses, cities have been surprisingly militant in their drive to push through creative new policies.

Nothing exemplifies this more than new utilities created at the municipal level in order to lower consumer prices for internet and electricity and to push for green energy.

In February [2015], along with coming out for net neutrality, the Federal Communications Commission (FCC) upheld the right of municipalities to create their own public internet utilities, reversing state laws that forbade this. This seems like a logical ruling. Yet in Wilson, North Carolina, residents had to fight to keep their newly-formed public internet after legal challenges from Time Warner.

Wilson created their public internet (called Greenlight Community Broadband) in order to better serve rural residents and to lower rates. Time Warner was so indignant with this action that they spent millions on litigation to challenge the legality of Wilson's program, as well as against a larger experiment in Chattanooga, Tennessee. Despite deep pockets and support from market-fundamentalist state legislatures, Time Warner lost.

Other communities are realizing their collective interests lie in increased direction over the energy market. Good examples of long-term models are San Antonio, Austin, and Sacramento, which all operate municipal power companies with competitive rates. They are inspiring other cities that gave up their utilities a generation ago.

Advocates like the Institute for Local Self Reliance maintain that municipal energy programs reverse the trend of privatization and corporate ownership, which helps reduce prices by removing profit motives. They also contend that many cities were actually losing money moving power regionally and maintaining a larger-than-necessary infrastructure. This is a viewpoint that should make a lot of sense to Republicans, who espouse the virtues of the Jeffersonian model of small government, with high participation at the community level.

Yet both Democrats and Republicans are beholden to check-writers: many of whom are in the energy or telecommunications businesses. But as grassroots coalitions for responsible energy and community internet show, people do want to get involved in local projects that produce tangible community goods. Many find this a welcome antidote to the usual forms of participation which concentrate on electoral campaigning.

Other cities have experimented with municipalization of their energy for more altruistic, less-budget-related reasons. Boulder in Colorado is a perfect example. Boulder, a college town which sits at the foot of the Rocky Mountains, is well-known for a progressive spirit and a strong sense of environmentalism. Citizens there recently approved two ballot measures that pave the way for de-privatizing the electricity grid in order to become less reliant on coal-burning and utilize more solar power.

This move was vociferously fought in court by the current energy provider, Xcel, a company from Minneapolis, which has spent millions of dollars contesting the city's right to buy the power grid and administer its own electricity. Boulder's attempt to wrestle back control of their power is not a protest against high bills, but against the pathetic status quo of green energy in the United States: even in Colorado ample sun and a powerful conservation movement has not made much impact on quitting carbon. Boulder is rated as the healthiest city in the country, with the most bike paths, and many people have wondered for years why their energy plan could not look more like them: fit, slightly unconventional, and environmentally attuned.

Now, with citizen-led movements that address energy, internet, and transport as collective goods—to be deliberated by communities—they have the opportunity.

Cities like Boulder, with high per capita income, are in a good position both to municipalize and to attract investors to buy municipal bonds in order to support future experimentation. Boulder has already spent 10 million dollars, approved by taxpayers, to assess the feasibility of a public alternative. The results are promising. Boulderites hope to finally harness the greenest energy available and not, like private utilities, to simply extract green dollars from bill-payers.

The fight for municipal utilities is an important kind of localism that dumps the fatuous proclamations of the Republican Congress on the subject of the glories of small town America and actually tries to get down to business.

Long before America's cities were demonized as paradises for crime and drugs (and consequently reborn for yuppies interested in grit and nostalgia) they were centers of policy experimentation. From Hull House's poverty alleviation in Chicago to the New Deal public works in Fiorello LaGuardia's New Deal New York, American cities have a strong history of experimental projects that utilize public control.

Some of these programs, like the much-maligned, now-destroyed public housing projects of Chicago and Saint Louis, did not work as planned. But the legacy of animosity toward all public ownership has been disproportionate to its failures. Also, the American anti-collectivist standpoint has never reckoned with the quieter, but no-less-pernicious, effects of the private sector squeezing all-profit-possible out of public services.

Cities, like New York under Mayor Bill de Blasio, have decided that there is no more standing on the sidelines and public investment in housing, infrastructure, and services must come now. They did not get to this point by accident. Rather, too many people felt the financial pinch of high bills or saw sooty skies and unclean water and wondered how this kind of neglect was possible. By taking community control, many cities have seen that they can move towards clean energy and fair prices for basic services independently without waiting for answers to "trickle-down" from Washington, DC.

Bibliography

"The Academy: Curriculum and Organization." *UPenn*. University of Pennsylvania University Archives & Records Center. 2004. Web. Aug 10 2015.

"Ambient (outdoor) Air Quality and Health." *WHO*. World Health Organization. Mar 2014. Web. Aug 3 2015.

"American Public Education: An Origin Story." *Education News*. Education News Inc. Apr 16 2013. Web. Aug 10 2015.

"Americans Say They Like Diverse Communities; Election, Census Trends Suggest Otherwise." *Pew Social Trends*. Pew Research Center. Dec 2 2008. Pdf. Aug 5 2015.

Ames, David L. "Interpreting Post-World War II Suburban Landscapes as Historic Resources." *NPS*. National Park Service. Web. Aug 4 2015.

Badenhausen, Kurt. "The Best Small Cities for Business and Careers 2015." *Forbes*. Forbes, Inc. Jul 29 2015. Web. Aug 6 2015.

Baskas, Harried. "Bike-Sharing Booming in US Cities." *CNBC*. CNBC News LLC. May 17 2014. Web. Aug 3 2015.

Bergal, Jenni. "Cities Forge Policy Apart from States." *Pew Trusts*. Pew Charitable Trusts. Jan 15 2015. Web. Aug 12 2015.

Blakeslee, Jan. "'White Flight to the Suburbs: A Demographic Approach." *Focus*. Institute for Research on Poverty Newsletter. Vol 3, Number 2: Winter 1978–79. Pdf. Aug 5 2015.

Bowles, Jonathan, and David Giles. "New City Tech." *NYC Future*. Center for an Urban Future. May 2012. Pdf. Aug 6 2015.

Boyer, Christine M. "Meditations on a Wounded Skyline and Its Stratigraphies of Pain," in Sorkin, Michael, and Sharon Zukin, Eds, *After the World Trade Center: Rethinking New York City*. New York: Routledge, 2002. Print.

Branson, Richard. "War on Drugs a Trillion-Dollar Failure." *CNN*. Cable New Network. Dec 7 2012. Web. Aug 7 2015.

"Busking It." *The Economist*. The Economist Newspaper Limited. Oct 12 2013. Web. Aug 12 2015.

Caprotti, Federico. *Eco-Cities and the Transition to Low Carbon Economies*. New York: St. Martin's Press, 2015. Print.

Carlyle, Erin. "America's Fastest-Growing Cities 2015." *Forbes*. Forbes Inc. Jan 27 2015. Web. Aug 5 2015.

Carlyle, Erin. "America's 20 Fastest-Growing Cities." *Forbes*. Forbes Inc. Feb 14 2014. Web. Aug 6 2015.

Carlyle, Erin, "America's Most Affordable Cities in 2015." *Forbes*. Forbes Inc. Mar 12 2015. Web. Aug 5 2015.

Carlyle, Erin. "San Francisco Tops Forbes' 2015 List of Worst Cities for Renters." *Forbes*. Forbes Inc. Apr 16 2015. Web. Aug 5 2015.

Census Bureau. "2010 Census Urban Area FAQs." *Census*. 2015. Web. Aug 8 2015.

"Charter Schools-Fast Facts." *NCES*. National Center for Education Statistics. U.S. Department of Education. 2014. Web. Aug 10 2015.

Chen, David W. "When Rent Control Just Vanishes; Both Sides of Debate Cite Boston Example." *New York Times*. Jun 15 2003. Web. Aug 26 2015.

Coleman-Jensen, et al. "Household Food Security in the United States 2011." *USDA*. United States Department of Agriculture. Sep 2012. Pdf. Aug 3 2015.

"Criminal Justice Fact Sheet." *NAACP*. National Association for the Advancement of Colored People. 2015. Pdf. Aug 7 2015.

Currid-Halkid, Elizabeth. "Evolving Perspectives on the Arts, Place, and Development," in Crane, Randall, and Rachel Weber, Eds, *The Oxford Handbook of Urban Planning*. New York: Oxford University Press, 2012, 373–392.

"The Death of Michael Brown." *New York Times*. New York Times Company. Aug 12 2014. Web. Aug 5 2015.

De Melker, Saksia. "'The History of American Graffiti:' From Subway Car to Gallery." *PBS*. PBS Newshour. Mar 31 2011. Web. Aug 12 2015.

Denvir, Daniel. "Voter Turnout in U.S. Mayoral Elections Is Pathetic, but It Wasn't Always This Way." *Citylab*. Atlantic Monthly Group. May 22 2015. Web. Aug 10 2015.

Desilver, Drew. "Chart of the Week: The Most Liberal and Conservative Big Cities." *Pew Research*. Pew Research Center. Aug 8 2014. Web. Aug 8 2015.

Desilver, Drew. "How the Most Ideologically Polarized Americans Live Different Lives." *Pew Research*. Pew Research Center. Jun 13 2014. Web. Aug 10 2015.

Douglas, George H. *Skyscrapers: A Social History of the Very Tall Building in America*. Jefferson, NC: McFarland & Company, Inc. 1996. Print.

Eisenstein, Paul A. "A Ban on Autos? Major Cities Consider Going Carless." *CNBC*. CNBC News LLC. Jan 26 2014. Web. Aug 3 2015.

"Environmental Performance Index." *Yale*. Yale University 2014 EPI. 2015. Web. Aug 3 2015.

"Eric Garner, Michael Brown Cases Spark 'Legitimate Concerns' About US Policing—UN Experts." *UN*. United Nations News Center. 2015. Web. Aug 7 2015.

Eversley, Melanie. "Hard-knocks Cities Are Working on a Comeback." *USA Today*. Gannett Media Company. Jul 24 2014. Web. Aug 15 2015.

Florida, Richard. "The Joys of Urban Tech." *The Wall Street Journal*. Dow Jones & Company. Aug 31 2012. Web. Aug 6 2015.

Frey, William H., and Zachary Zimmer. "Defining the City," in, Paddison, Ronan, Ed. *Handbook of Urban Studies*. London: Sage Publications, 2001. Print.

Gearty, Robert, and Corky Siemaszko. "NYPD Stop-and-Frisk Policy Yielded 4.4 Million Detentions but Few Results: Study." *NY Daily News*. New York Daily News. Apr 3 2013. Web. Aug 7 2015.

Glaeser, Edward L., and Andrei Shleifer. "The Curley Affect: The Economics of Shaping the Electorate." *The Journal of Law and Economics*. Vol. 21, No. 1 2005.

"Going Native." *NCSU*. NC State University. Benefits of Going Native. Forest Service NC. 2013. Web. Aug 3 2015.

"Green Roofs." *EPA*. Environmental Protection Agency. 2013. Web. Aug 3 2015.

Hargreaves, Steve. "America's Jobs Are Moving to the Suburbs." *CNN Money*. Cable News Network, Inc. Time Warner. Apr 18 2013. Web. Aug 6 2015.

Heath, Brad. "Racial Gap in U.S. Arrest Rates: 'Staggering.'" *USA Today*. Gannett Media. Nov 19 2014. Web. Aug 7 2015.

Hesson, Ted. "Why American Cities Are Fighting to Attract Immigrants." *The Atlantic*. Jul 21 2015. Web. Aug 27 2015.

"Highlights from PISA 2009: Performance of U.S. 15-Year-Old Students in Reading, Mathematics, and Science Literacy in an International Context." *NCES*. Naitonal Center for Education Statistics. U.S. Department of Education. 2011. Pdf. Aug 10 2015.

Hinton, Elizabeth. "Why We Should Reconsider the War on Crime." *Time*. Time, Inc. Mar 20 2015. Web. Aug 7 2015.

Hogan, Marc. "How Much Is Music Really Worth?" *Pitchfork*. Pitchfork Media Inc. Apr 16 2015. Web. Aug 10 2015.

Hollingsworth, Mary. *Art in World History*. Farenze, Milan, Italy: Giunti. 2003. Print.

Hook, Janet. "Liberals Make Big Comeback in 2015, Poll Analysis Finds." *Wall Street Journal*. Dow Jones & Company. Jun 7 2015. Web. Aug 10 2015.

Hudson, Kris. "Generation Y Prefers Suburban Home of City Condo." *Wall Street Journal*. Dow Jones & Company. Jan 21 2015. Web. Aug 5 2015.

Hurdle, Jon, "Philadelphia Raises Stakes with Plan to Reverse Blight." *New York Times*. New York Times Company. Sep 22 2013. Web. Aug 6 2015.

"Indego." *Ride Indigo*. 2015. Web. Aug 3 2015.

Ingraham, Christopher. "White People Are More Likely to Deal Drugs, but Black People Are More Likely to Get Arrested for It." *Washington Post*. Nash Holdings. Sep 30 2014. Web. Aug 7 2015.

Jackson, Kenneth T. *Crabgrass Frontier: The Suburbanization of the United States*. New York: Oxford University Press, 1985. Print.

Jensen, Eric. *Teaching with Poverty in Mind*. Alexandria, VA: ASCD, 2009. Print.

Juday, Luke J. "The Changing Shape of American Cities." *Cooper Center*. Weldon Cooper Center for Public Service. University of Virginia. Demographics Research Group. March 2015. Pdf. Aug 5 2015.

Kansas State University. "Poverty Is Rooted in US Education System, Research Finds." *Science Daily*. Science Daily Inc. May 5 2009. Web. Aug 10 2015.

Koebler, Jason. "On 10th Anniversary, a Look Back at 'No Child' Legacy." US News. *U.S. News and World Report*. Jan 4 2012. Web. Aug 11 2015.

Kolko, Jed. "Urban Headwinds, Suburban Tailwinds." *Huffington Post*. The Huffington Post, Inc. Apr 13 2015. Web. Aug 5 2015.

Kopp, Wendy. "Do American Schools Need to Change? Depends What You Compare Them To." *Atlantic*. Atlantic Monthly Group. Oct 25 2013. Web. Aug 10 2015.

Kotkin, Joel. "The Rustbelt Roars Back from the Dead." *The Daily Beast*. The Daily Beast Company LLC. 2014. Web. Aug 26 2015.

Kron, Josh. "Red State, Blue City: How the Urban-Rural Divide Is Splitting America." *The Atlantic*. Atlantic Monthly Group. Nov 30 2012. Web. Aug 10 2015.

Kushner, David, *Levittown: Two Families, One Tycoon, and the Fight for Civil Rights in America's Legendary Suburb*. New York: Walker Publishing, 2009.

"Large-Scale Offshore Wind Power in the United States: Assessment of Opportunities and Barriers." *NREL*. National Renewable Energy Laboratory. Sep. 2010. PDF.

Levy, John M. *Contemporary Urban Planning*. New York: Routledge, 2013. Print.

Lind, Dara. and German Lopez. "16 Theories for Why Crime Plummeted in the US." *VOX*. Vox Media. May 20 2015. Web. Aug 7 2015.

Mathis, Sommer. "Overall, Americans in the Suburbs Are Still the Happiest." *Citylab*. Atlantic Monthly Group. Aug 25 2014. Web. Aug 10 2015.

McBride, Alex. "Brown v. Board of Education (1954)." *PBS*. Public Broadcasting Station. The Supreme Court. Landmark Cases. 2006. Web. Aug 10 2015.

McKenzie, Brian. "Modes Less Traveled—Bicycling and Walking to Work in the United States: 2008–2012." *Census.gov*. United States Census Bureau. May 2014. Web. 17 Nov. 2014.

Mendoza, Martha. "U.S. Drug War Has Met None of Its Goals." *NBC News*. NBC. May 13 2010. Web. Aug 9 2015.

Mieszkowski, Peter, and Edwin S. Mills. "The Causes of Metropolitan Suburbanization." *Journal of Economic Perspectives*. Vol 7, No. 3, 1993. Pp. 135–147. Print.

"Millennials: Breaking the Myths." *Nielsen*. The Nielsen Company. Jan 27 2014. Pdf. Aug 5 2015.

"Millennials Prefer Cities to Suburbs, Subways to Driveways." *Nielsen*. The Nielsen Company. Mar 4 2014. Web. Aug 5 2015.

Morley, Neville. "Population Size and Structure," in Erdkamp, Paul. *The Cambridge Companion to Ancient Rome*. New York: Cambridge University Press, 2013. Print.

Moyers, Bill. "The Great American Class War." *Huffingtonpost*. Huffington Post. Dec 11 2014. Web. Aug 12 2015.

"NYC Parks: The High Line." *Museum of the City*. 2015. Web. Aug 10 2015.

Pagar, Devah. *Marked: Race, Crime, and Finding Work in an Era of Mass Incarceration*. Chicago: University of Chicago Press. 2007. Print.

Pentland, William. "Top 16 U.S. Cities for Solar Power." *Forbes*. Forbes Inc. May 22 2015. Web. Aug 3 2015.

"Population—Current Population Estimates." *NYC*. Department of City Planning. City of New York. July 2014. Web. Aug 9 2015.

"The Postwar Economy: 1945–1960." *Rutgers*. Rutgers University. American History. 2012. Web. Aug 6 2015.

"The Prison Crisis." *ACLU*. American Civil Liberties Union. ACLU Foundation. 2015. Web. Aug 7 2015.

"Public and Private Schools: How Do They Differ." *NCES*. National Center for Education Statistics. 1997. Pdf. Aug 28 2015.

Quinton, Sophie. "States Battle Cities over Minimum Wage." *Huff Post Politics*. Huffington Post. Jul 13 2015. Web. Aug 12 2015.

"Raleigh Demographics." *City of Raleigh*. Feb 25 2015. Web. Aug 9 2015.

Reese, William J. *American Public Schools: From 'Common Schools' to 'No Child Left Behind.'* Baltimore, MD: Johns Hopkins University Press, 2011. Print.

"Rental Housing Affordability." *Harvard*. Harvard University Press. 2011. Pdf. Aug 5 2015.

"Rise of Industrial America, 1876–1900." *LOC*. Library of Congress. City Life in the Late 19th Century. Classroom Materials. 2015. Web. Aug 8 2015.

Roose, Kevin. "The Tech Sector's New, Urban Aesthetic." *NYMag*. New York Magazine. New York Media, LLC. May 13 2014. Web. Aug 5 2015.

Rotman, Michael. "Cuyahoga River Fire." *Cleveland Historical*. Center for Public History + Digital Humanities. 2015. Web. Aug 3 2015.

Sanchez, Claudio. "The Charter School vs. Public School Debate Continues." *NPR*. National Public Radio. Jul 16 2013. Web. Aug 11 2015.

Schlesinger, Robert. "The 2015 U.S. and World Populations." *U.S. News*. U.S. News and World Report. Dec 31 2014. Web. Aug 8 2015.

Scribner, Christopher MacGregor, *Renewing Birmingham: Federal Funding and the Promise of Change, 1929–1979*. Athens: GA: University of Georgia Press, 2002. Print.

Solli, Christian. *Global Carbon Footprints*. Copenhagen, Denmark: Nordic Council of Ministers. Nov 1, 2010. Print.

"Sources of Greenhouse Gas Emissions." *EPA*. Environmental Protection Agency. Jun 21 2015. Web. Aug 3 2015.

"Statue of Liberty." *UNESCO*. United Nations Educational, Scientific and Cultural Organization. World Heritage Convention. World Heritage List. 2014. Web. Aug 9 2015.

Straughn, Celka, and Howard Gardner. "Goodwork in Museums Today. . . And Tomorrow," in Marstine, Janet, ed. *Routledge Companion to Museum Ethics: Redefining Ethics for the Twenty-First Century*. New York: Routledge, 2011, pp. 41–54. Print.

Strauss, Valerie. "Poll: What Americans Say About Public Education." *The Washington Post*. Nash Holdings. Aug 22 2012. Web. Aug 10 2015.

"Sustainable Cities Index." *Arcadis*. Arcadis Global. 2015. Pdf. Aug 3 2015.

"U.S. Cities Commit to 100 Percent Renewable Energy." *EESI*. Environmental and Energy Study Institute. 2015. Web. Aug 3 2015.

Urban Ecology. "History." *Urban Ecology*. 2013. Web. Aug 3 2015.

"Uruk: The First City." *Met Museum*. Metropolitan Museum of Art. Heilbrunn Timeline of Art History. 2015. Aug 9 2015.

Van Horn, Carl E., and Herbert A. Schaffner. *Work in America*. Santa Barbara, CA: ABC-CLIO, Inc. 2003.

Wacquant, Loic. *Urban Outcasts*. Malden, MA: Polity Press, 2008. Print.

"War Comes Home: The Excessive Militarization of American Policing." Jun 2014. Pdf. Aug 7 2015.

Weber, Lauren. "Companies Say Goodbye to the 'Burbs." *Wall Street Journal*. Dow Jones & Company. Dec 4 2014. Web. Aug 6 2015.

Westcott, Lucy. "More Americans Moving to Cities, Reversing the Suburban Exodus." *The Wire*. Atlantic Monthly Group. Mar 27 2014. Web. Aug 6 2015.

"What Is Gentrification?" *PBS*. Public Broadcasting Station. POV. Jun 17 2003. Web. Aug 15 2015.

"What Is Green Infrastructure?" *EPA*. Environmental Protection Agency. American Rivers. 2014. Web. Aug 3 2015

Williams, Cole. "Why Pittsburgh Is a Front-Runner in Sustainable Development." *Evolve EA*. EvolveEA. 2015. Web. Aug 14 2015.

Williams, Jeffrey J. "Is There a 'Liberal Bias' in Academia?" *Salon*. Salon Media Group. Jun 18 2013. Web. Aug 10 2015.

Williams, Wendy, and Robert Whitcomb. *Cape Wind: Money, Celebrity, Energy, Class, Politics, and the Battle for Our Energy Future*. New York: PublicAffairs Press, 2007. Print.

Wilson, James Q. "Hard Times, Fewer Crimes." *The Wall Street Journal*. Dow Jones & Company. May 28 2011. Web. Aug 7 2015.

Wilson, Jill H., and Nicole Prchal Svajlenka, "Immigrants Continue to Disperse, with Fastest Growth in the Suburbs." *Brookings*. Oct 29 2014. Web. Aug 5 2015.

"With Baltimore Unrest, More Debate Over 'Broken Windows' Policing." *NPR*. National Public Radio. May 4 2015. Web. Aug 7 2015.

Woodward, Christopher. "The Age of Flower Towers." *FT*. Financial Times. Financial Times LTD. Oct 7 2011. Web. Aug 9 2015.

Zhang, Haifeng. "School Desegregation and White Flight Revisited: A Spatial Analysis from a Metropolitan Perspective." *Urban Geography*. Vol 32, No 8, pp.1208–1226. 2011. Pdf. Aug 10 2015.

Websites

Brookings Institution's Metropolitan Policy Program

http://www.brookings.edu/about/programs/metro

The mission of the Metropolitan Policy Program is to deliver research to metropolitan leaders from public, private, and nonprofit sectors and to help those leaders put into practice economic solutions to foster the growth of their communities.

Center for an Urban Future

https://nycfuture.org/

The Center for an Urban Future is a NYC-based think tank dedicated to highlighting the critical opportunities and challenges facing New York and other cities, and providing fresh ideas and workable solutions to policymakers. The Center's primary focus is on growing and diversifying the local economy, expanding economic opportunity and targeting problems facing low-income and working-class neighborhoods.

City of Philadelphia Mural Arts Program

http://www.muralarts.org/

This organization employs local artists to create public murals throughout the city of Philadelphia, with the goals of building community, empowering both amateur and experienced artists, and beautifying the city in the process.

Institute for Local Self-Reliance

http://ilsr.org/

The Institute's mission is to provide innovative strategies, working models and timely information to support environmentally sound and equitable community development. To this end, ILSR works with citizens, activists, policymakers and entrepreneurs to design systems, policies and enterprises that meet local or regional needs; to maximize human, material, natural and financial resources; and to ensure that the benefits of these systems and resources accrue to all local citizens.

Mayors Innovation Project

http://www.mayorsinnovation.org/

The Mayors Innovation Project is a network of American mayors interested in innovative policy and governance. Committed to pressing social issues of the day, these mayors are taking the lead on such important social and environmental issues as climate change, infrastructure, economic revitalization, health care, prison reentry, to name a few. This group helps participating mayors put policies into action, share their experiences with peers, and make the case for the leading roles of cities to the rest of the nation. This website discusses various works underway by participating members and lists meetings the organization holds in cities around the country.

The Municipal Arts Society of New York

www.mas.org

With a network of urban planners, architects, elected officials, activists, and developers, MAS has helped shape the future of New York for over 120 years in areas such as building and public space development, culture, and the arts.

National League of Cities

http://www.nlc.org/

The National League of Cities (NLC) is dedicated to helping city leaders build better communities. Working in partnership with the 49 state municipal leagues, NLC serves as a resource to and an advocate for the more than 19,000 cities, villages and towns it represents.

Next Cities

https://nextcity.org/

Next City is a nonprofit organization with a mission to inspire social, economic, and environmental change in cities by creating media and events around the world.

Project for Public Spaces

http://www.pps.org/

Project for Public Spaces (PPS) is a nonprofit planning, design, and educational organization dedicated to helping people create and sustain public spaces that build stronger communities.

Regional Planning Association

http://www.rpa.org/

At Regional Planning Association professional researchers and regional planners seek to improve the prosperity, sustainability, and quality of life in the New York–New Jersey–Connecticut metropolitan region through work in transportation, economic development and real estate, environment and open space and more. This organization also provides leadership on transportation, environmental and economic-development issues in the Northeast and across the U.S.

Sustainable Cities Collective

http://www.sustainablecitiescollective.com/

Sustainable Cities Collective is a community that gathers content and provides resources for all who work in or are interested in urban planning, sustainable development, and urban economics. Looking at issues such as transportation, building practices, community planning and development, education, water, health and infrastructure, they hope to create a community where people can get involved and learn about the advances in how cities are becoming smarter and greener in the 21st century.

U.S. Conference of Mayors

http://www.usmayors.org/

The United States Conference of Mayors (USCM) is the official nonpartisan organization of cities with populations of 30,000 or more, of which there are currently 1,407. The primary roles of the U.S. Conference of Mayors are to promote the development of effective national urban/suburban policy, strengthen federal-city relationships, ensure that federal policy meets urban needs, provide mayors with leadership and management tools, and create a forum in which mayors can share ideas and information.

Index